A People for His Name

A CHURCH-BASED MISSIONS STRATEGY

A People for His Name

A CHURCH-BASED MISSIONS STRATEGY

Paul A. Beals

William Carey Library

PASADENA, CALIFORNIA 91104

Published by William Carey Library, P.O. Box 40129, 1705 N. Sierra Bonita Ave., Pasadena, California 91104. Telephone: (818) 798-0819.

International Standard Book Number 0-87808-336-7
Library of Congress Catalog Card Number 84-73488

PRINTED IN THE UNITED STATES OF AMERICA

To VIVIAN

suitable helper *par excellence*

and

beloved mother of Lois, Stephen, Samuel, and Timothy

Contents

PART 6
The Divine Imperative in Missions Strategy

Figures

Foreword

Dr. Paul Beals has produced the most easy-to-read, all-encompassing source book on his subject that I have yet encountered. Dr. Beals' years of personal experience as a missionary in Africa enable him to understand the viewpoint both of missionaries and of the national churches they establish. Yet his years spent promoting the role of North American churches as senders of missionaries qualify him equally to appreciate the viewpoint of pastors and missions committees here at home. Further, his long tenure as a seminary professor has given him intimate knowledge of theological and academic perspectives on missions.

Though Dr. Beals writes as a scholar, he is also a very warm, sensitive human being—and that warmth comes through in every chapter. I was charmed by his comment that "missionaries live like fish in an aquarium" with home supporters looking in on one side and the nationals among whom and with who they work looking in on the other. He also manifests an appealing ability to keep concepts in balance. For example, discussing the need for local church leaders to interview potential missionaries before, during and after their appointment to field service, Dr. Beals cautions against "interviewing missionaries to death," and advises that "missionaries also evaluate the performance of the home church toward [them] . . . Evaluation should work both ways" (p. 92).

Again, affirming Michael Griffith's emphasis that missionaries on furlough should spend "quality time" with their supporting churches, Dr. Beals adds the important condition that this is possible "only if the number of supporting churches [per missionary] is kept within reason" (p. 92).

Also apt are his cautions to missionaries regarding goal setting, warning that "pet projects are more dangerous than a pet python. If worse comes to worse, the python can be donated to a zoo. Projects of one's own making can become tangential to field purposes" (p. 141).

Nuggets of both theoretical and practical wisdom abound and seem to become even more frequent as one progresses chapter by chapter. Now that I've read this book once and finished this foreword, I'm going to go back and read it again!

And I plan to keep a copy of it close at hand at all times, as a help to my ministry. I recommend that all who are concerned with the forwarding of the cause of missions do the same.

Don Richardson

Preface

In only a few years we will start dating our checks with the year 2000. Ongoing technological breakthroughs already make Buck Rogers seem outdated. Still, in the midst of high tech and megabytes, the church of Jesus Christ continues to pursue its unchanging mission of world evangelization.

Never in the history of the Church have believers had such a realistic possibility of evangelizing the world as does this generation. Even so, some things remain unchanged in our fast-changing global city, such as the unrelenting truth of Scripture, the yet-to-be-completed commission, and the ever-increasing numbers of people.

People. God is taking out from among them "a people for His name" (Acts 15:14). How can churches around the world get the gospel message to those yet unreached, frontier peoples in the Fourth World? This question underlies the material in the following pages.

My thesis is this: in world missions, the local church is the biblical sending body through which missionaries serve world-wide, aided by the mission agency and the Christian school. I place emphasis upon the practical outworking of the missions responsibilities of local churches, as well as their relationship to mission agencies, missionary personnel, and Christian schools.

In articulating a church-based missions strategy, I will direct attention to these topics:

- a biblical model for carrying out world missions
- a biblical base for world missions
- the local church's centrality as the sending body in world missions
- the mission agency's role in helping the local church implement its world mission
- the career missionary's duties as one sent to participate in the church's mission
- the Christian school's task of teaching church leaders and career missionaries biblical missions principles
- the divine imperative of the Holy Spirit and of Christ's coming, which propel the church on its mission.

I want to express appreciation to my students, both former and present, who had a part in motivating the contents of this book. Gratitude goes to the Grand Rapids Baptist Seminary for a sabbatical leave to give attention to study and writing. I am also grateful to David Shaver and Robert

Martin, William Carey Library editors, for their Christian camaraderie and publishing professionalism. My thanks also go to Cyndie Walstra for her careful work on my diagrams, to Sherri Van Belkum for technical assistance, to Tim Beals for his professional help with the manuscript, and to Don Trott for his effective encouragement to publish. David Egner, author-editor and friend, gave wise counsel and on a number of occasions used his sharp pencil to strengthen the manuscript. I bear responsibility for the final product.

My children and their spouses kept me at the task by their concern and support. Vivian, my "suitable helper," not only encouraged me, but sat where I sat, preparing the manuscript in meticulous fashion on the word-processor. The project was a team effort from beginning to end.

Paul A. Beals
January, 1985

Part 1

Biblical Basis of Missions Strategy

Our Mission Defined

1

In the waning years of the twentieth century, mission leaders continue to debate the church's mission in the world today. What is included in our mission? What is excluded? Have we defined our mission too broadly? Are we guilty of settling for simplistic answers? Are we inconsistent? Inflexible?

Mission scholars are found at both ends of the spectrum. " 'Mission,' " states John R. W. Stott, "describes . . . everything the church is sent into the world to do. 'Mission' embraces the church's double vocation of service to be 'the salt of the earth' and 'the light of the world.' "[1] This "double vocation"—usually spoken of as the cultural mandate and the evangelistic mandate—has stirred considerable debate in recent days.

George W. Peters represents the other side of the issue. He writes: "It is . . . unscriptural to confuse these two mandates and speak of them on equal terms as missions and church ministries. Only the second mandate is considered missions in the strict biblical sense."[2] The author also holds this position, which we will consider later. Is there valid middle ground between these views? Does the question boil down to a matter of semantics? Or do we need to consider the relationship between these positions more carefully?

Before pursuing the question further, let us explore some scriptural guidelines for defining and describing the church's mission. Paul's ministry and writings are the basis of our inquiry.

The Pauline Model for the Church's Mission

Paul's model for carrying out his God-appointed mission to the Gentiles is found in Acts 14:21-23. The historical setting of this passage places it at approximately 48 A.D., some eighteen years after Pentecost.[3] Paul was nearing the end of his first missionary journey. The church, the body of Christ, began at Pentecost with the baptism of the Holy Spirit (Matt. 16:18; Acts 1:4-5; 2:1-13; 1 Cor. 12:12-14). The Holy Spirit's baptizing ministry was new and unique, never having occurred in God's dealing with His people throughout the Old Testament.

The geographical setting is southern Galatia, in the region of Pisidia and Lycaonia, where the cities of Antioch, Inconium, Lystra, and Derbe were located. Although he always preached to the Jews where possible (Acts 13:14-43), Paul launched out to reach the Gentiles, his primary target people (Acts 9:15; Rom. 11:13; Gal. 2:7-9; Eph. 3:8; 2 Tim. 4:17).

3

Paul and Barnabas proclaimed the gospel to both Jews and Gentiles in Antioch. They then moved on to Iconium, where their successful witness stirred up opposition by both the Gentile and Jewish communities (Acts 14:5). They travelled on to Lystra where both receptivity and rejection intensified (Acts 14:6-20). The Jews from Antioch and Iconium stirred up the opposition as a high wind fans a grass fire. The people stoned Paul and dragged him out of the city, convinced that he was dead. Paul got up, however, and returned to Antioch. After a night's sleep, the two apostles left for Derbe (Acts 14:19-20).

The account in Acts 14:21-23 presents information about Paul's missionary strategy that serves as a model for us today. He saw missionary activity as a threefold process. We will look at each of them in detail. See figure 1.

FIGURE 1

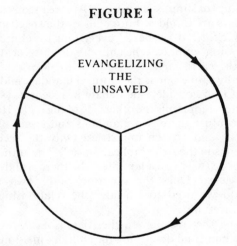

EVANGELIZING
THE
UNSAVED

Evangelizing the Unsaved

Paul and Barnabas' strategy began with the preaching of the good news. Luke tells us, "They preached the good news in that city and won a large number of disciples" (Acts 14:21).

Paul's first step, therefore, was to preach the gospel. The word used in this context is *euangelizo* meaning "to proclaim good tidings," or "to evangelize." *Euangelizo* is used fifty-four times in the New Testament. The related word *euangelion*, "good news" or "gospel," is used seventy-six times throughout the New Testament.

This term *euangelizo* is by no means the only word used to describe the communication of the gospel. Michael Green states that there are "three great words used for proclaiming the Christian message."[4] One of these words is *euangelizo*; the second is *kerusso,* translated "proclaim" or "preach." When the believers were scattered from Jerusalem, for example, "Phillip went down to the city of Samaria, and *preached* Christ unto them" (Acts 8:5 KJV). This term is used sixty-one times with respect to preaching the gospel.

The third term used for communicating the gospel is *martureo,* often translated "testify" or "witness" when used in reference to making Christ known. In his defense before Agrippa, Paul affirmed, "I continue unto this day, *witnessing* both to small and great . . . that Christ should suffer, and that he should be the first that should rise from the dead . . ." (Acts 26:22-23 KJV). These are the primary words used for gospel preaching, but David Hesselgrave warns against reductionism in speaking of gospel proclamation. He lists thirteen additional terms used for it throughout the apostolic ministry.[5] Most of those have a direct bearing on gospel witness.

It is evident, then, that gospel proclamation takes many forms. But what is the gospel we preach? What is the irreducible message people must hear before they can make a knowledgeable decision for or against receiving Christ as Savior?

The term *euangelion,* translated "good news" or "gospel," is distinctively a New Testament word. It is a joyous expression relating to the redemptive work of God through Christ. The "good news" has both historical and theological dimensions, as well as an appeal to faith in Christ's finished work. Robert H. Mounce summarizes the gospel message this way:

> In briefest outline, this message contained: (1) A historical proclamation of death, resurrection, and exaltation of Jesus, set forth as the fulfillment of prophecy and involving man's responsibility; (2) A theological evaluation of the person of Jesus as both Lord and Christ; (3) A summons to repent and receive the forgiveness of sins.[6]

This is the message Paul and Barnabas preached at Derbe. Wherever Paul went throughout his entire ministry, his all-consuming desire was to preach that same good news (Rom. 1:14-17; 11:13-14; 15:16-19).

Paul's second step in evangelizing the unsaved was *to gather in the results of his witness.* The text states that the apostles preached the good news and "won a large number of disciples" (Acts 14:21). The New Testament clearly teaches that wherever faithful witnesses preached the good news, they always had results. Paul never proclaimed the gospel without winning converts. The most meager response on record was at Athens, but even here, Spirit-prepared hearers believed (Acts 17:34).

The expression, "and won . . . disciples" (*matheteusantes*), is the same word used in Matthew 28:19 "and *make disciples* of all nations" (*matheteusate*). Both passages distinctly teach that when a person hears the gospel and believes it, he becomes a disciple. Becoming a disciple of Christ is not dependent on "discipling" subsequent to placing one's faith in Christ. The kingdom is not made up of two kinds of believers—some who are disciples and some who are not. Acts 11:26 states, "The disciples were first called Christians at Antioch." C. Peter Wagner comments, "This is the heart of the matter, and the most forthright definition of disciples. A disciple is as true Christian. A disciple is a person who has been born again by the Holy Spirit."[7] Wagner continues:

Be cautious therefore, of the Christian worker who says, "My ministry is not so much winning people to Christ as it is *discipling Christians.*" The thought behind this is noble, but since this [is] not a biblical use of the word "discipling" the phrase tends to be confusing. *Matheteusate* is a command to bring unbelievers to a commitment to Christ. Feeding or edifying those who respond, helping them to move forward on the road of growing discipleship, is a different matter. It relates more to the didactic ministry of the church, not the kerygmatic function.[8]

In brief, Paul preached the good news clearly and won disciples. This biblical pattern of the primacy of evangelism is all well and good, but a word of caution must be sounded. Not only should evangelism have a primary place biblically, but it must be practiced *worldwide.*

Evangelism on broken ground must continue with informed vigor, but what of the thirsty and parched ground where the gospel seed has yet to be sowed and watered? A ground swell of witness to hidden, unreached peoples is beginning, and it must surge ahead if we are to reach our generation. More than three out of four people on planet earth today have yet to hear the gospel, or they have not heard it clearly enough to make an understanding decision for or against Jesus Christ as Savior.

We cannot continue to ignore this crying challenge to witness. For further discussion on these people on the frontiers of witness, see Chapter 17 where we discuss the priorities of both unreached and responsive people.

Preaching the good news and winning disciples was only the first step in Paul's model for missions. With Paul evangelism never stood alone.

Edifying the Believers

The Acts 14 narrative continues, "Then they returned to Lystra, Iconium

FIGURE 2

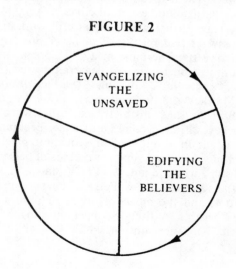

and Antioch, strengthening the disciples and encouraging them to remain true to the faith. 'We must go through many hardships to enter the kingdom of God,' they said"(Acts 14:21-22). Paul now retraced his steps to solidify the gains made through gospel preaching. See figure 2.

After having passed through bitter trials, Paul and Barnabas returned home through Lystra, Iconium, and Antioch to build up the believers. The afflictions had made an indelible impression on Paul. He said to Timothy toward the end of his life:

> You, however, know all about my teaching, my way of life, my purpose, faith, patience, love, endurance, persecutions, sufferings— what kinds of things happened to me in Antioch, Iconium and Lystra, the persecutions I endured. Yet the Lord rescued me from all of them (2 Tim. 3:10-11).

The overland route back to their home church in Syrian Antioch was much quicker and shorter. Indeed, Paul and Silas took this road when they set out on their second journey (Acts 15:41-16:1). Yet much remained for Paul to do among the fledgling groups of disciples now growing in these cities. Refer to map (figure 3) on page 8.[9]

First, the apostles moved among the churches "strengthening the disciples." The word translated "strengthening"(*episterizontes*) means "to build up with additional (*epi*) strength." The term is found in the New Testament only in Acts 14:22; 15:32, 41; and 18:23. In each instance it refers to building up believers in the faith. In fact, Paul's two subsequent journeys started with "strengthening " ministries among the churches. At the beginning of his second journey, Paul "went through Syria and Cilicia, *strengthening* the churches"(Acts 15:41). After furloughing in Antioch, he initiated his third journey "and traveled from place to place throughout the region of Galatia and Phrygia, *strengthening* all the disciples"(Acts 18:23).

Second, the apostles went about "encouraging" the believers (*parakalountes*). This term conveys the thought of pleading, exhorting, or beseeching. A sense of urgency prevailed. Paul wrote to the Philippian church, "I *plead* with Euodia and I *plead* with Syntyche to agree with each other in the Lord (Phil. 4:2). Again Paul reminds Timothy, "As I *urged* you when I went into Macedonia, stay there in Ephesus . . ."(1 Tim. 1:3). The encouragement to remain true to the faith was doubly urgent because of the hardships that come in the Christian life.

The text indicates a direct quote from the apostle's exhortation: "We must go through many hardships to enter the kingdom of God" (Acts 14:22). Mention of the kingdom of God in this context is typical of the apostolic use of the term. Other instances of its use in preaching or teaching occur as well in Acts (8:12; 19:8; 20:25; 28:23). Charles C. Ryrie comments as follows concerning its meaning in apostolic preaching:

> Chiefly . . . the idea seems to be the basic idea of kingdom; i.e., the sovereign ruling power of God. Thus the phrase used in the apostolic preaching means the things concerning the power and plan of God

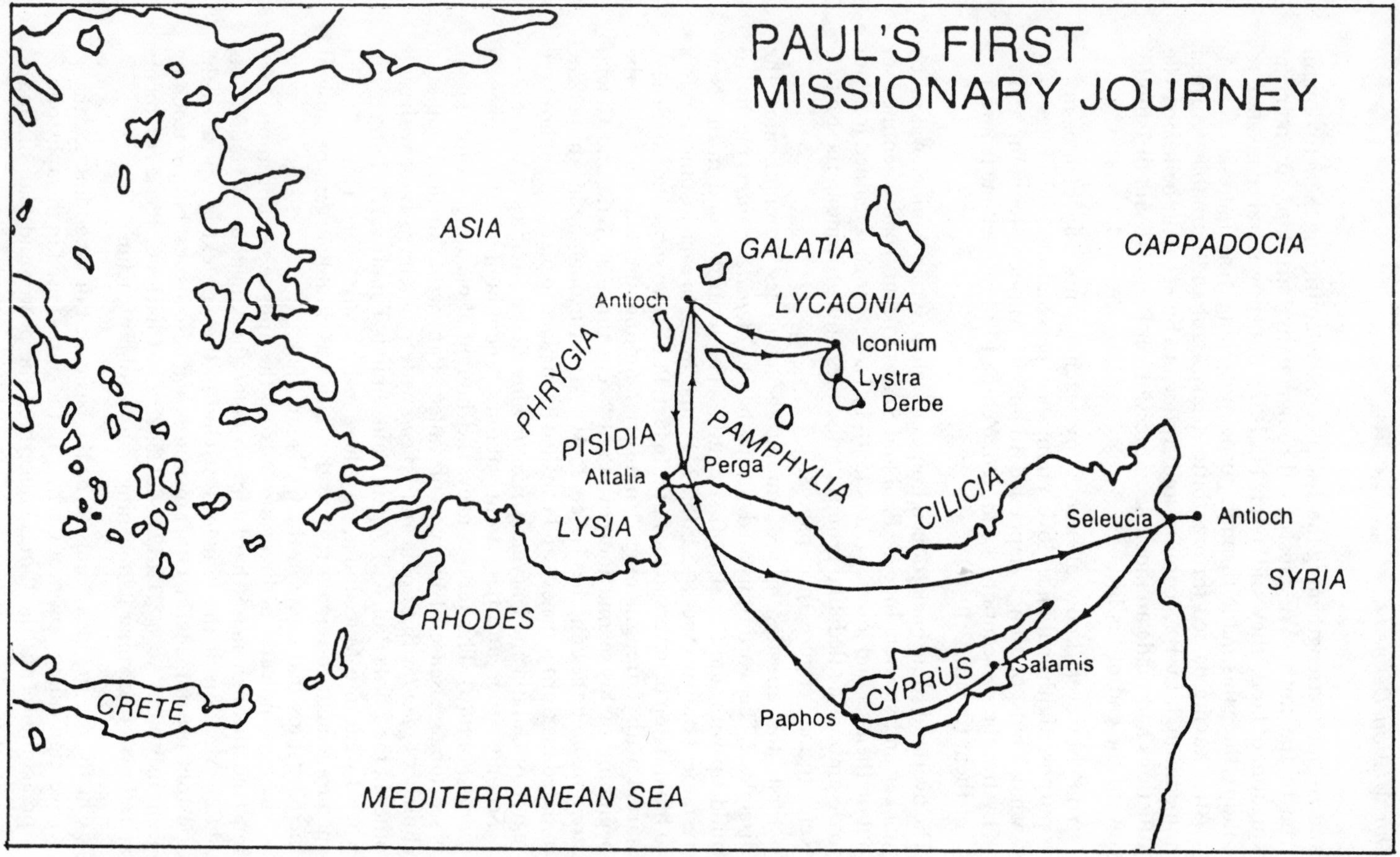
PAUL'S FIRST
MISSIONARY JOURNEY
ASIA
GALATIA
CAPPADOCIA
Antioch
LYCAONIA
Iconium
Lystra
Derbe
PHRYGIA
PISIDIA
PAMPHYLIA
Perga
Attalia
CILICIA
Seleucia
Antioch
LYSIA
SYRIA
RHODES
CYPRUS
Salamis
Paphos
CRETE
MEDITERRANEAN SEA

FIGURE 3

working to bring salvation through Jesus the Messiah, which salvation will consummate in future glory. It is closely akin to the Jewish idea of the universal kingdom.[10]

Paul's edifying ministry was centered in doctrinal instruction and exhortation to victorious Christian living. His entire work models for us a biblical pattern of soul care. Roland Allen was bold to say that Paul's missionary success is attributed to his ministry to convert. He wrote, "Indeed, I think we may say that it is in his dealing with his converts that we come to the heart of the matter and may hope to find one secret of his amazing success."[11]

So we see that the Pauline model for missions centers on evangelizing the unsaved and edifying those who believe. A third, and crucial, element remains.

Establishing Local Churches

The narrative continues, "Paul and Barnabas appointed elders for them in each church and, with prayer and fasting, committed them to the Lord in whom they had put their trust" (Acts 14:23). See figure 4.

FIGURE 4

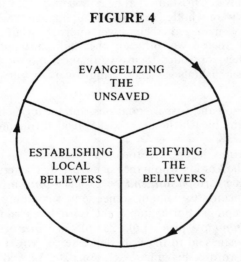

There were now groups of believers in Lystra, Iconium, and Antioch, but they were not organized and had no appointed leaders. The apostles first assisted these groups by setting men apart for leadership roles. Then they commended each church into God's care.

First, the apostles *appointed* (*cheirotonesantes*) *elders* in each church. This is an intriguing compound word "that originally meant to vote by show of hands."[12] This term does not mean "ordain" in the sense in which it is understood today. Paul used this word later when he said of Titus, "What is more, he *was chosen* by the church to accompany us as we carry the offering . . ." (2 Cor. 8:19). No explicit evidence appears in the text, but circumstances indicate that these men were chosen as elders by the believers. Then they were set apart by the apostles for their duties. No doubt these men had demonstrated leadership qualifications while the apostles were absent.

The principal lesson here is that spiritual men manifested gifts for leadership and accepted the appointment of the believers and the apostles. It would be folly, however, to establish a form of church polity on this passage alone. A stalwart missiologist of his day, Robert E. Speer, commented:

> All was life and motion and freedom. Neither did Barnabas and Paul employ a helper and place him over the group. They hit upon a perfectly simple, natural, self-supporting arrangement, designed to secure liberty, growth and the sense of responsibility.[13]

These churches were grounded in the faith and founded in the culture. They were part and parcel of the culture while being at the same time local personifications of the total body of Christ. Roland Allen commended Paul's wisdom in church planting:

> The little groups of Christians that he established in towns like Lystra or Derbe . . . were wholly composed of permanent residents in the country. They managed their own internal affairs under the leadership of their own officers, they administered their own sacraments, they controlled their own finance, and they propagated themselves, establishing in neighboring towns or village Churches like themselves.[14]

Paul had laid soil and wise foundations, and the local churches became the natural means by which the gospel spread throughout the Roman Empire.

The second action the apostles took was to *commit these churches and their leaders* to the Lord in whom they had trusted. The term "committed" (*parethento*) is the verb *paratithemi* (v. 23). The form in which it occurs (middle voice) means "to commit someone or something to another for protection or keeping." For example, the Lord Jesus said, "Father, into your hands I *commit* my spirit" (Luke 23:46). On a later occasion in Paul's ministry, the apostle said to the Ephesian elders, "Now I *commit* you to God and to the word of his grace . . ." (Acts 20:32). And what a solemn event it was! This commitment of the churches was "with prayer and fasting." Paul cast them entirely on God for their personal and corporate life. He would not have them tied to his apron strings. He visited them, wrote to them, and sent some of the missionary team to encourage them, but Paul never made the churches dependent on him. Because he was confident that God would keep the newly formed churches, Paul could establish them to exercise complete independence. This, then, is the Pauline model for the church's mission. Both in the historical record of Acts and in the teaching of Paul's letters to the churches, the essence of Paul's work is in (1) evangelizing the unsaved, (2) edifying the believers, and (3) establishing local churches. The following diagram summarizes the Pauline model.

FIGURE 5

THE PAULINE MODEL FOR THE CHURCH'S MISSION		
Evangelizing the Unsaved Acts 14:21	Edifying the Believers Acts 14:22	Establishing Local Churches Acts 14:23
Action: Preaching gospel Making Disciples	Action: Strengthening Encouraging	Action: Appointing Committing
Proclaiming	Perfecting	Planting

Paul did many other good things in the course of his ministry, but his apostolic *mission* was to win the lost, teach the saved, and plant churches. We can do no less if we wish to follow a biblical model for missions today.

The church's mission moves forward in cultural contexts that are as varied as humankind itself. Paul the Jew discovered this fact head-on when he accepted divine appointment as apostle to the Gentiles. Paul serves as our biblical model for missions today.

Wrap-Up

The purpose of this chapter has been to define the church's mission using the Apostle Paul's ministry as our biblical model. With this purpose in mind, we crystallize some conclusions.

• The *sine qua non* (indispensable essential) of the church's mission is to evangelize the lost, to edify the believers, and to establish local churches (Acts 14:21-23). If these elements are not present in our missionizing, we are not involved in biblical missions in the truest sense. This is not to say that in its mission the church does not do other things. These will be discussed when we consider the cultural mandate.

• Evangelism in the New Testament never stands alone. Winning people to Christ, or "making disciples," is the *initial* step in the church's mission.

• The Apostle Paul sets the pattern for the ongoing ministry of strenthening believers.

• Believers must be gathered into local churches for edification and service. Planting churches is essential to New Testament missions.

• Spirit-prepared leaders are basic to the church-planting process. Church leaders were always a special concern for Paul.

Notes to Chapter 1

1. John R. W. Stott, *Christian Mission in the Modern World* (Downers Grove: InterVarsity Press, 1975), p. 30.

2. George W. Peters, *A Biblical Theology of Missions* (Chicago: Moody Press, 1972), p. 170.

3. George T. Purves, *Christianity in the Apostolic Age* (Grand Rapids: Baker Book House, 1955), pp. 112, 315.

4. Michael Green, *Evangelism in the Early Church* (Grand Rapids: Eerdmans, 1970), p. 48.

5. David J. Hesselgrave, *Communicating Christ Cross-Culturally* (Grand Rapids: Zondervan Publishing House, 1978), pp. 20-21. The thirteen terms listed are: *syngcheo* (confound, Acts 9:22); *symbibazo* (prove, Acts 9:22); *diegomai* (declare, Acts 9:27); *syzeteo* (dispute, Acts 9;29); *laleo* (speak, Acts 9:29); *dialegomai* (reason with, Acts 18:4); *peitho* (persuade, Acts 18:4); *noutheteo* (admonish, warn, Acts 20:31); *katecho* (inform, instruct, Acts 21:20-24); *deomai* (beg—beseech, 2 Cor. 5:20); *elengcho* (reprove, 2 Tim. 4:2); *epitimao* (rebuke, 2 Tim. 4:2); *parakaleo* (exhort, urge, 1 Peter 2:11).

6. Robert H. Mounce, "Gospel," in *Baker's Dictionary of Theology,* ed. Everett F. Harrison (Grand Rapids: Baker Book House, 1960), p. 257.

7. C. Peter Wagner, "What Is 'Making Disciples'?" *Evangelical Missions Quarterly* 9 (Fall 1973): 292.

8. Ibid. See also Donald A. McGavran, "How About that New Verb 'To Disciple'?" *Church Growth Bulletin* 15 (May 1979): 265-70.

9. *The Expositor's Bible Commentary,* ed. Frank E. Gaebelein, 12 vols. (Grand Rapids: Zondervan Publishing House, 1981), 9:248. Used by permission of Zondervan Publishing House.

10. Charles C. Ryrie, *Biblical Theology of the New Testament* (Chicago: Moody Press, 1959), pp. 126-27.

11. Roland Allen, *Missionary Methods: St. Paul's or Ours?* (Grand Rapids: Eerdmans, 1962), p. 82.

12. Archibald T. Robertson, *Word Pictures in the New Testament* (New York: Harper & Brothers, 1930), 3:216.

13. Robert E. Speer, *Missionary Principles and Practice* (New York: Fleming H. Revell, 1902), p. 262.

14. Roland Allen, *Education in the Native Church* (London: World Dominion Press, n.d.), p.4.

Paul's Cultural Milieu Described

2

Evangelizing the lost, edifying the converts, and establishing local churches are not done in a vacuum. *People* are up front! *People* are weaving their own cultural fabric. *People* are putting their own indelible cultural stamp on either receptivity or resistance to the gospel. The teaching of scriptural truth to people is marked by their built-in learning patterns, educational levels, literacy or illiteracy, age, concept of sex roles in their culture, ongoing religious tradition in their culture, and many other integrating factors. Efforts to plant churches in a given culture are affected by the people's concept of leadership, respect or lack of respect for age, patterns of decision-making, and ideas about such things as worship and music.

Humanly speaking, Paul was a most unlikely candidate for the position, "apostle to the Gentiles"! (See Galatians 2:8) How could there have been a more bigoted Jew—both theologically and culturally? Paul expressed it himself in this passage in Philippians:

> If anyone else thinks he has reasons to put confidence in the flesh, I have more: circumcised on the eighth day, of the people of Israel, of the tribe of Benjamin, a Hebrew of Hebrews; in regard to the law, a Pharisee; as for zeal, persecuting the church; as for legalistic righteousness, faultless (Phil. 3:4-6).

Talk about being culture-bound! And Paul knew what he believed, too! But meeting Jesus on the Damascus road made all the difference (Acts 9:1-19). Paul believed Christ's claims, was born again by the Spirit, and now "walked in newness of life" (Rom. 6:4 KJV). He viewed all religious and cultural heritage as "rubbish, that I may gain Christ and be found in him ... " (Phil. 3:8-9).

God turned Paul about-face from persecuting churches to planting churches. All this happened in the space of twelve to fifteen years.

The Pauline Model in Relation to the Cultural Milieu

Paul pursued his church-planting ministry in a diversity of cultural contexts. He proclaimed the gospel to Jews, to "country" Gentiles, to "cultured" Gentiles, and to all shades between. As he taught converts from these various groups, he faced multiple questions about such issues as circumcising, law keeping, offering of meat to idols, wearing the veil, covering and uncovering heads, and many more. The members of the churches he planted represented people with backgrounds in Judaism, idol worship, slavery, and slaveholding. Former alcoholics and prostitutes graced many worship services (Acts 14:11-13; 1 Cor. 11:21; Eph. 5:3-5; 5:18; 6:5-9; Col. 3:5-11; 3:22-4:1; Philemon 8-16). See figure 6.

FIGURE 6

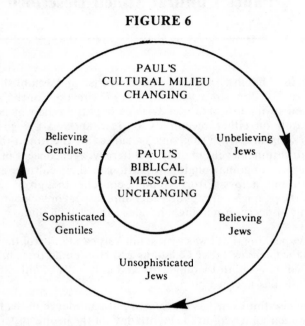

In short, God was calling out for Himself a people for His name (Acts 15:14). And all of these people were still part and parcel of their varied cultures. How did Paul deal with these human elements of his church planting role? Two answers are clear. Paul took a high view of Scripture, and he took a high view of culture. Donald McGavran argues that this is the only reasonable position we can take in Christian missions today and be true to both Scripture and culture.[1]

Paul Took a High View of Scripture
Without a firm anchor in the propositional truth of God's Word, Paul would have been awash in the cultural seas of his day. The application to our present-day situation is obvious.

1. *Paul held to the divine authority of Scripture.* What is said of Paul, of course, can be said of other New Testament writers as well. Together they understood that God was the author of the Old Testament.

Paul argued for his apostolic right to live by the gospel in his first letter to the Corinthian believers. He posed the question:

> Do I say this merely from a human point of view? Doesn't the Law say the same thing? For it is written in the Law of Moses: "Do not

muzzle an ox while it is treading out the grain." Is it about oxen that God is concerned? Surely he says this for us, doesn't he? (1 Cor. 9:8-10).

Paul equated the words of Moses with God's words. Paul understood the words of Moses to be those of God Himself. S. Lewis Johnson comments, "Thus what we have here, as elsewhere throughout the Bible, is the double authorship of Scripture, with God the source of the Word and man the means by which it comes to us."[2] There was no question in Paul's mind about the source and authority of the Word: it came from God. In turn he preached the gospel as the power of God unto salvation for both Jews and Gentiles (Rom. 1:16; 1 Cor. 1:23-24).

In addition, numerous quotations from the Old Testament appear in Paul's account of Israel's past, present, and future (Rom. 9-11). He made some thirty-five direct references to the Old Testament with passages ranging from "the Law of Moses, the Prophets and the Psalms" (Luke 24:44). The authors are mentioned by name in a number of these passages (Rom. 9:27, 29; 10:19, 20; 11:9). Benjamin B. Warfield took account of this phenomenon by writing:

> It is to be noted that when thus Scripture is adduced by the names of its human authors, it is a matter of complete indifference whether the words adduced are comments of these authors or direct words of God recorded by them. As the plainest words of the human authors are assigned to God as their real author, so the most express words of God, repeated by the Scripture writers, are cited by the names of these human writers . . . To say that "Moses" or "David says," is evidently thus only a way of saying that "Scripture says," which is the same as to say that "God says."[3]

2. *Paul held to the divine inspiration of Scripture.* Paul's high view of Scripture included the divine inspiration of the written text. In his second letter to Timothy, Paul reminded him "how from infancy you have known the holy Scriptures, which are able to make you wise for salvation through faith in Christ Jesus. All Scripture is God-breathed . . ." (2 Tim. 3:15-16). The "holy Scriptures" were the Old Testament books.

What body of truth could make Timothy "wise for salvation" unless it had a divine author? No doubt Timothy's grandmother Lois and his mother Eunice taught him the Scriptures and encouraged him to memorize them. This was the custom of the day in godly Jewish homes. Ralph Earle adds:

> These OT Scriptures were able to make him "wise" in preparation "for salvation through faith in Christ Jesus." They disciplined him in obedience to God and also pointed forward to the coming Messiah, through whom salvation by faith would become available.[4]

The phrase, "All Scripture is God-breathed," is a faithful rendering of the text. As Earle states, "That is exactly what the Greek says. The adjective *theopneustos* (only here in the NT) is compounded of *theos,*

'God,' and the verb *pneu,* 'breathe.' This is one of the greatest texts in the NT on the inspiration of the Bible."[5] Paul, writing under the inspiration of the Holy Spirit, took the highest possible view of the divine inspiration of Scripture. Benjamin B. Warfield concluded:

> When Paul declares, then, that "every scripture," or "all scripture" is the product of the Divine breath, "is God-breathed," he asserts with as much energy as he could employ that Scripture is the product of a specifically Divine operation.[6]

No wonder Paul could preach the gospel in any audience with power! He had a message from God. Whether speaking to the Jews in the synagogue or Zeus worshippers in Lystra, Paul had a "Thus saith the Lord" to back him up.

Paul Took a High View of Culture

This does not mean that Paul, or any other apostle, saw Scripture and culture on the same plane. When faith in Christ produces a new creature in Christ, the lifestyle of that person changes. A new value system takes over. A Christ-centered life results in cultural changes as well as spiritual. When faith in Christ clashes with the former lifestyle of the new believer, some cultural features must give way. Only Scripture is absolute.

What is culture? In this discussion, culture is viewed as the "totality of man's learned, accumulated experience which is socially transmitted."[7] For Paul, the Jews in Pisidian Antioch, the Lystrans in Lycaonia, the philosophers in Athens, as well as many other groups of people made up the cultural mosaic of his day. The Roman Empire was not, as some assume, a cultural monolith. The Banglas in Bangladesh, the Bostonians in Boston, and the Bandas in Bambari are a part of our mosaic today. Perhaps the marvel is that the gospel is communicated at all!

By acknowledging cultural differences, Paul was not condoning sin. He did everything he could to emphasize and identify with those with whom he shared Christ. Paul stated this principle of identification in 1 Corinthians 9:19-23, where he discussed his relationship to the Jews, Gentiles, and the weaker brethren.

1. *Paul identified with the Jews.*

> Though I am free and belong to no man, I make myself a slave to everyone, to win as many as possible. To the Jews I became like a Jew, to win the Jews. To those under the law I became like one under the law (though I myself am not under the law), so as to win those under the law (1 Cor. 9:19-20).

Indeed, Paul was proud of his Jewish heritage. Such boldness nearly cost him his life (1 Cor. 9:23-25), but concern for his people prodded him on. He *was* a Jew. The statement in 1 Corinthians 9:20, "To those under the law I became like one under the law ...," is taken by some to refer to God-fearing Gentile proselytes who voluntarily placed themselves under the law. More likely, however, this statement is simply an explanation of Paul's previous reference to Jews.

Paul's heart for his Jewish heritage is strongly expressed in his letter to the Romans (9:2-4; 10:1-2). "I have great sorrow," he said, "and unceasing anguish in my heart. For I could wish that I myself were cursed and cut off from Christ for the sake of my brothers, those of my own race, the people of Israel" (Rom. 9:2-4). Paul anguished in his soul for his people. Try as he might, the cross-cultural communicator can never erase his personal cultural ties.

2. *Paul identified with the Gentiles.*

To those not having the law I became like one not having the law (though I am not free from God's law but am under Christ's law) so as to win those not having the law (1 Cor. 9:21).

As the apostle to the Gentiles, his ministry carried him far and wide not only geographically, but also culturally. Some people he went to were quite unsophisticated, while others were the intelligentsia of their day. Jews, of course, made up a part of the churches that were planted as well.

The New Testament record indicates that Paul effectively preached the gospel and planted churches among varied pieces of the Gentile mosaic. Examples of his ministry in Lystra and Athens are two cases in point. Paul was always ready to share the gospel with people regardless of their culture or creed. He wrote to the Romans, "I am obligated both to Greeks and non-Greeks, both to the wise and the foolish" (Rom. 1:14). We now explore these two contrasting examples of his approach with the gospel.

Paul communicated Christ to the unsophisticated: his experience in Lystra. On their first journey, Paul and Barnabas went to Pisidian Antioch where they preached primarily to Jews (Acts 13:13-14:3). For the most part, the Jews of Antioch violently opposed the Messianic message, although some of them accepted the truth (13:43), and a few Gentiles joined them (13:48). In Iconium "a great number of Jews and Gentiles believed" (Acts 14:1). However, great opposition soon exploded, and the apostles departed for the cities of Lystra and Derbe (14:6). As Paul's preaching progressed through the years, he learned to keep his bags packed when he entered a city. Revivals he could handle; riots were quite another thing. A missionary could get separated from his senses rather quickly as he soon learned in Lystra.

No one had ever said to a lame man in Lystra, "Stand up on your feet!" (Acts 14:10). What's more, when the man actually jumped up and walked, the attending crowd jumped to some bizarre conclusions. Barnabas was the older and more dignified of the two, so they concluded he was surely Zeus. Paul, the fiery and effective speaker, was surely Hermes. And all of this discussion was going on in the Lycaonian language! What kind of people were these Lystrans anyway?

Apparently there were few Jews in Lystra. No mention is made of a synagogue, at any rate. The city was a frontier town in southern Galatia in the district of Lycaonia. The temple of Zeus was a landmark just outside the city gate (Acts 14:13). Conybeare and Howson described the situation:

We are brought in contact . . . with Heathen superstition and mythology; yet not the superstition of an educated mind, as that of Sergius Paulus,—nor the mythology of a refined and cultivated taste, like that of the Athenians,—but the mythology and superstition of a rude and unsophisticated people. Thus does the Gospel, in the person of St. Paul, successively clash with opposing powers, with sorcerers and philosophers, cruel magistrates and false divinities.[8]

What an invitation to apostleship in the provinces! The Old Testament covenant promises were of no avail here. Paul demonstrated time and again that he started with people *where they were* in their God-understanding. He approached them where they were religiously, culturally, and socially.

In this tense setting, Paul's message was threefold: (1) all men had a common human heritage—"We too are only men, human (*anthropoi*) like you" (Acts 14:15), (2) the living God, Creator of all things, is the only one worthy of worship (14:16), and (3) the living God, provider of all things, sends rain, harvest, food, and joy (14:17). These were people of the soil. The elements dictated their very lives and livelihoods. Paul met them where they were and brought them good news.[9] The cultural milieu determined his approach. Yet he never compromised the biblical message.

Paul communicated Christ to the sophisticated: his experience in Athens. This is the setting: Paul was on his second journey, and he was waiting in Athens for Silas and Timothy to join him (Acts 17:16-34). Although he preached to Jews first whenever possible (17:17), Paul's main confrontation in Athens was with the Epicurean and Stoic philosophers. They invited him to reason with them on the Areopagus. Paul started with the known—idolatry. He then led them to the unknown—the Creator and sovereign God who sent His now-resurrected Son to judge the world. F.F. Bruce comments, "Paul starts with his hearers' belief in an impersonal divine essence, pantheistically conceived, and leads them to the Living God revealed as Creator and Judge."[10] The inscription on one particular altar had attracted Paul's attention. For good reason, he used this altar as his point of contact. Paul began:

Men of Athens! I see that in every way you are very religious. For as I walked around and observed your objects of worship, I even found an altar with this inscription: TO AN UNKNOWN GOD. Now what you worship as something unknown I am going to proclaim to you (Acts 17:22-23).

"To an unknown God" (*agnosto theo*)! Who could this "unknown God" be? Bruce summarizes the historical background:

According to Diogenes Laertius . . . the Athenians during a pestilence sent for Epimenides the Cretan . . . , who advised them to sacrifice sheep at various spots . . . , and to commemorate the occasion altars to unnamed gods . . . were set up.[11]

Don Richardson adds:

> Diogenes Laertius himself does not mention that the words *agnosto theo* were inscribed upon Epimenides' altars. He states only that "altars may be found in different parts of Attica with no name inscribed upon them, which are memorials of this atonement!"

> Two other ancient writers, however—Pausanias in his *Description of Greece* (vol. 1, 1:4) and Philostratus in his *Appolonius of Tyana*—refer to "altars to an unknown god" implying that an inscription to that effect was engraved upon them.[12]

A teacher somewhere in Paul's background, possibly Gamaliel, must have given him some assigned reading! He knew not only the history behind the altar in question, he could even quote Epimenides' poetry! (Titus 1:12). He met these philosophers on their own ground and proclaimed the gospel to them. When God called Paul to minister to the Gentiles, He equipped him to do it. Paul, a converted Pharisee, reasoned with Greek philosphers on their home territory. He boldly claimed, "Now what you worship as something unknown I am going to proclaim to you" (Acts 17:23). Richardson poses the question:

> Was the God whom Paul proclaimed really a *foreign god* as the philosophers surmised? Not at all! By Paul's reasoning, *Yahweh*, the Judeo-Christian God, was anticipated by Epimenides' altar. He was therefore a God who had already intervened in the history of Athens. Surely He had a right to have His name proclaimed there![13]

The philosophers listened carefully until Paul spoke of Christ's resurrection. At this point the audience divided three ways: some sneered, some wanted more discussion, and others believed (Acts 17:32-34). This response is illustrative of many who hear the gospel today.

The point is clear: God prepared Paul for his ministry both biblically and culturally. The lesson is clear as well: Paul's biblical and cultural models of church-planting evangelism provide valid patterns for us today.

3. *Paul identified with the weak.* The apostle continued his principle of identification by saying:

> To the weak I became weak, to win the weak. I have become all things to all men so that by all possible means I might save some. I do all this for the sake of the gospel, that I may share in its blessings (1 Cor. 9:22-23).

To this point we have listened while Paul developed his model for missions in various cultural milieus. He identified with the Jews both by racial heritage and by appeal to Old Testament truth about Messiah. He identified with the Gentiles, both the unsophisticated and sophisticated— quick-tempered Lystrans and philosophical Athenians.

What did Paul mean when he said, "To the weak I became weak, to win the weak" (1 Cor. 9:22)? The context helps us here. In the previous chapter,

Paul raised the question about food offered to idols (1 Cor. 8:1-4). His conclusion: "We know that an idol is nothing at all in the world and that there is no God but one" (8:4).

When a Corinthian believer strolled through the marketplace, he knew that the sides of beef and lamb hanging there had arrived by way of the idol temples. His conscience dictated whether or not he would enjoy prime rib for dinner that evening (1 Cor. 8:7). If he had a weak conscience concerning food offered to idols, he walked past with eyes straight ahead. If he should try to sneak home with a succulent tenderloin "just this once," he defiled his conscience concerning the idols. "But," Paul reasons, "food does not bring us near to God; we are not worse if we do not eat, and no better if we do. Be careful, however, that the exercise of your freedom does not become a stumbling block to the weak" (1 Cor. 8:8-9).

Although Paul could enjoy eating any food in the marketplace, his weaker brothers could not. Paul's position was that "if what he ate caused his brother to fall into sin, he would never eat meat again" (1 Cor. 8:13).

No doubt both Jews and Gentiles were among these "weaker brethren." Paul's identification here is both cultural and spiritual. He wished to "win" or "gain" the weak. F. Godet comments:

> No doubt the term *gain* does not apply to them in the same sense as to the Jews and Gentiles of whom Paul has been speaking; but the consequence of their weakness, if one should scandalize them, by making them return to their Gentile or Jewish life, might yet be to *destroy* them as is shown by passages of the Epistle to the Corinthians and to the Hebrews. Paul did not regard them as gained till they were secured against such lapses.[14]

Paul deals with the principle of accommodating to the weaker brother in other contexts, such as Romans 14:1-15:4. He constantly wished to win the weak believer.

Paul then summarized his principle of identification with his hearers. He was willing to "become all things to all men so that by all possible means I might save some. I do all this for the sake of the gospel" (1 Cor. 9:22-23). In matters of scriptural principle Paul was adamant. He would not budge when "false brothers" insisted on Titus' being circumcised (Gal. 2:3-5). On the other hand, he readily circumcised Timothy "because of the Jews who lived in that area, for they all knew that his father was a Greek" (Acts 16:3). Godet concludes, "No observance appeared to him too irksome, no requirement too stupid, no prejudice too absurd, to prevent his dealing tenderly with it in the view of saving souls."[15]

In today's terms, Paul "contextualized" the gospel. The "in" word today in missions is "contextualization," a term that obviously means different things to different people. One's theological position determines the extent to which he will contextualize. Will it include the message as well? One's cultural background bears on practices that are accepted or a anathema. Shall we keep looking for new words to describe what missionaries, beginning with Paul, have tried to do these many years? Shall we rewrite our hermeneutics? Have missiologists become a bit esoteric—a bit "heavy"? Suppressing the urge to debate these questions further, let us agree with James F. Engel that our goal in contextualization "is not to make the gospel relevant but to *communicate the relevance of the gospel.*"[16] This is the heart of the matter.

Wrap-Up

Our purpose in this chapter has been to describe the approaches Paul took to communicate the relevance of the gospel in various cultural contexts. He has taught us the following principles.

• The "good news" never changes. Whatever the cultural milieu of the audience, the message is absolute.

• We must reach people where they are religiously, culturally, and socially. Each piece of human mosaic is unique and must be prayerfully studied and understood. The unchanging message is proclaimed in an ever-changing milieu.

• We must identify with people in order to gain a hearing for the gospel—"all things to all men" (1 Cor. 9:22).

• The gospel messenger is an agent of cultural change. When hearers become believers and doers of the Word, *both* lives and cultures undergo change. What better way to be "salt" and "light" (Matt. 5:13-16) than to proclaim the gospel to obedient hearers?

• Local churches in turn become centers of gospel witness—lighthouses—that reach out into local cultures and societies first and then throughout the world. This is the end result of the New Testament model for mission. A church-oriented strategy of missions is biblical.

Notes to Chapter 2

1. Donald A. McGavran, *The Clash Between Christianity and Cultures* (Washington, D.C.: Canon Press, 1974), pp. 51-74.

2. S. Lewis Johnson, *The Old Testament in the New: An Argument for Biblical Inspiration* (Grand Rapids: Zondervan Publishing House, 1980), p. 49.

3. Benjamin B. Warfield, *The Inspiration and Authority of the Bible* (Philadelphia: The Presbyterian and Reformed Publishing Company, 1948), p. 152.

4. Ralph Earle, "1 Timothy," *The Expositor's Bible Commentary,* ed. Frank E. Gaebelein, 12 vols. (Grand Rapids: Zondervan Publishing House, 1978), 11:409.

5. Ibid.

6. Warfield, *The Inspiration and Authority of the Bible*, p. 133.

7. Felix M. Keesing, *Cultural Anthropology: The Science of Custom* (New York: Holt, Rinehart and Winston, 1965), p. 18.

8. W.J. Conybeare and J.S. Howson, *The Life and Epistles of St. Paul* (Grand Rapids: Eerdmans, 1957), p. 150.

9. F.F. Bruce, *The Acts of the Apostles* (Grand Rapids: Eerdmans, 1960), p. 282. Bruce observes that this is the first recorded incident of gospel preaching to a "pagan audience." Paul appealed to them on the basis of natural revelation.

10. Ibid., pp. 335-36.

11. Ibid.

12. Don Richardson, *Eternity in Their Hearts* (Ventura, CA: Regal Books, 1981), p. 21. Richardson begins his book with a well-documented account of the Athenians and their altar to the unknown God, pp. 14-28.

13. Ibid., p. 24.

14. F. Godet, *Commentary on the First Epistle of St. Paul to the Corinthians* (Grand Rapids: Zondervan Publishing House, 1957), p. 39.

15. Ibid., p. 40.

16. James F. Engel, *Contemporary Christian Communication: Its Theory and Practice* (New York: Thomas Nelson Publishers, 1975), p. 276. His section on contextualization is found on pages 272-84.

The School of World Mission and Evangelism of Trinity Evangelical Divinity School has held three consultations on Theology and Mission in which contextualization was discussed. The third of these, held March 18-20, 1982, concentrated on "Contextualization: Truth in Context." Published volumes are available for the first two Consultations.

The Bible: A Missionary Book
The Old Testament

3

The Pauline model for missions does not stand alone on the horizon like a silo rising out of an Iowa prairie. It is an integral part of the biblical panorama in which the triune God reveals Himself as a missionary God. He pleads "Come" in the Old Testament. He commands "Go" in the New Testament. Jehovah said to Israel, "You are my witnesses . . ." (Isa. 43:10). Christ instructed His followers, ". . . you will be my witnesses . . ." (Acts 1:8). The Old Testament prepares the way for Messiah's coming. The New Testament presents Messiah as God's remedy for sin. The church, the body of Christ, now propagates the gospel to the ends of the earth, with accompanying good works, for man's good and God's glory.

The Bible is a missionary book. Scripture in its entirety declares God's purpose of making His person and work known throughout humankind by His people—Israel in the Old Testament and the church in the New. Confirming this understanding of Scripture in our thinking, however, is quite another matter. George W. Peters points out:

> The study of Christian missions has been for centuries a separate and distinct discipline not usually considered to be material for the theologian or the pastor. In fact most theologians and pastors passed by the courses in missions and ignored mission literature and matters of mission organization. The church, the pastor and the theologian often remained detached if not aloof from mission studies and mission movements.[1]

Even today we tend to disassociate our study of theology from that of missions. The theology we inherited from the Reformation strongly established the *majesty* of God but sadly neglected His *mission.* Peter observes that Reformation Protestant theology:

> . . . has bypassed the biblical concept of *the living God,* the God of purpose, the God of history, action and existential relationships, the God of here and now; the God who presently is working out His plan and program, the God who is an outgoing God, a God of mission"[2]

It is time to establish a new integration of biblical, theological, and missiological studies. We need a holistic understanding of Scripture. Our purpose in this chapter is to summarize, in a series of vignettes, the teaching of the Old Testament about the God of mission.

God's Mission in the Old Testament

Evidence in the Pentateuch

The foundation of God's mission (*Missio Dei*) is laid in the five books of Moses. God's purposes clearly focus on four features.

1. *God predicted Messiah's coming to deal with sin.* After man's fall, the Lord said to the serpent, ". . . I will put enmity between you and the woman, and between your offspring and hers; he will crush your head, and you will strike his heel" (Gen. 3:15). This pristine prediction of Satan's judgment is God's solution to the sin question. Long ago this statement earned the title *protevangelium*, meaning "the first gospel proclamation."[3] God is the author of salvation through His suffering Redeemer who stepped into history at the divinely appointed time (Gal. 4:4). This Redeemer destroyed Satan and his works (John 16:11; 1 John 3:8). The promise of the Messiah was universal in scope. Peters concludes:

> The universality of the protevangelium is basic to Old Testament revelation. It is the soteriological leitmotif (dominant, unifying, all-inclusive thrust and intent) and hermeneutical principle governing Old Testament interpretation. It cannot be revoked or modified, for it rests on the unconditional "I will" of the eternal God in whom there is no variableness. It becomes the guiding star throughout history and prophecy of the Old Testament until it finds its fulfillment in Christ, the seed of the woman.[4]

The God-Satan confrontation in the Garden of Eden was the first step of a progressive revelation that leads to the cross.

2. *God provided for restored fellowship for man.* The fall of man resulted in spiritual and physical death (Gen. 2:17). For those who die in their sin, it terminates in the second death (Rev. 20:14). Because of Adam's sin, "death came to all men, because all sinned" (Rom. 5:12). As Lewis Sperry Chafer explains, "The initial, single sin of Adam is the cause, or occasion, for the penalty of death in all its forms falling universally upon all members of the human race."[5] Who can measure the enormity of the fall?

God's provision of animal skins to cover the naked bodies of our first parents is a picture of His supply of Christ's righteousness for the believing sinner. The Genesis account is straightforward: "The Lord God made garments of skin for Adam and his wife and clothed them" (Gen. 3:21). Isaiah gives us an example of a garment provided by God. "For he has clothed me with garments of salvation and arrayed me in a robe of righteousness . . ." (Isa. 61:10).

Paul went beyond the picture to the reality when he wrote, "It is because of him that you are in Christ Jesus, who has become for us wisdom from God—that is, *righteousness,* holiness and redemption" (1 Cor. 1:30). By His obedience unto death, He met the demands of God's justice (2 Cor. 5:21; Rom. 1:17). The whole sacrificial system of the Old Testament foreshadows Christ in His finished work.

3. *God promised universal blessing in the Abrahamic Covenant* (Gen. 12:1-3). This covenant is the foundation of all covenants Jehovah made with His people. Further confirmation and features of the covenant make clear Jehovah's unconditional promises not only to Israel but to the nations (Gen. 13:14-17; 15:4-21; 17:4-16; 22:15-18). The only condition to the execution of the covenant was Abraham's willingness to leave his country and go to the promised land (Gen. 12:1, 4). Abram believed God, "and he credited it to him as righteousness" (Gen. 15:6; Rom. 4:3; Gal. 3:6).

The Abrahamic Covenant is a missionary text par excellence, and it sets the stage for the missionary character of the entire Bible. After the "I will" promises (Gen. 12:1-3a), Jehovah boldly stated the universal promise of the Covenant. Walter C. Kaiser, Jr. points out that "the writer of Genesis adds a purpose clause, while shifting the tense of the verb, so that a fuller statement of his purpose can be given. Now it was *'so that* in you all the families of the earth might be blessed.' "[6]

Kaiser continues:

> The message and its content, in fact the whole purpose of God, was that He would make a nation, give them a "name," bless them *so that* they might be light to the nations and thereby be a blessing to all the nations . . . . The mission has not changed in our own day. Abraham and Israel were not intended to be passive transmitters of the "seed" any more than we are to be passive.[7]

In the same vein, Don Richardson in his intriguing book, *Eternity in Their Hearts,* states:

> The Abrahamic Covenant . . . is the very spinal column of the Bible. Bible teaching which is unrelated to that spinal column has a certain spinelessness about it . . . . And it will tend to leave Christians less than motivated to pass on the blessings they have received, not merely to their own kind of people, but to *all* peoples on the earth.[8]

The Abrahamic covenant provides a continuum between the Old and New Testaments. Our God is a missionary God, and His missionary purposes do not change with time as we shall see from Paul's letter to the Galatians.

In his thoroughgoing discussion of the Abrahamic Covenant, George N.H. Peters discusses thirteen promises Jehovah made to Abram.[9] Our interest is in the last of these, His guarantee of universal blessing on the nations. Genesis 12:3 concludes, "and all peoples on earth will be blessed through you." This promise was reaffirmed to Abram (Gen. 18:18; 22:18) and repeated to Jacob (Gen. 28:14). The apostle Paul clarified it in his argument about law observance and faith. Let us listen to him reason with the Galatian believers.

> Understand, then, that those who believe are children of Abraham. The Scripture foresaw that God would justify the Gentiles by faith, and announced the gospel in advance to Abraham: "All nations will

be blessed through you." So those who have faith are blessed along with Abraham, the man of faith (Gal. 3:7-9).

What good news! God is calling out from the Gentiles a people for His name (Acts 15:14). And to think that this good news was preached before (*proeueggelisato*) to Abraham! This Greek word appears only here in the New Testament. The good news in the Abrahamic Covenant for the Gentiles is that Jehovah includes them in His redemptive plan. Robert G. Gromacki reminds us:

> Just as all Jews do not qualify to be known as the children of Abraham (3:7), so all nations will not automatically receive the universal blessings of the covenant. There is a difference between provision and appropriation. The blessing only comes to "they which be of faith."[10]

4. *God purposed to proclaim His name in all the earth.* The God of the Bible is a missionary God. Further evidence is given in the plagues in Egypt. After the sixth plague, Jehovah addressed Pharaoh through Moses, "But I have raised you up for this very purpose, that I might show you my power and that my name might be proclaimed in all the earth" (Ex. 9:16). Even though the word "earth" (*erets*) in this context can be translated "land," meaning Egypt, we learn from Romans 9:17, where Paul quoted the verse, that it has universal meaning. Paul, arguing for God's purpose in election (Rom. 9:10), said in verse 17: "For the Scripture says to Pharaoh: 'I raised you up for this very purpose, that I might display my power in you and that my name might be proclaimed *in all the earth (en pase te ge).*'" This same word translated "earth" appears in Acts 1:8, ". . . unto the uttermost part of the earth" (KJV). Jehovah's purpose for the universal proclamation of His name is clear. As Keil and Delitzsch observe:

> The report of this glorious manifestation of Jehovah spread at once among all the surrounding nations . . . , and travelled not only to the Arabians, but to the Greeks and Romans also, and eventually with the Gospel of Christ to all the nations of the earth . . . .[11]

The Pentateuch, then, contains predictions about Messiah's coming (Gen. 3:15) and about God's provision of righteousness through blood sacrifice (Gen. 3:21; 4:3-5). Jehovah promised universal blessing for Gentiles in the Abrahamic Covenant (Gen. 12:3; Gal. 3:8). His sovereign purpose is that His name "might be proclaimed in all the earth" (Ex. 9:16; Rom. 9:17).

Evidence in the historical books
After the conquest of the land, Israel slowly took her place among the nations. Her insistence on having a king like the other nations (1 Sam. 8:6-9) led to a checkered history of good and evil kings, a divided kingdom, and eventual dispersion to Assyria and Babylon. Throughout this time Jehovah used the Jews, even in division and weakness, as a witness to the true and living God.

1. *God displayed His power to the nations through Israel.* After crossing the Jordan, Joshua set up the twelve stones taken from the riverbed as a testimony to future generations. These stones had special significance for both Israel and the nations. Joshua explained:

> For the LORD your God dried up the Jordan before you until you had crossed over. The LORD your God did to the Jordan just what he had done to the Red Sea when he dried it up before us until we had crossed over. He did this so that all the peoples of the earth might know that the hand of the LORD is powerful and so that you might always fear the LORD your God (Josh. 4:23-24).

The biblical writers frequently mention Israel's Red Sea experience (Neh. 9:9; Ps. 106:7-9, 22; 136:13, 15; Jer. 49:21; Acts 7:36; Heb. 11:29). The psalmist says that even though Israel rebelled at the Red Sea, "Yet he saved them for his name's sake, to make his mighty power known" (Ps. 106:8). The Red Sea event became a touchstone for Israel in recalling Jehovah's mighty dealings with her.

But the display of God's power at the Red Sea was not only for Israel's benefit. "He did this," says Joshua, "so that all the peoples of the earth might know that the hand of the LORD is powerful . . ." (Josh. 4:24). The immediate impact on the people of the land was evident. Rahab said to the spies:

> We have heard how the LORD dried up the water of the Red Sea for you when you came out of Egypt . . . . When we heard of it, our hearts sank and everyone's courage failed because of you, for the LORD your God is God in heaven above and on the earth below (Josh. 2:10-11).

When the kings in the land heard that Jehovah brought His people dry shod across the Jordan, "their hearts sank and they no longer had the courage to face the Israelites" (Josh. 5:1). Even when the Gibeonites deceived Joshua, they displayed genuine awe at the power of Jehovah. They answered Joshua, "Your servants have come from a very distant country *because of the fame of the LORD your God.* For we have heard reports of him: all that he did in Egypt . . ." (Josh. 9:9). Looking beyond his own time, Joshua viewed the stones as a memorial for future generations as well. He said to the people, "In the future when your descendants ask their fathers, 'What do these stones mean?' tell them, 'Israel crossed the Jordan on dry ground'" (Josh. 4:21-22). The true and living God etched the reality of His power on the minds of earth's peoples.

2. *Jehovah preserved His people from destruction.* The words "Kept by the power of God," stand out boldly over Israel's history from Abraham to the present. Hated by the nations and decimated by repeated bloodbaths, Israel seemed doomed to extinction. But she is God's people. Her judges, prophets, kings, priests, and governors came to her rescue. And what would the Jews have done without Esther? Mordecai pleaded, "And who knoweth whether thou art come to the kingdom for such a time as this" (Esth. 4:14 KJV)?

One event in Israel's early history serves as a testimony to Jehovah's preservation of His people. The scene was in the Valley of Elah, some eleven miles southwest of Jerusalem. David was staring up into the eyes of Goliath, a bona fide heavyweight from the Philistine ranks (1 Sam. 17:4-7). After a verbal attack by the champion, David fired back:

> This day the Lord will hand you over to me, and I'll strike you down and cut off your head. Today I will give the carcasses of the Philistine army to the birds of the air and beasts of the earth, and the whole world will know that there is a God in Israel. All those gathered here will know that it is not by sword or spear that the LORD saves; for the battle is the Lord's and he will give all of you into our hands (1 Sam. 17:46-47).

This was no local skirmish. David put Jehovah's reputation right on the line before "the whole world." The rest is history. Through this event the world's peoples have an eternal testimony of Jehovah's power to preserve His people. Because he kept them safe, the channel remained open for the coming of Messiah.

3. *Jehovah welcomed the worship of proselytes.* These proselytes were from among the peoples of the earth. They sought out the living God, much like the God-fearers of the New Testament times. In his prayer of dedication, Solomon called these proselytes "the foreigner" (1 Kings 8:41). Solomon prayed:

> As for the foreigner who does not belong to your people Israel but has come from a distant land because of your name . . . when he comes and prays toward this temple, then hear from heaven, your dwelling place, and do whatever the foreigner asks of you, so that all the peoples of the earth may know your name and fear you, as do your own people Israel, and may know that this house I have built bears your Name (1 Kings 8:41-43).

The "peoples of the earth" in this passage are in contrast to "your own people of Israel." The Hebrew word for "people" (*'am*) has a more particular sense than the word "Gentiles" or "nations" (*goim*), though they both refer to those outside of God's covenant people. Solomon views "the peoples of the earth" in their infinite variety, asking Jehovah that they may know His name and fear Him. He closed his prayer by saying, ". . . so that all the peoples of the earth may know that the Lord is God and that there is no other" (1 Kings 8:60).

We seldom think of the missionary impact of the temple on the Gentile world. However, Solomon clearly requested Jehovah to hear and respond when the foreigner "comes and prays toward this temple" (1 Kings 8:42). Peters comments:

> We may seriously question whether Solomon realized the full implication of his prayer. Nevertheless, the Holy Spirit directed him to include the stranger in his prayer and to point out the missionary significance of the temple. The temple was God's monument of His

relationship to the earth and of the accessibility to God by all nations.[12]

In brief, Jehovah constantly demonstrated His power to Israel during her long history. He preserved her from multiplied enemies, and He continues to do so to this very day. Though Israel was not always faithful in her witness (Isa. 43:10), proselytes from among the peoples of the earth did come to worship Jehovah.

Evidence in the Poetic Books

These books, Job, Psalms, Proverbs, Ecclesiastes, and Song of Solomon, are also known as the wisdom literature of the Old Testament. Except for Job, these books were written when Israel was in her glory. David and Solomon figure heavily in their authorship.

In the midst of suffering, Job rejoiced in the hope of redemption and resurrection. He exclaimed:

I know that my Redeemer lives, and that in the end he will stand upon the earth. And after my skin has been destroyed, yet in my flesh I will see God; I myself will see him with my own eyes—I, and not another. How my heart yearns within me! (Job 19:25).

The Messanic Psalms provide distinct evidence of Jehovah's purposes to redeem and to reign. Messiah's two advents are the major themes of the Messianic Psalms.

1. *Messiah came first as Savior.* Psalm 22 describes the suffering Savior. Death by crucifixion is depicted. Reading the Gospel accounts, especially Matthew chapter 27, leave no doubt that David was describing Messiah's death. David spoke also of Messiah's resurrection (Ps. 16:9-10). Peter cited this passage in his Pentecost sermon (Acts 2:25-28).

2. *Messiah will return as Sovereign.* Reference to Christ's future universal reign is a dominant theme of the Messanic Psalms. Jehovah said to the Son, "Ask of me, and I will make the nations your inheritance, the needs of the earth your possession. You will rule them with an iron scepter; you will dash them to pieces like pottery" (Ps. 2:8-9). Psalm 72 relates Solomon's prayer for a righteous, peaceful, and prosperous reign. Fulfillment of his prayer, of course, can only come through the coming King, Jesus Christ.

Many other glimpses of Messiah appear in the Psalms (See Psalms 40:7-8; 41:9; 45:6; 69:9, 21; 109:8; 110:1, 4; and 118:22, 26).

Nor do the Psalms leave us without a call to witness. We read:

Declare his glory among the nations, his marvelous deeds among all peoples . . . . Say among the nations, "The Lord reigns." The world is firmly established, it cannot be moved; he will judge the peoples with equity" (Ps. 96:3, 10).

Evidence in the Prophetic Books

As we look at this extensive body of prophetic teaching, we will first highlight the lives of two of the prophets. Then we will let Isaiah help us further define the missionary thrust of the Old Testament.

Most of the prophets were "home missionaries" among their own people. They served in both Judah and Israel and spoke out under both good and evil rulers. Measured by human standards, they did not experience outstanding success. There is no evidence, for example, that *anyone* listened to Jeremiah. Two of the prophets were cross-cultural communicators—Jonah and Daniel—and we will look at them more closely.

1. *Jonah was at best a reluctant missionary.* Jehovah did accomplish through Jonah his goal of bringing Nineveh to repentance. However, Jonah was quite unhappy about the response to his preaching. Apparently he had not heard of the importance of empathetic identification with one's hearers!

Actually, Jonah's book is a historical account of his ministry in Nineveh. How does the book further our understanding of the God-mission? Leon J. Wood believed "there was a need for people to know that God has a real interest in Gentiles of the day." He continued:

> God had chosen Israel as a special people for Himself centuries earlier and thus had segregated His word for a time, but this was not because of a desire to forget the nations of the world at large. In fact it was to the end of making possible a gospel message that might be extended to all nations in due time. In the Book of Jonah God was showing that He maintained His interest in Gentiles even while He was working with His own people to this end.[13]

Although Jonah's message won the day, he is hardly a model missionary.

2. *Daniel was a "tentmaker" missionary.* He made his living in a cross-cultural situation using his God-given skill as government administrator. The Babylonian Empire paid the bills while Daniel consistently witnessed in high places for the God of Israel. And because he was going to be there seventy years, he did not have to worry about being transferred out! True he did experience shaky situations such as interpreting Nebuchadnezzar's forgotten dream and the lions' den episode, but they only tended to result in promotions. He even weathered the change of government under the Persians. Daniel was more than eighty years old, and the work kept coming in. Wood stated, "This work could well have been to bring influence on King Cyrus to issue the decree that permitted the Jews to return to their land."[14] No doubt about it—both Babylon and Persia received a consistent witness from Daniel in word and deed.

3. *Isaiah, prince of the prophets, proclaimed a Messianic message.* Wood calls our attention to Isaiah's personal training and gifts when he declares, "It seems fair to say that God told him more regarding the Messiah than He did to any other man in the Old Testament."[15] New Testament writers directly quote Isaiah twenty-one times. Two of his prophetic statements are particularly striking, and they are both "servant" passages.

First, Isaiah describes the character of Jehovah's servant (Isa. 42:1-7). Matthew quoted the first part of this prophecy (Matt. 12:17-21; Isa. 42:1-

4). This humble, suffering Servant "will bring justice to the *nations"* (*goim*) (42:1). Again, Jehovah will make Him "to be a covenant for the people and a light for the *Gentiles"* (42:6). In both of these passages the *goim* are in view. Robert B. Girdlestone informs us that *goi*, generally used in the plural, is the only word translated either "Gentile" or "heathen" in the Old Testament.[16] Referring to the passages before us, Girdlestone continues:

> The *goim* were to seek after the Messiah, the son of Jesse (Isa. 11:10); God's Chosen One was to minister judgment to them (Isa. 42:1); He was to be not only a covenant to the *people* (of Israel), but also a light to the *goim* (42:6), and a salvation to the ends of the earth (49:6).[17]

As a light to the Gentiles, Messiah's work was "to open the eyes that are blind, to free captives from prison and to release from the dungeon those who sit in darkness" (Isa. 42:7). Jehovah's provision for the Gentiles is evident. Messiah will bring the light of salvation to *all* men. Christ is the light of the world. "Whoever follows me," Jesus said, "will never walk in darkness, but will have the light of life" (John 8:12). Appropriating the light is man's responsibility.

Paul remembered another of Isaiah's statements when he was opposed by the Jews in Pisidian Antioch. The Jews caused a near riot and did all they could to destroy Paul's ministry (Acts 13:45). As a result, Paul and Barnabas turned to the Gentiles, saying, "For this is what the Lord has commanded us: 'I have made you a light for the Gentiles, that you may bring salvation to the ends of the earth'" (Acts 13:47). When Paul's life was threatened, God gave him the prophecy from Isaiah 49:6. The Jews knew this passage as well as Paul did. Messiah would minister to the Jewish nation, but He would also be a "light for the Gentiles." And this prophecy was being fulfilled before their eyes! The Gentiles rejoiced in Paul's message, "and all who were appointed for eternal life believed" (Acts 13:48).

Jehovah revealed His purpose for Israel to be His witnesses through Isaiah. In a passage in which Jehovah argues for His exclusive position as Savior, He challenges Israel, "You are my witnesses . . . and my servant whom I have chosen (Isa. 43:10). This statement was repeated in Isaiah 43:12. This was Israel's call to witness. H.C. Leupold summarizes the passage as follows:

> Israel is not to be a mighty worldly power dominating other nations and exercising world-empire. She is to be witness to what God has done for her, witness by her very existence and witness by the testimony that she can bear orally. By thus witnessing she fulfills her calling of being God's "servant," whom he has chosen.[18]

Jehovah's universal concern and provision for *all* men are prominent upon the pages of the Old Testament. From the first prophecy of Messiah's coming (Gen. 3:15) through the Abrahamic Covenant (Gen. 12:1-3) and to the last word of the prophets, the message is clear, "Messiah is coming!" This is evident in the following chart.

FIGURE 7

LAW	HISTORY	POETRY	PROPHETS
PREDICTION Gen. 3:15	POWER OF GOD Josh. 4:22-24	MESSIAH AS SAVIOR Psalm 22	MEN Jonah Daniel
PROVISION Gen. 3:21	PRESERVATION BY GOD 1 Sam. 17:45-47	MESSIAH AS SOVEREIGN Psalm 2	MESSAGE Isa. 42:1-7 Matt. 12:17-21 Isa. 49:6 Acts 13:44-49 Isa. 45:20-22
PROMISE: ABRAHAMIC COVENANT Gen. 12:1-3 Gal. 3:6-9	PROSELYTES 1 Kings 8:41-43 8:59-60	MESSIANIC Psalms 8, 16, 22, 22-24 40, 41, etc.	CALL TO WITNESS Isa. 43:10-12 44:8
PROCLAMATION Ex. 9:14-16 Rom. 9:17		CALL TO WITNESS Ps. 96:3, 10	
MESSIAH IS COMING!!!			

Preparation—Old Testament

Wrap-Up

The purpose of this chapter has been to demonstrate from the Old Testament that the Bible is a missionary book. Here are some concluding observations.

• The Old Testament proclaims a *Messianic* message. All other revelation bends to this central theme. Jehovah will send Messiah to crush Satan (Gen. 3:15) and to be light to the Gentiles (Isa. 42:6-7; 49:6).

• The Old Testament presents a *universal* message. Jehovah provided for Gentile blessing in the Abrahamic Covenant (Gen. 12:1-3; Gal. 3:8). God's concern for the nations is evident throughout the Old Testament. History shows that the gospel can be understod in any language.

• The Old Testament witnesses to *the true and living God*. Jehovah constantly warned His people against false Gods (Exod. 20:1-7). He said, "Before me no God was formed, nor will there be one after me. I, even I, am the Lord, and apart from me there is no Savior (Isa. 43:10-11).

• Throughout the Old Testament *Israel* was Jehovah's chosen witness among the nations (Isa. 43:10, 12).

Notes to Chapter 3

1. George W. Peters, *A Biblical Theology of Missions* (Chicago: Moody Press, 1972), p. 25.
2. Ibid., p. 26.
3. H.C. Leupold, *Exposition of Genesis* (Grand Rapids: Baker Book House, 1975), 1:164.
4. Peters, *A Biblical Theology of Missions,* p. 86.
5. Lewis Sperry Chafer, *Systematic Theology* (Dallas: Dallas Seminary Press, 1948), 7:113.
6. Walter C. Kaiser, Jr., "Israel's Missionary Call," *Perspectives on the World Christian Movement,* ed. Ralph D. Winter and Steven C. Hawthorne (Pasadena, CA: William Carey Library, 1981), pp. 27-28.
7. Ibid., p. 28.
8. Don Richardson, *Eternity in Their Hearts* (Ventura, CA: Regal Books, 1981), p. 129. For further discussion of "The Abraham factor" see chapter Four, "The Four-Thousand-Year Connection."
9. George N.H. Peters, *The Theocratic Kingdom* (Grand Rapids: Kregel Publications, 1978), 1:293-94.
10. Robert G. Gromacki, *Stand Fast in Liberty: An Exposition of Galatians* (Grand Rapids: Baker Book House, 1979), pp. 87-88.
11. C.F. Keil and F. Delitzsch, *Biblical Commentary on the Old Testament,* 25 vols. (Grand Rapids: Eerdmans, 1968), 1:490-91.
12. Peters, *A Biblical Theology of Missions,* p. 117.
13. Leon J. Wood, *The Prophets of Israel* (Grand Rapids: Baker Book House, 1979), p. 293.
14. Ibid., p. 347.
15. Ibid., p. 303.
16. Robert B. Girdlestone, *Synonyms of the Old Testament: Their Bearing on Christian Doctrine* (Grand Rapids: Eerdmans, 1956), p. 256.
17. Ibid., pp. 256-57.
18. H.C. Leupold, *Exposition of Isaiah* (Grand Rapids: Baker Book House, 1971), 2:84.

The Bible: A Missionary Book
The New Testament

4

The New Testament is more familiar territory for most Christians than the Old Testament. We must remember that Scripture *in its entirety* records God's purpose to make known universally Christ's finished work. The Old Testament *prepares* the way for Messiah's coming, while the New Testament *presents* Messiah as He comes to do the Father's will. We will summarize the missionary purpose of the New Testament as demonstrated in the Gospels, the Book of Acts, the epistles, and the Book of Revelation. In conclusion we will review the cultural and commission mandates and our relation to them.

God's Mission in the New Testament

Evidence in the Gospels

Christ's own *mission* comes immediately to mind, when we think of the Gospels. He addressed His disciples about servanthood, reminding them that whoever wants to be first must be a servant of all. He concluded, "For even the Son of Man did not come to be served, but to serve, and to give his life as a ransom for many" (Mark 10:45; see Matt. 20:28). Jesus said to Zacchaeus, "Today salvation has come to this house, because this man, too, is a son of Abraham. For the Son of Man came to seek and to save what was lost" (Luke 19:9-10). In His discourse on the bread of life, Jesus said, "For I have come down from heaven not to do my will but to do the will of him who sent me" (John 6:38). The long-awaited Savior was among men. There is no mistaking it—Christ came to do the Father's will, and that will involved the supreme act of ministry (Ps. 40:7-8).

After his resurrection, Christ *commissioned* His disciples to carry on the God-mission (Matt. 28:19-20; Mark 16:15; Luke 24:44-49; John 20:21). Harry R. Boer discussed the relation of the Great Commission to the Church's witness as follows:

> The kerugmatic activity of the Church is an expression of the law that governs the discharge of her task in the world. *This law is the Great Commission.* At Pentecost this law went into effect. The Great Commission is a mandate to *witness,* and it is a mandate to witness *universally.*[1]

Each of the Gospel writers makes a unique contribution to stating the commission left by Christ. Because the commission account of Matthew

28:19-20 is the best known, we will stop for a more careful look. After declaring the authority he received from the Father, Christ said:

> Therefore go and make disciples of all nations, baptizing them in the name of the Father and of the Son and of the Holy Spirit, and teaching them to obey everything I have commanded you. And surely I will be with you always, to the very end.

The Commission contains the command, "make disciples," and is supported by three participles, "going," "baptizing," and "teaching."

The aorist tense of the first participle, (*poreuthentes*), translated "go," gives it the sense of a command. J.B. Phillips translates, "You, then, are *to go* and make disciples . . . ." Kenneth S. Wuest translates quite literally, "*Having gone* on your way therefore . . . ." The imperative itself, "make disciples" (*mateteusate*), means to win converts to Christ. The word occurs again in Acts 14:21, "and won disciples" (*matheteusantes*), where it has the same meaning of winning people to Christ. We discussed the significance of the term in chapter one. "Baptizing them" (*baptizontes*), identifies the believers with the community of converts and with Christ. "Teaching them" (*didaskontes*), is the ongoing ministry of strengthening the believers. (See also Acts 14:22.)

Present in this passage, then, are these four features: extension (going), conversion (make disciples), identification (baptizing), and instruction (teaching). These features were evident in the work of the early church whenever they took the gospel to their world.

The Gospel writers leave no doubt about Christ's mission and the commission He left for us. *Obedience* to that commission is the key to world evangelism.

Evidence in the Book of Acts

In the scheme of progressive revelation, Acts records the beginning and early history of the church. The major contribution of the book is the transitional picture it presents of the setting aside of Israel and the introduction of God's purpose through the church today. It shows the change from the dispensation of law to that of grace, and the progress in making known God's purposes to both Israel and the church. The book records the continuation of Christ's works and words, now to be accomplished through the apostles (Acts 1:1-2).

The central theme of the Book of Acts is found in the phrase, ". . . you will be my witnesses . . ." (1:8). Viewing this verse demographically rather than geographically, the book depicts a progressive witness to the Jews and Gentiles. The major divisions are:

- Witnessing to the Jews—Acts 1:1-8:3
- Witnessing to the Jews and Gentiles—Acts 8:4-12:25
- Witnessing to the Gentiles—Acts 13:1-28:31

I believe the greatest event recorded in Acts is the birth of the church at Pentecost. The waiting company of believers were baptized into the church, the body of Christ (Acts 2:1-4). Christ had promised He would build His church (Matt. 16:18). After His resurrection, He instructed the disciples: "Do not leave Jerusalem, but wait for the gift my Father promised, which you have heard me speak about. For John baptized with water, but in a few days you will be baptized with the Holy Spirit" (Acts 1:4-5; Luke 24:49; 1 Cor. 12:13). The Great Commission could never have been carried out without Pentecost. Peters states:

> The great dividing line in the lives of the twelve is Pentecost, the watershed of evangelical missions. Here New Testament missions began a progressive course of realization. Therefore, the missionary significance of Pentecost is beyond human estimation.[2]

Luke traces in Acts the ministries of Philip (Acts 8:5-40), Peter (9:32-11:18), and Paul (13:1-28:31). Paul's work dominates the record, for he focused his primary attention on the Gentiles. As time went on both believers and churches multiplied, and the stage was set for an Empire-wide witness.

Evidence in the Epistles

Paul wrote these letters to churches founded by his own effort and that of his team. Apparently the believers in Colosse had not seen him personally (Col. 2:1). He knew many of these churches intimately. He prayed for them, wept over them, visited them, and wrote to them. He said to the Thessalonians, "We loved you so much that we were delighted to share with you not only the gospel of God but our lives as well, because you had become so dear to us" (1 Thess. 2:8). The church in Philippi sent him financial support. We must read the epistles with an understanding of their place in history. Timothy and Titus served with Paul on the missionary team. Paul sent them to minister to the churches and then recalled them for other tasks.

The epistles, both Paul's and those of other authors, set forth and clarify the position, order, privileges, and duties of the churches and individuals addressed. The Spirit of God designed these letters to bring repentance and faith to the sinner and spiritual maturity to the saint.

The New Testament epistles burst with new light. God now carries forward His purpose to reach a lost world through a new people—the church. The barrier is broken down between Jew and Gentile. "His purpose," states Paul, "was to create in himself one new man out of the two, thus making peace, and in this one body to reconcile both of them to God through the cross, by which he put to death their hostility" (Eph. 2:15-16). The mystery of Christ now revealed by the Spirit is "that through the gospel the Gentiles are heirs together with Israel, members together of one body, and sharers together in the promise in Christ Jesus" (Eph. 3:6)

The church in Thessalonica put reality into this oneness and demonstrated the seriousness with which its members advanced the gospel. Paul commended them for their *example* to other churches: "And so you became a model to all the believers in Macedonia and Achaia" (1 Thess. 1:7).

This was the only church Paul called a "model" (*tupos*). They led the way so that others could follow.

Paul also commended them for the clear *evidence* of their faith. He continued, "The Lord's message rang out from you not only in Macedonia and Achaia—your faith has become known everywhere" (1 Thess. 1:8). In view of the Jewish-led riot when Paul was in Thessalonica, it is doubly amazing to see the boldness with which they witnessed throughout the whole region (Acts 17:5-9).

Paul commended them as well for the *expression* of their faith. He concluded, "They tell how you turned to God from idols to serve the living and true God, and to wait for his Son from heaven, whom he raised from the dead . . ." (1 Thess. 1:9-10). They forsook their pagan past in order to serve God and to wait for His Son to return. Every church across the Roman Empire could learn some lessons from the believers in Thessalonica. And their example is not lost on us today.

Evidence in the Book of Revelation

The Gospels reveal Christ's *mission* (Mark 10:45) and our *commission* (Matt. 28:19-20). The Book of Acts records the *beginning* of the early church; the epistles depict the *development* of the first-century church. Taking us to the end of the first century, the Book of Revelation relates the *testimony* of seven churches in the province of Asia. Through these testimonies, we get a glimpse of the strengths and weaknesses of the churches some two generations after Pentecost.

A great body of biblical literature today views these seven churches and their respective letters as pictures of the progress of church history from the first century to the present. However, it is doubtful that this was the primary purpose of the Spirit of God in penning these messages through John. Leon Morris states:

> It seems much more probable that the letters are letters to real churches, all the more so since each of the messages has relevance to what we know of conditions in the city named. John has addressed himself to the needs of the little churches but has dealt with topics which have relevance to God's people at all times and all places.[3]

These churches were selected from a number of churches in the province of Asia at the time. Geographically they lay along an arc made by the main trade roads of the day. The letters follow a common sevenfold format, each ending with the exhortation, "He who has an ear, let him hear what the Spirit says to the churches" (Rev. 2:7, 11, 17, 29; 3:6, 13, 22). Obviously each church needed a particular message, yet these addresses met the needs of other churches as well. The Spirit talks to the "churches." John F. Walvoord observes:

> The selection of the churches was . . . governed by the fact that each church was in some way normative and illustrated conditions common in local churches at that time as well as throughout later history . . . . Along with the messages to the churches were

exhortations which are personal in character constituting instruction and warning to the individual Christian."[4]

By the end of the first century, churches were flourishing throughout the Roman Empire. They needed these closing words from the venerated apostle John. A great deal had happened since the birth of the church at Pentecost. The remainder of the New Testament records progressive revelation about the church, the body of Christ, as well as about local church government and order. Through the scattered church and the ministry of the apostles, the gospel message reached both Jew and Gentile, both city and village. God's mission in the world was alive and well. Consult the following summary chart.

FIGURE 8

GOSPELS	ACTS	EPISTLES	REVELATION
CHRIST'S MISSION Luke 19:10 Mark 10:45 John 6:38	BEGINNING OF EARLY CHURCH Acts 1:8	DEVELOPMENT OF EARLY CHURCH	TESTIMONY OF EARLY CHURCH Ch. 2-3
	Witness to Jews Ch. 1-7	Pauline Epistles Churches Individuals	"I know thy works. . . ."
OUR COMMISSION Matt, 28:18-20 Mark 16:15 Luke 24:44-48 John 20:21	Witness to Jews and Gentiles Ch. 8-12	GENERAL EPISTLES	SUMMARY TIME PERIOD
	Witness to Gentiles Ch. 13-28		PROGRESSION
MESSIAH HAS COME			

Presentation—New Testament

We have traced the biblical record as it relates to God's mission from the Garden of Eden to the end of the first century A.D. As we observed in chapter one, God's missionary purposes are carried out in a multiplex mosaic of cultural milieus. But a lingering question is being asked today: "Is that *all* there is to God's missionary purposes? What about a cultural mandate? Does not "mission" constitute even more than evangelizing, teaching believers, and planting churches? We will deal with these questions before pursuing our study further.

God's Mission and the Cultural Mandate

The First Mandate
This mandate is usually spoken of as the cultural mandate. God commanded Adam, "Be fruitful and increase in number; fill the earth and subdue it. Rule over the fish of the seas and the birds of the air and over

every living creature that moves on the ground" (Gen. 1:18). After God formed man from the dust of the ground, He "put him in the Garden of Eden to work it and take care of it" (Gen.2:15). After the flood, God repeated the mandate to Noah (Gen. 9:1, 7). In short, the first mandate was God's command to man to multiply, subdue, dominate, cultivate, and preserve. It relates to man in his varied cultural and societal relationships including family, occupation, environment, and all interpersonal relationships common to the human condition.

Stephen R. Spencer observes that this first mandate: (1) is addressed to man *as man,* (2) is oriented toward the created order, (3) manifests God's character in the development of His created order, (4) becomes a preservative in a fallen world, and (5) is nonredemptive.[5]

The Second Mandate

This mandate is sometimes referred to as the Great Commission or evangelistic mandate. It is found in the Great Commission passages in the Gospels and Acts (Matt. 28:19-20; Mark 16:15; Luke 24:44-49; John 20:21; Acts 1:8), and it is demonstrated in the Pauline model of missions (Acts 14:21-23). The first mandate relates to man as man; the second relates to believers as members of the body of Christ. The first mandate deals with societal relationships; the second mandate: (1) is addressed to members of the kingdom of God, (2) is fulfilled by the proclamation of the "good news" of Christ's person and work, (3) is thus oriented toward individuals, not the created order, (4) is fulfilled by the believer in obedience to God's command, and (5) is redemptive.[6] Figure 9 illustrates the relationships and the distinctives of the mandates.

FIGURE 9
The Two Mandates

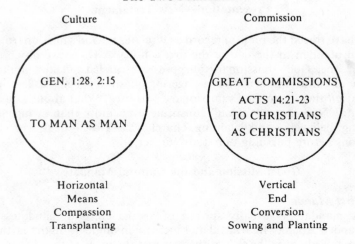

Culture

Commission

GEN. 1:28, 2:15

TO MAN AS MAN

GREAT COMMISSIONS
ACTS 14:21-23
TO CHRISTIANS
AS CHRISTIANS

Horizontal
Means
Compassion
Transplanting

Vertical
End
Conversion
Sowing and Planting

Our Relationship to the Two Mandates

The believer does have a responsibility to both mandates. Jesus told His disciples that they were both "salt" and "light" (Matt. 5:13-16). By his very presence in society the believer is a positive preservative for right in the moral order. He dispels darkness in a fallen world. Jesus concludes, "In the same way, let your light shine before men, that they may see your good deeds and praise your Father in heaven" (Matt. 5:16). The believer is "created in Christ Jesus to do good works, which God prepared in advance for us to do" (Eph. 2:10). Paul encourages the believer not to become weary in doing good. "Therefore," he concludes, "as we have opportunity, let us do good to all people, especially to those who belong to the family of believers" (Gal. 6:10). Both James and John remind believers to care for one another (James 2:14-17; 1 John 3:17-19).

The question before us does not demand an either/or answer. Rather, it is a question of priority. While the second mandate is *missions* in the biblical sense, the first mandate cannot be ignored. Donn W. Ketcham, missionary-surgeon in Bangladesh says:

It seems, then, that the responsibility for meeting the societal needs of man is *not* the responsibility of the *church*. *Members* of the church share this responsibility with the rest of mankind because they are part of mankind but not because they are part of the church. Would it not be a good synthesis of the Christian's dual responsibility to participate in the solution to the societal needs of man in such a way the mandate of the church can be carried out with more facility?[7]

In brief, the first mandate is a *corollary* to the church's mission, but it is not an *integral* part of it.

Wrap-Up

The New Testament is a missionary book. Revelation about the church's mission permeates its pages. We summarize some of the pertinent characteristics of New Testament missions.

• The New Testament leaves us with a commission. From the beginning of time, God has not been without a witness. Christ's mandate to the church is crystal clear; it is not to be decided by congregational vote (Matt. 28:19-20; Mark 16:15; Luke 24:44-49; John 20:21; Acts 1:8).

• The church was born on the Day of Pentecost by Spirit baptism (Acts 1:4-5; 2:1-4). New Testament missions also began at Pentecost with Peter's sermon (Acts 2:14-41).

• The New Testament's message has harvest as its goal. It is not enough to search for the sheep; we must find them. We cannot be content with the proclamation of the gospel. The harvest may be meager—a hundredfold, sixtyfold, or thirtyfold—but harvest there will be (Matt. 9:37-38; 13:23; 28:19).

• The New Testament helps us define our priorities. Although believers, as a part of humankind, have valid societal responsibilities to perform good deeds, these duties must not take priority over their mission (Acts 14:21-23). Indeed, meeting societal needs should contribute to carrying out our commission.

Notes to Chapter 4

1. Harry R. Boer, *Pentecost and Missions* (Grand Rapids: Eerdmans, 1961), p. 119.

2. George W. Peters, *A Biblical Theology of Missions* (Chicago: Moody Press, 1972), p. 134.

2. Leon Morris, "The Revelation of St. John," *The Tyndale New Testament Commentaries,* ed. R.V.G. Tasker, 20 vols. (Grand Rapids: Eerdmans 1978) 20:57-58.

4. John F. Walvoord, *The Revelation of Jesus Christ* (Chicago: Moody Press, 1966), p. 51.

5. A written statement by Stephen R. Spencer, fellow faculty member, June 5, 1981, concerning the content and interrelationship of the two mandates.

6. Ibid.

7. Donn W. Ketcham, *The World Hurts!* (Cherry Hill, NJ: Association of Baptists for World Evangelism, 1981), p. 40.

Part 2

Strategic Role of the Home Church

The Church Defined

5

The church, both universal and local, is central to God's purposes today. Inherent in the nature of the church is gospel proclamation and progressive growth. In discussing the goal of evangelism, Edward R. Dayton and David A. Fraser correctly observe:

> Any approach to evangelization that does not deal with the reality of the Church is deficient. Evangelization is a process which grows out of the nature of the church as a redeemed community of people who have been made stewards of the grace of God. While it may not be true that there is no salvation outside the Church, there is no salvation that is unrelated to the Church. Those who share the Good News and those who embrace it are members of one body, fellow participants in a wider solidarity of people who share the same life and Lord.[1]

Because God commissioned the church to carry out His purpose of world evangelization, we must understand biblical teaching about the church. This segment of our study, then, begins with establishing the biblical nature and function of the church. Let us define the church, both universal and local.

• The universal church in its earthly pilgrimage is the spiritually united, called-out, worldwide assembly of all believers whose Head is Jesus Christ. It began at Pentecost by the baptism with the Holy Spirit and continues its God-given mission during successive generations throughout the world. It will be caught up to be with Christ at His coming.

• The local church is an autonomous, organized assembly of baptized believers, together with their elected leaders, who gather for worship, edification, and the practice of the ordinances, and who, functioning as salt and light, go out into their communities to practice good works and to witness to the unbelieving world.

The Church is God's Instrument for World Evangelization

The Greek word *ekklesia* refers to both the universal and the local church. While the term is a compound expression meaning "to call out," it primarily applies to an "assembly." When this word is used in the New

Testament in its technical sense, it designates a Christian assembly of believers such as "the church of the Thessalonians" (1 Thess. 1:1). Robert L. Saucy writes:

> Through use, it became so completely identified with the specific Christian assembly that the term took on that particular meaning itself and could stand for that assembly without being confused with others. The majority of the New Testament references have this technical meaning.[2]

The word *ekklesia* occurs 115 times in the New Testament primarily referring to a local assembly of believers. When used of the universal church, the spiritual unity of believers is in view. As Saucy states, "The *ekklesia* was therefore all those spiritually united in Christ, the Head of the church."[3] In the New Testament *ekklesia* refers only to believers either in the sense of a local assembly of believers or as believers united in Christ in the universal church. The following questions will help us understand the nature and function of the church, the body of Christ, as related to the God-mission (Acts 15:14).

When Did the Church Begin?

The church began at Pentecost when believers were baptized with the Holy Spirit.

Christ predicted the origin of the church when he said to Peter, "And I tell you that you are Peter, and on this rock I will build my church, and the gates of Hades will not overcome it" (Matt. 16:18). When Christ spoke to Peter, the founding of the church was yet future.

When Christ instructed His disciples during His postresurrection ministry, they had not yet been baptized with the Holy Spirit (Luke 24:49; Acts 1:4-5). Jesus commanded His disciples, "Do not leave Jerusalem, but wait for the gift my Father promised, which you have heard me speak about. For John baptized with water, but in a few days you will be baptized with the Holy Spirit" (Acts 1:4-5). At Pentecost the Father's promise was fulfilled.

On the Day of Pentecost the Spirit rested upon each believer. The text states, "All of them were filled with the Holy Spirit . . ." (Acts 2:4). This event fulfilled the Father's promise (Acts 1:5). In the case of Cornelius' household, Peter recalled:

> As I began to speak, the Holy Spirit came on them as he had come on us at the beginning. Then I remembered what the Lord had said, "John baptized with water, but you will be baptized with the Holy Spirit" (Acts 11:15-16).

The "beginning" refers to Pentecost. The book of Acts records the historical account of the church's origin.

Paul explained the doctrinal significance of Pentecost to the Corinthians, "For we were all baptized by one Spirit into one body— whether Jews or Greeks, slave or free—and we were all given the one Spirit to drink" (1 Cor. 12:13). The expression "by one spirit" may be translated "in one Spirit." John the Baptist used the same construction when he said, "I baptize you with (*en*) water . . . . He will baptize you with (*en*) the Holy Spirit" (Matt. 3:11). Saucy comments:

> As believers are placed in the sphere of the Spirit, they are fused into the spiritual body which is identified as the church (Eph. 1:22-23; 5:30; Col. 1:18). Christ, who promised to send the Spirit, is the Baptizer who baptizes His people with the Spirit. The Spirit, however, being a personal Being, actively indwells the members of the church, uniting them together in Himself.[4]

The baptizing work of the Holy Spirit is His new ministry in the New Testament. The church began on the Day of Pentecost.

Who Makes Up the Church?

The universal church is people, both Jews and Gentiles, who are children of God through saving faith in Jesus Christ.

Through His blood Christ destroyed "the dividing wall of hostility" between Jew and Gentile (Eph. 2:13-14). "His purpose," says Paul, "was to create in himself one new man out of the two, thus making peace" (Eph. 2:15). The "new man" is new not simply in time (*neos*) but in quality (*kainos*). Believing Jews remain Jews, and believing Gentiles remain Gentiles—but they are now united in Christ.

Today the remnant of Israel is preserved by believing Jews. Paul reminds us, "So too, at the present time there is a remnant chosen by grace" (Rom. 11:5). Paul speaks of unity in diversity in Galatians 3:28: "There is neither Jew nor Greek, slave nor free, male nor female, for you are all one in Christ Jesus." Robert G. Gromacki states:

> This is positional oneness and equality. In Him there is no spiritual superiority or inferiority. All mundane divisions are eliminated: racial ("Jew of Greek"), social ("bond nor free"), and sexual ("male nor female"). The man is not more accepted in Christ than the woman nor is the Jew more justified than the Gentile. All share the same standing before God.[5]

Through the centuries since Pentecost the gospel has progressively penetrated into the world of men. Although many unreached people groups remain, the universal message of Christ has been "preached among the nations" (1 Tim. 3:16). The church universal is as diverse in its composition as humanity itself.

Several metaphors appear in the New Testament describing the universal church in its unity and diversity. One of these is the figure of the church as a building or temple (1 Cor. 3:11; Eph. 2:20-22). Christ is the foundation (1 Cor. 3:11). The apostles and prophets are foundational as well. The church's foundation is the person and work of Christ. He is the ultimate foundation. The apostles and prophets were God's gift to the first-century church. They received revelation from God, and they taught the truth of that revelation to the churches. They were the means by which Christ was revealed to men.

Christ is also "the chief cornerstone" (Eph. 2:20). J.B. Philipps translates, ". . . the actual foundation-stone being Christ Jesus himself." Peter quoted Isaiah, calling him the "precious cornerstone" (1 Pet. 2:6; Isa. 28:16). The cornerstone gives the building unity, harmony, and design. Christ performs these functions for the church. For, as Paul continues, "In him the whole building is joined together and rises to become a holy temple in the Lord" (Eph. 2:21). The "whole building" relates to the universal church in all its diversity. The picture here is one of ongoing activity and growth. The expression "joined together" (*sunarmologoumene*) is a present passive participle. Each stone is being shaped and formed for a perfect fit in relation to the others. Paul used the word only one other time concerning Christ and the church. Ephesians 4:16 states, "From him the whole body, *joined* and held together by every supporting ligament . . . ."

Continuing growth is inherent in the nature of the church. Paul continued, ". . . and rises to become a holy temple in the Lord" (Eph. 2:21). The word translated "rises" (*auxei*) is in the present tense indicating ongoing growth. This growth will continue until God completes His program with the church. Through worldwide proclamation of the gospel, believers are responsible for the church's growth. Using the figure of the body, Paul said to the Colossians, ". . . from whom the whole body, supported and held together by its ligaments and sinews, *grows* as God causes it to grow" (Col. 2:19). Church growth is not only imperative; it is scriptural!

Growth deals with quality of life as well as increase in numbers. Paul pictures the church as a "*holy* temple in the Lord" (Eph. 2:21). The word for "temple" (*naos*) refers to the temple itself, the Holy Place and the Holy of Holies.[6] The lifestyle of the church, both universal and local, is to be holy, pleasing to God. Paul concluded his word picture of the church by saying that we ". . . are being built together to become a dwelling in which God lives by his Spirit" (Eph. 2:22). Jews and Gentiles are now one "new man" in Christ. The corporate body of believers, as well as each believer's body, is the temple of the Holy Spirit (1 Cor. 3:16-17; 6:19; Eph. 2:21-22). We are God's dwelling place on earth.

The people who make up the universal church include all those who are children of God through faith in Christ's finished work from Pentecost to the present. The "holy temple" will continue to grow until Christ's coming for the church.

What Is the Church's Mission?

The *sine qua non* of the church's mission is to evangelize the unsaved, to edify those who believe, and to establish local churches (Acts 14:21-23). Today God carries His kingdom purposes forward through the church, both universal and local. What is God's purpose in the world today? This question was debated and answered at the Jerusalem council.

The issue before the council was clearly stated by believers from among the Pharisees: "The Gentiles must be circumcised and required to obey the law of Moses" (Acts 15:5). Those gathered at the council listened intently first to Peter and then to Barnabas and Paul. Peter concluded that the

Gentiles were saved by faith alone (Acts 15:6-11). Barnabas and Paul recounted the miracles God performed through them among the Gentiles. James then addressed Peter's testimony directly, "Simon has described to us how God at first showed his concern by taking from the Gentiles a people for his name. The words of the prophets are in agreement with this, as it is written: 'After this I will return...'" (Acts 15:14-16). God's purpose today is to take "from the Gentiles a people for his name." He is also calling out a believing remnant of Jews (Eph. 2:14-16). When this process is complete, Christ will return to restore his program with Israel.

Israel's "hardening in part" is directly related to God's purpose of taking a people from among the Gentiles. Paul explains, "I do not want you to be ignorant of this mystery, brothers, so that you may not be conceited: Israel has experienced a hardening in part until the full number of the Gentiles has come in" (Rom. 11:25).

How is God accomplishing His purpose of "taking out" from among the peoples of the world a people for His name? He is doing it through the members of the body of Christ, the church. Paul modeled the church's mission throughout his ministry (Acts 14:21-23). Today we must continue this ongoing process. Obedience is our only choice. Paul said, "I am obligated both to Greeks and non-Greeks, both to the wise and the foolish" (Rom. 1:14). He exclaimed to the Corinthian church, "Woe to me if I do not preach the gospel!" (1 Cor. 9:16). And woe to us today if we do not give ourselves wholly to the mission Christ left us! The church *is* God's instrument for world evangelization.

We have reviewed together the origin, composition, and mission of the church, the body of Christ. See figure 10.

FIGURE 10

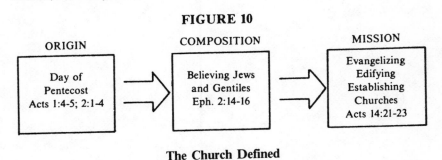

The Church Defined

Wrap-Up

By its very nature, the church is missionary. Our purpose in this chapter was to focus on the church in God's missionary purposes. Some final observations are in order.

● Today God is creating in Himself "one new man" from both Jews and Gentiles (Eph. 2:15).

● God is taking out "from the Gentiles a people for himself" (Acts 15:14).

Together with believing Jews, these redeemed Gentiles make up "the church, which is his body . . ." (Eph. 1:22-23).

• By its very nature the church is designed to grow. Scripture teaches that the church grows both numerically and in spiritual maturity (Eph. 2:21; 4:14-16).

• God is using the church, both universal and local, to carry out His kingdom purposes.

Notes to Chapter 5

1. Edward R. Dayton and David A. Fraser, *Planning Strategies for World Evangelization* (Grand Rapids: Eerdmans, 1980), p. 350.

2. Robert L. Saucy, *The Church in God's Program,* (Chicago: Moody Press, 1972), p. 16.

3. Ibid., p. 17.

4. Ibid., p. 65.

5. Robert G. Gromacki, *Stand Fast in Liberty: An Exposition of Galatians* (Grand Rapids: Baker Book House, 1979), p. 114.

6. Richard Chenevix Trench, *Synonyms of the New Testament* (Grand Rapids: Eerdmans, 1948), p. 11.

The Church and Its Missionaries:
The Pastor

6

A careful look at what is expected of a pastor is mind boggling. His duties demand great versatility. In addition to the usual functions we identify as "pastoral," he must be "missions minded." Speaking of the pastor's responsibilities in the church's mission program, Reginald L. Matthews said that he must:

(1) face the issue of God's call in his own life; (2) study missionary passages in Scripture and preach on them; (3) read missionary books, literature and history; (4) become acquainted with missionary personnel and agencies; (5) pray that his church will become a missionary-minded church; (6) possess a knowledge of missionary principles in the light of God's Word and seek to implement them.[1]

The pastor must lead his people in their missions interest. As Harold R. Cook comments:

The life of any missionary program in a local church depends largely on the leadership. Someone has to have the interest, the vision, the initiative to inaugurate a program, plus the persistence to carry it through. Normally the pastor should be that leader. People usually look to him for leadership, and in this matter they expect him to be much better informed than the members.[2]

Putting these job descriptions in perspective, we now focus on several functions of a pastor as he leads his people in their missions commitments. See figure 11.

FIGURE 11

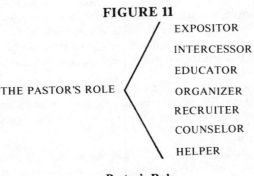

THE PASTOR'S ROLE

- EXPOSITOR
- INTERCESSOR
- EDUCATOR
- ORGANIZER
- RECRUITER
- COUNSELOR
- HELPER

Pastor's Role

The Pastor Leads the Missions Program

He Is an Expositor

Paul charged Timothy, "Preach the Word . . ." (2 Tim. 4:2). The pastor has many duties, but first and foremost he proclaims the gospel (1 Cor. 1:17; 9:16) and declares the whole counsel of God to his people. Paul reminded the Ephesian elders, "For I have not hesitated to proclaim to you the whole will of God" (Acts 20:27). The word translated "will" (*bouten*) means "counsel" or "purpose." Peter used this term in his Pentecost sermon when he said, "This man was handed over to you by God's set *purpose* and foreknowledge . . ." (Acts 2:23). In Pisidian Antioch Paul declared, "For when David had served God's *purpose* in his own generation, he fell asleep . . ." (Acts 13:36).

A part of God's whole purpose today is to take out from among the Gentiles a people for His name (Acts 15:14; Rom. 11:25). The pastor's duty is to declare from the entire Bible God's redemptive purposes. The pastor will make clear from both the Old and New Testaments God's missionary purposes.

By virtue of being a faithful expositor, the pastor will be a careful exegete of the texts that deal with God's missionary purposes. To exegete (*exegeomai*) means to "lead out of" a text its real meaning. This word is translated "to declare" or "tell" and occurs six times in the New Testament (Luke 24:35; John 1:18; Acts 10:8; 15:12; 15:14; 21:19). For example, Walter C. Kaiser comments:

> Paul and Barnabas "exegeted" what the "signs and wonders God had done through them among the Gentiles" meant (Acts 15:12); Peter "exegeted" how God first visited the Gentiles (Acts 15:14); and Paul "exegeted in detail" what God had accomplished through his ministry to the Gentiles (Acts 21:19).[3]

These first-century missionaries set a good example for the pastor's preaching ministry. Preaching on the subject of God's missionary purposes demands careful work on the text.

In planning his preaching schedule, the pastor needs to include missions-related messages. These messages should be used in services when he will reach the most people, usually on Sunday mornings. A series of missions messages may be in order. A regularly scheduled missions Sunday may provide the needed missions emphasis. Book studies will provide many opportunities to highlight the church's mission. The Bible is a missionary book.

In his reading the pastor will find missions-related illustrations that will enhance his messages. Missionary biographies are especially helpful for illustrative purposes. Books of missionary stories are available as well.

He Is an Intercessor

The apostles in the Jerusalem church gave their "attention to prayer and the ministry of the word" (Acts 6:4). These two facets of ministry are prominent on the pages of the New Testament. Paul emphasized prayer both in his own ministry and in the churches (Acts 13:3; 14:23; 16:25; Rom. 15:30-32; Col. 1:9; 1 Thess. 5:17).

First, the pastor sets an example for his people in *private* prayer for the church-supported missionaries. Because many missionaries and a number of needs are ever before the church, the pastor must structure his daily prayer so that all prayer needs are met on a regular basis. A church prayer calendar or booklet simplifies the planning procedure. Current prayer letters keep the needs in focus. A pastor with a consistent prayer ministry for the church's missionaries will be more effective in leading the church in its missionary interests.

Second, the pastor is an example to the church in *public* prayer for missionaries. Scheduling prayer for missionaries in the morning worship service is important. Perhaps it will be necessary to pray specifically for several missionaries each Sunday remembering particular needs. Listing the names, fields, and mission agencies in the bulletin keeps the missionaries before the congregation. Brief excerpts from current missionary letters are helpful as well. Stamped, addressed airforms to the missionaries should also be made available to people. This service makes it convenient for individuals to write reminders to their missionary friends that they are being remembered in prayer.

The prayer interest of the people will probably not exceed that of the pastor. He must set the pace.

He Is an Educator

First, in order to lead his people knowledgeably in the church's missionary program, the pastor must take every means available to inform himself about the church-supported missionaries. He can gain much helpful information by taking time (1) to read prayer letters carefully and (2) to correspond personally with missionaries. Exchanging information with missionaries by cassette tapes keeps the pastor current on field progress and problems. Direct contact with missionaries by ham radio is increasingly available. Of course, the pastor should spend time with furloughing missionaries learning about many facets of the work that can only be shared in person. By keeping in touch with the mission boards through whom the church sends its missionaries, the pastor gains a broader base of information that only the boards can supply. The pastor should make it a point to be present when missionaries present their work. Missionary Sunday is no time for a pastor's vacation!

Mission-related books and articles are spinning off the press in unparalleled volume. Not all missions literature is of equal value or interest. Good reading material abounds to keep the pastor well informed. A well-read pastor is bound to reflect this in his preaching and teaching ministries.

This information-gathering process is a formidable task. Goals and priorities must be set to carry out the process for gaining missionary information. It will be worth the effort, because an informed, praying pastor leads to a better-informed, praying congregation.

Second, an informed pastor will lead his people into a better understanding of their own missionaries. Generalizations are one of the greatest enemies of missionary understanding. Individual missionaries, their families, fields, ministry, problems, and progress, must be brought into sharp focus. Missions is people: those sent, those to whom the gospel is proclaimed, and those who hold the ropes. Missionaries are too often the landscape at which the church gazes, nice to have as part of the "program," but not real people. Or they may be looked upon as machinery, carrying out their given tasks on their given fields being maintained by the dutiful gifts of the church. If they do not function well, they may be repaired or replaced.

In like manner the "nationals" are simply a blur in the minds of many people. These far-away people are fortunate to have the gospel preached to them at all.

No, these people are *real* people, and the educational wing of the local church has its work cut out to restore reality concerning church-supported missionaries and those to whom they minister.

Third, the pastor is the initiator in a missions-informed church. He is the idea person. He will lead his people in formulating a missions strategy of the total church. Others, such as the missionary committee, will help, but the pastor is ultimately responsible for the missions commitment of his church. Such responsibility demands time, commitment, prayer, thought, creativity, and faith. No church dares to settle for the status quo today. The pastor initates the missionary outreach of the church, while his people join him in implementing their outreach at home and abroad.

To be informed is a good beginning for a pastor. But for educational goals to come to fruition, information must issue in knowledgeable prayer, in creative planning, and in all-church implementation.

He Is an Organizer

The pastor cannot assume sole responsibility for carrying out the church's missions program. Learning to delegate duties to others is imperative. But in delegating, the pastor does not divest himself of ultimate responsibility. There must be a leader in all corporate effort whatever the task, and the pastor is that leader in the church.

First, the pastor takes the leadership in formulating a missions committee if one does not exist. The committee leadership should be in the hands of capable and committed people. The pastor is an *ex-officio* committee member.

Second, if there is no written missions policy in the church, the pastor should take the lead in seeing that such a policy is formulated. The present missions committee can help write the policy. If a missions committee does not exist, the pastor can call upon some members of the church board who work with him. Unless he delegates much of the responsibility in drawing up the policy, it will become *his* policy in the eyes of the people. For this to happen is to write "Ichabod" over the whole project!

Third, the pastor is responsible for seeing that the missionary conference, or any other missions emphasis, is planned throughout the church's calendar year. The missions committee will work closely with him. Congregational interest and particpation is a direct reflection of the pastor's leadership.

Fourth, the pastor will organize structured prayer for missionaries. Varied missions interest depend upon the pastor's concern. God's people need direction as they corporately intercede for their misssionaries. The pastor can help by praying publicly for particular missionaries and their needs. He can encourage other means of effective prayer, such as prayer prompters and daily prayer reminders. These prayer aids are discussed further in another section.

He Is a Recruiter

The local church is the missing link in missionary recruitment. By default, recruiting is now mostly in the hands of the training schools and the mission agencies. And woe betide them if they fail!

Primary responsibility for enlistment in career Christian service must return to the local churches. Pastors have a leading role to play.

First, the pastor can present to his people the *options* open to them in career Christian service. Because of his position, he knows those options better than anyone else in the church. The field is constantly expanding today. Career missionary service is not the only option, nor should it be presented as the "highest."

Second, the *opportunities* for career Christian service should be presented by the pastor. Mission agencies can supply lists of opportunities both by vocation and location.

Third, the pastor can acquaint his people with the *expectations* of various careers in Christian service. These expectations involve necessary spiritual gifts, personal aptitudes, and educational requirements. The pastor might lead in planning a "Christian Service Career Day" and invite those who can help his people. The local church is an ideal location for such a seminar.

Fourth, the pastor should take steps to *preserve* commitments made through the church's ministry. These commitments may be made at camps, retreats, or through other direct ministry of the church. At any rate, periodic seminars on Christian service careers or even a Career Club will provide the information, camaraderie, and continuity often needed to bring these commitments to fruition.

He Is A Counselor

The pastor's counseling ministry is multifaceted, of course. His missions-related counseling is fourfold. First, he is often sought out by those who are seeking God's will for their lives. Counseling those whose life's direction will be affected is an awesome task. Only the wisdom of the Holy Spirit is sufficient. Missionary service may or may not be God's will for the one seeking counsel, but that possibility is always present. If the pastor does not believe the person has proper motivation or gifts for missionary service, he should deal frankly and graciously with the counselee. Other options are open for Christian service.

Second, many believers today are faced with midlife vocational choices. Perhaps early retirement makes another career possible. Again, God may deal in His own way in leading mature Christians into a Christian service career. Through prayer and biblically based counsel the pastor can render great service to these people.

Third, appointees from the home church need the listening ear and ministry of their pastor. Any number of problems arise—the arduous deputation trail, obtaining meetings, separation of the father from his family while traveling, balance between deputation and employment—and on. An understanding pastor can often take steps to help the appointee, if he is aware of the problems.

Fourth, the furloughing missionary needs a listening ear. Often it is enough for the pastor just to listen. The missionary's problems are often peculiar to the missionary situation itself. The pastor may not have specific solutions, but he can listen, sympathize, and pray more understandingly than before. Open communication must be maintained between pastor and missionary so that mutual problems can be freely shared.

He Is a Helper

First of all, the pastor can help the new appointees by personally introducing them to area pastors. Deputation meetings are often the result of these introductions. As the time approaches to prepare for departure, the home church has special opportunities to help. The pastor can encourage people to assist with babysitting, preparing the appointee's home for rent or sale, packing, making crates, obtaining steel drums for packing, and finding storage for household goods left behind. These tasks and many more face appointees before their trip to the airport. These matters are seldom talked about, but they become very real in those last hectic weeks before departure.

Second, the pastor is a helper to furloughing missionaries. Briefing them on the current status of affairs in the church will help them update their understanding. Several years may have passed, and it has been virtually impossible for missionaries to keep up. Even a new pastor may have come to the home church since they left for the field. If the missionaries do not own a home, the church can be of great service in providing housing or finding a home to rent. The chances are that they will have to start over including securing household goods. A veteran missionary once said, "I dreaded coming home each time. We never knew where we were going to live." The pastor can lead in taking this kind of pressure off a missionary family.

Third, the pastor can help the mission agencies with which church-supported missionaries serve. He can publicize their personnel needs both for career missionaries and short termers. Often people in the church can meet particular short-term needs if they only know about them. Mission agencies sometimes have special or emergency financial needs that the church can meet on a one-time basis. Here again, the pastor can be used as an informer of needs.

Indeed, the pastor plays a key role in the local-church missions outreach. He can be the greatest asset a church has in fulfilling its mission.

Wrap-Up

Paul wrote to Timothy, "If anyone sets his heart on being an overseer, he desires a noble task" (1 Tim. 3:1). One of the pastor's roles as overseer relates to the missions outreach of his church. Some concluding thoughts about this role are in order.

• Basic to all of his ministry is the pastor's servant role. While Christ talked to the disciples about His impending death, they argued about who would be the greatest (Mark 9:30-37; 10:32-45). When James and John asked for favored positons in the kingdom, Christ said, "For even the Son of Man did not come to be served, but to serve, and to give his life as a ransom for many" (Mark 10:45). The pastor has the potential of a global ministry, and he must bring it his best as a servant.

• The pastor must also assume the leadership role in the missions program. The success of the church's missions outreach will usually be in direct proportion to the leadership provided by the pastor.

• Both in attitude and in action, as servant and leader, the pastor can be God's instrument far beyond the confines of his congregation.

Notes to Chapter 6

1. Reginald L. Matthews, *Missionary Administration in the Local Church* (Schaumburg, IL: Regular Baptist Press, 1970), p. 51.

2. Harold R. Cook, *An Introduction to Christian Missions* (Chicago: Moody Press, 1971), p. 222.

3. Walter C. Kaiser, Jr., *Toward an Exegetical Theology: Biblical Exegesis for Preaching and Teaching* (Grand Rapids: Baker Book House, 1981), p. 44.

The Church and Its Missionaries:
Initial Steps

7

In the final analysis, God's people in the local church hold the key to reaching both the community and the world with the gospel message. The scripture record gives evidence to this fact. To demonstrate, let us look at three first-century churches.

The church in Jerusalem saw many thousands come to Christ (Acts 2:41-47; 4:4, 32; 5:42; 6:1, 7). Because of persecution, believers were scattered and "preached the word wherever they went" (Acts 8:4). As a result, Gentiles began to hear and believe the gospel.

The church in Antioch was the first church to send some of its number to proclaim the gospel in other cities and countries. As a result of the prompting of the Holy Spirit, Barnabas and Saul were chosen to go. After the believers fasted, prayed, and laid their hands on them, they "sent them off" (Acts 13:3). The church obeyed the Spirit's command and made their brethren available for His direction. Thus the church in Antioch became the first sending church outside the land of Palestine, and this opened the door to Gentile evangelization throughout the empire.

Paul established a church in Thessalonica on his second tour (Acts 17:1-9). This is the only church Paul recommended as an example to others (1 Thess. 1:7). He commended their zeal for spreading the gospel by saying, "The Lord's message rang out from you not only in Macedonia and Achaia—your faith in God has become known everywhere. Therefore we do not need to say anything about it" (1 Thess. 1:8). This first-century church continues to be an example to churches today.

Twenty centuries later, the centrality of local churches in mission endeavor has not diminished. However, their relationship to parachurch organizations such as theological schools and mission agencies is a new dimension. These organizations were nonexistent in the first century. Missionaries in the sense of the apostolic missionary team were well known, but many of the current relationshiips between churches and their missionaries were unknown in those early days. Today the local church maintains an interdependent relationship with the theological school, mission agency, and missionary. See figure 12.

In subsequent chapters we will consider the role of the mission agency, the missionary, and the theological school. Our present purpose is to delineate the place of the home church in missions strategy.

The local church is the hub of the wheel of missions. The pastor plays a key role in world evangelism. A mission-minded pastor will eventually

FIGURE 12

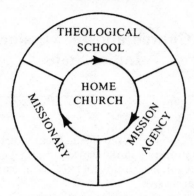

A Church-Based Mission Strategy

have a mission-minded congregation. These are the most crucial days since Pentecost for discipling all peoples (Matt. 28:19), and Bible-believing churches must understand their responsibility. See figure 13.

FIGURE 13

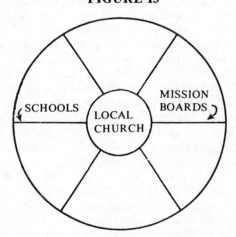

The Wheel of Missions

In an effort to place the local church in proper perspective, our study now turns to the question, "How can the home church have a biblical and meaningful relationship with the missionary and the mission agency?" The relationship of the home church to the theological school is discussed only as these two organizations are involved in the life and work of the missionary. The mutual concern of church and school for enlisting missionary personnel is a case in point. The terms "home church," "local church," and "sending church" are used interchangeably. "Home church" means the local church of which the missionary is a member.

The Home Church Co-Sends Its Missionaries

Although sending the missionary occurs only after many other matters are cared for, we must identify the senders at the outset. A familiar passage, Acts 13:1-4, gives us direction. As the prophets and teachers in the church in Antioch were worshipping and fasting, the Holy Spirit instructed them to set apart Barnabas and Saul for work to which He had called them (13:1-2). That the Holy Spirit had a balanced missionary team in mind is clear from the Greek text. It is quite evident that Barnabas was classified as a "prophet" and Saul as a "teacher." Richard N. Longenecker points out:

> At Antioch there were five "prophets and teachers" in the church. The Greek particle *te* (untranslatable) was used in antiquity to connect word pairs, coordinate clauses, and similar sentences, thereby often distinguishing one set of coordinates from another. Probably, therefore, we should understand Barnabas, Simeon, and Lucius, who are introduced by the first *te*, as the prophets, and Manaen and Saul, who are grouped by the second *te*, as the teachers . . . .[1]

Barnabas, the prophet, and Saul, the teacher, had already served well in Antioch. They are credited with both the numerical and spiritual growth of that group of believers (Acts 11:22-26). In fact F.F. Bruce comments, "It is worth noting that the two men to be released for missionary service were the most gifted and outstanding in the church."[2]

After fasting, praying, and laying their hands on Barnabas and Saul, the leaders of the church sent them off (Acts 13:3). Although there is no clear antecedent to the expression "they . . . sent them off," it is likely that this was a whole church affair rather than a unilateral action by the leaders.[3] At any rate, when the apostles returned to Antioch, "they gathered the church together" for their report (Acts 14:27).

The Holy Spirit directed Luke to use the word *apoluo* meaning "to dismiss, release, or send off." Pilate uses this word concerning Christ, ". . . it is your custom for me *to release* to you one prisoner at the time of the Passover" (John 18:39). Later Pilate said to Jesus, "Don't you realize I have power either *to free* you or to crucify you?" (John 19:10). It is used of Peter and John before the Sanhedrin, "After further threats they *let them go*" (Acts 4:21). This was simply an act of obedience by the Antiochan believers.

The prime mover in sending Barnabas and Saul was the Holy Spirit. The narrative states, "So they, being sent forth by the Holy Sirit, departed unto Seleucia . . . ." (Acts 13:4).The word used for "send" here is *ekpempo* which, as a compound verb, is almost synonymous with *apostello*. The term means "to send away" or "to send out." It appears only here and in Acts 17:10, which states, "As soon as it was night, the brothers sent Paul and Silas away to Berea."

The Holy Spirit is still the prime mover in calling and sending His servants to the work of His choice. He does, however, use the ministry of the local church to carry out His purposes. Harold R. Cook concluded:

> Who, then, does send the missionaries? Acts 13:4 leaves us in no doubt: the Holy Spirit. Looking at other instances, note that it was the Holy Spirit who sent Philip to the Ethiopian eunuch (Acts 8:29). He sent Peter to Cornelius (Acts 11:12). He kept Paul from going into Bithynia (Acts 16:7), but led him to Macedonia (v. 10).[4]

Ultimately, God the Holy Spirit is the sending agent in the church's mission. This is the vertical aspect of sending. The church at Antioch through their spiritual leaders let Barnabas and Saul go their way at the Spirit's prompting. This is the *horizontal* aspect. Our churches today need to recapture the vitality of this divine-human plan for sending missionaries.

The Home Church Enlists Its Missionaries

Missionary enlistment can be thought of in military terms. This concept fits well because the local church should be the place where God's people are challenged to Christian service. No doubt the parents of young people have a primary responsibility in conjunction with the church, in encouraging missionary understanding and interest.

Christian parents play a key role in enlisting harvesters in the local church. Through both attitudes and activities, moms and dads introduce their children to the world of missions as no one else can. Several methods may be used to create missionary interest in the home.

● Extending hospitality is a successful way to have children and teens give their first serious thought to missionary involvement. Many people on the field today can trace their first interest in missions to a visiting missionary who showed concern for them in their home.

● Parents can build meaningful prayer interest in missionaries into their family devotional life. Systematic prayer for missionary friends makes a lasting impression on young lives. Prayer can be particularized by using prayer prompters from the church, prayer cards, and current prayer letters received in the home.

● Visuals make missions come alive for the family. A prayer card bulletin board or album, curios from family missionary friends, maps, a globe help children identify with missionaries they know. When a nine-year-old asks, "Where does Cindy live?" Dad can help find Brazil on the globe. This kind of geography lesson is not soon forgotten.

● Letters written to missionaries are a source of encouragment difficult to measure. Letters full of family news are like a cooling breeze to a busy missionary. And, of course, missionary response gives reality to names, places, and various facets of the work.

● A family can take on a special project for a missionary friend. Purchasing a piece of equipment, Christmas, anniversary, or birthday gifts, providing clothing for missionary children—all are concrete reminders that missionaries are people just like we are.

- Some have found family missions interest highly increased by participating in short-term missionary service. At any given time missionary families in supportive roles can be found in cross-cultural situations around the world.

Churches can encourage their own people to consider career Christian service. A good deal is being written today about voluntarism as the means by which the ranks of Christian workers are filled. Enlistment goes one step further, however, by actively challenging promising people in the church to consider Christian service as their life's vocation. This applies as well, of course, to those who can serve for shorter periods of time to fill a particular need on a given field.

One Baptist pastor has made it a point to spend time with promising young people on a one-to-one basis, encouraging them to give serious thought to Christian service. If this example of concerned strategy for enlistment were to be multiplied throughout our churches, the ranks of missionary appointees would swell. Cook asks:

> What are you doing with the young people in your church? Do you have any definite aims and programs for them? Not just for missions. That will come if your spiritual program is a vital one. But are you paying serious attention to your young people? Do you have goals that you are earnestly trying to help them reach?[5]

Active enlistment for Christian service is also a serious concern for summer camping programs. But aside from camp report time on the following Sunday evening, how many of these sincere young people have been followed up with a structured strategy to preserve the results?

Christian colleges and seminaries are valuable recruiting grounds for Christian service. Mission candidate secretaries make an annual pilgrimage to campuses, armed with the latest in statistics, well-honed messages, and four-color literature, hoping to enlist much-needed personnel for their paticular fields.

School and candidate secretaries have a legitimate place in the enlistment process. But whatever happened to the local church? How long will we allow parachurch organizations to do our recruiting? "The aplication to the issue and answer of personnel for worldwide missions," states Ken Kilsinki, "is to go to the churches. Churches need to be sensitive to the Holy Spirit and challenge men and women for the Great Commission."[6]

The local church has two chief concerns in enlisting people for career Christian service. The first of these relates to *vocation.* Without being pushy and overanxious, local church leaders need to help their young people become familiar with vocational options in order to make wise decisions. People in our churches need to know that their leaders *care* what they do with their lives. If they are given opportunities to serve in the church, they will get a taste of Christian activities. Honest evaluation about spiritual gifts will be of great encouragement to the person seeking God's will in life.

The second of these concerns relates to *direction*. God's people need sympathetic counsel from church leaders in two areas. First, our people need direction concerning Christian service. It is no coincidence that some churches over a number of years see an unusual proportion of their number answering the call to Christian service. Back of this is a pastor or concerned church leader who is challenging these people to look to career Christian service as a viable option for their lives. In proportion to the harvest, the laborers will always be few (Matt. 9:37). Never can there be too many harvesters for the harvest. The local church is the most fruitful recruiting ground for new workers.

Second, those called into a church-related ministry need wise counsel concerning preparation for Christian service. Pastors and youth leaders naturally want their young people to attend their own alma mater. And indeed, this may be in God's providence for them. They would be wise, however, to present the young person with several options of various schools that are faithfully upholding the fundamentals of the faith and that take the same doctrinal stand as the local church. Individual interests and gifts can be better cultivated in some schools than others. It helps the interested young people to visit various Christian schools, or to have school representatives present the schools in the local church. Caution should be taken not to have schools represented that would influence people toward mission boards that the church could not approve.

The mission agency has a role in enlistment as well. This role is twofold, namely, providing guidance concerning *location* and *participation* in missionary service. The agencies are in a position to suggest a variety of options for missionary involvement. Both mission board personnel and prospective recruits must ever be sensitive to God's will in each choice made. What a sobering task—taking part in the life decisions that others make!

The home church, then, has the primary role in enlisting missionaries. The school and mission agency play a part as well. See figure 14.

FIGURE 14

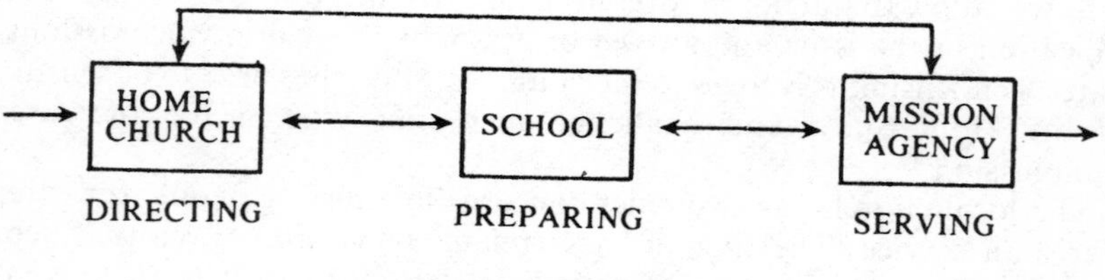

Enlistment Roles

Happy is the pastor who can look back on his ministry with the knowledge that God has used him in challenging others to serve in the worldwide ministry of the Word.

The Home Church Selects Its Missionaries

Not all those enlisted for Christian service are *missionary* material. When thinking specifically about missionary service, Cook warns, "Don't say, 'You can probably be used somewhere.' Could you use them at home? . . . Don't make the mission candidate secretaries do all the weeding out. You know your young people better than they do."[7]

Two principles are involved in selecting missionaries. The first is the person's presentation, or the *principle of availablity*. The second is the church's confirmation, or the *principle of selectivity.*

The principle of availablity was in operation on the road to Damascus when Paul said, "What shall I do, Lord?" (Acts 22:10). Paul was not volunteering for a good solid stoning at Lystra or a night and a day in the deep (Acts 14:19; 2 Cor. 11:25). He was not volunteering for missionary service at all. He was simply saying, "Lord, I'm available. What's next?" Indeed, this is all we ever have a right to ask of anyone—a willingness to do God's will whatever it may be.

We do not see people volunteering for missionary service in the New Testament. Michael C. Griffiths reminds us that "the emphasis made by Scripture is never upon an individual volunteering or upon his own subjective sense of call, but always upon the initiative of others."[8]

This brings us to our second principle, namely, the church's confirmation or the principle of selectivity. Barnabas went to Tarsus to find Paul and took him to Antioch (Acts 11:25-26). Barnabas and Saul were selected from among the other Antiochan leaders when the Holy Spirit said, "Set apart for me Barnabas and Saul . . ." (Acts 13:2). The text states that when Paul prepared to leave on his second journey, he "chose Silas" (Acts 15:40). Timothy had a good report among the brethren, and Luke tells us, "Paul wanted to take him along on the journey . . ." (Acts 16:2-3). In the waning days of his work, Paul instructed Timothy, "Get Mark and bring him with you, because he is helpful to me in my ministry" (2 Tim. 4:11).

Edwin L. Frizen observes:

> It is apparent that New Testament congregations were consulted and involved in the sending role. It seems evident from scripture that in the New Testament church the Holy Spirit used the corporate initiative of congregations or the initiative of missionaries in selecting people. The New Testament church selected, commended, commissioned, supported, and prayed. There is no evidence that the missionary volunteered, or that the great commission was the motivating force in missionary witness. The Holy Spirit given at Pentecost was the motivator, the undergirder, the empowerer in the missionary witness of the early church.[9]

This is not always the procedure today. The prospective missionary is often away from the home church for an extended period of preparation. Consequently, a close affiliation no longer exists between the students and their home church. Besides, the church may change pastors, so that when the students return to the home church they need a period of reacquaintance. Frizen says, "Often the local church is not involved until after his training is completed and the mission society has been selected."[10] This lack of home church involvement indicates a lack of understanding of the central role of the local church in world missions. This will be considered in the next chapter.

Let us look at an actual case of local church confirmation for missionary service. John and Gail Lillis are now serving in Thailand. Before they approached the mission agency, they went to their pastor and their missions committee and expressed their desire to enter misssionary service. The Lillises asked the church to consider seriously their proposal. If the church did not believe that they had proper motivation or gifts, the Lillises were willing to abide by the church's decision and seek another avenue of ministry. After deliberation and prayer, this motion was presented to the congregation by the missions committee:

> Because, we as a church have a responsibility to recognize and search out the gifts and qualifications of members of our congregation; and because we are commanded to bear one another's burdens; and because we appreciate the sensitivity of the Lillises to the leading of the Spirit of God in their lives; and because we as a local assembly of believers want also to be sensitive to the Spirit's leading—

> I move that we, as a body of believers, go on record to express to John and Gail Lillis, that we concur with their expression and desire to serve the Lord as missionaries:

> That we express love and encouragement to them to pursue the leading of the Lord as He opens doors to them.[11]

Upon approval by the congregation, the pastor initiated the candidate procedure with the mission agency for the Lillises. When candidature neared completion, he was on hand for their final oral examination by the mission.

Griffiths summarizes the idea of personal presentation and corporate confirmation by saying, "The most that an individual can do is express his *willingness*. Others must determnine his *worthiness*. The individual may be *free* to go, but only his church knows if he is really *fitted* to go."[12]

To summarize, home churches must take the initiative if they wish to pursue a biblical pattern of missionary sending.

Wrap-Up

The following recommendations answer the question, "How can the home church have an effective relationship with its missionaries?" Of course, recommendations are only helpful to the extent that they are put into practice.

• Because the home churches and the Holy Spirit co-send missionaries, pastors and church leaders need to give priority to enlisting qualified people for missionary service.

• Christian parents should provide a structured missionary education in the home.

• The home church should consider establishing a "Career Ministry Club," or a similar organization to encourage young people committed to career Christian service.

• The church must maintain regular communication with students who are preparing for ministry.

Notes to Chapter 7

1. Richard N. Longenecker, "The Acts of the Apostles," *The Expositor's Bible Commentary,* ed. Frank E. Gaebelein, 12 vols. (Grand Rapids: Zondervan Publishing House, 1981), 9:416.

2. F.F. Bruce, *The Acts of the Apostles* (Grand Rapids: Eerdmans, 1960), p. 253.

3. Longenecker, "The Acts of the Apostles," p. 417.

4. Harold R. Cook, "Who Really Sent the First Missionaries?" *Evangelical Missions Quarterly* 11 (October 1975): 238.

5. Harold R. Cook, *An Introduction to Christian Missions* (Chicago: Moody Press, 1971), p. 261.

6. Ken Kilinski, "How Churches Can Follow Antioch's Model," *Evangelical Missions Quarterly* 15 (January 1979): 21.

7. Cook, *An Introduction to Christian Missions,* p. 267.

8. Michael C. Griffiths, *Who Really Sends the Missionary?* (Chicago: Moody Press, 1974), p. 12.

9. Edwin L. Frizen, Jr., "Missionaries and Their Sending Churches," *Evangelical Missions Quarterly* 16 (April 1980): 71.

10. Ibid., p. 73.

11. A resolution approved by Berean Baptist Church, Grand Rapids, MI on October 7, 1979.

12. Griffiths, *Who Really Sends the Missionary?,* pp. 15-16.

The Church and Its Missionaries:
Further Steps

8

During His last days with the disciples, Jesus said, "All authority in heaven and on earth has been given to me" (Matt. 28:18). He is the ultimate authorizer of workers. The Book of Acts indicates that the Holy Spirit separates and sends men (Acts 13:1-4). It is equally plain that the local church is the "mediating sending authority."[1] Peters writes:

> We believe that we are not out of line with New Testament thinking if we state that the local congregation of believers stands in a unique relationship to Christ and that the local assembly becomes the mediating and authoritative sending body of the New Testament missionary. This is a vital, biblical principle and we dare not weaken, minimize or disregard it.[2]

The Home Church Authorizes It's Missionaries

This principle of sending authority is demonstrated in Paul's relationship with the church at Antioch. This was the first sending church outside the land of Palestine. Paul returned to this church after his first two journeys to give a full report of his ministry (Acts 14:26; 18:22). The brethren at Antioch had identified themselves with Barnabas and Saul by laying their hands on them (Acts 13:3). Luke states in Acts 14:26, "From Attalia they sailed back to Antioch, where they had been committed to the grace of God for the work they had now completed." The expression "committed" is *paradidomi*, which in this context means "to commit someone to perform a given task." The word was used again when Paul and Silas began the second journey. The text states, "But Paul chose Silas, and left, *commended* by the brothers to the grace of the Lord" (Acts 15:40).

In brief, *ultimate* authority for missionary sending rests with God. The home church is the *mediating* authority. Where does the present-day mission agency fit into the picture? It has an *implementing* ministry, helping both church and missionary carry out their task. See figure 15.

FIGURE 15

Ultimate Authority: CHRIST	→	Mediating Authority: HOME CHURCH	→	Implementing Authority: MISSION AGENCY

Authorizing Chain of Command

On the functional level this procedure is difficult to implement. Often the prospective missionary has been away from the home church for schooling. He may commit himself to missionary service and prepare to go, without informing his home pastor or church. He may even begin the candidate procedure with the mission agency without consulting his home congregation. In pleading for a proper relationship of the missionary candidate to his church, George H. Slavin explains the dilemma at hand:

> During youth, up to and including high school, the pastoral and church relationship is fairly close with guidance and direction. It is during the years of higher education away from home that the relationship tends to be broken. If the young person is spoken to by the Lord during his years away at school, the usual procedure is to make application to some mission board. The pastor and church usually learn about this step when reference papers are receieved. Sympathize with the pastor, if you will. Neither he nor the church have seen the young person for four years, except occasionally.[3]

This procedure has become so well established that it is now accepted as normal. In order to establish the home church as the initiating and authorizing body, however, a statement should be included in the mission agency's intial application form. This form is referred to here as the Preliminary Information Questionaire (PIQ). I believe that this statement should declare that the applicant has been interviewed, authorized, and recommended by the home church *before* he takes the first step of application to the mission agency. This is illustrated in figure 16 (page 72).

The candidate procedure is pictured in two stages, the first being related to the home church. The procedural approach may vary from church to church. However, both church leaders and the congregation should be involved in decisions about the potential candidate. If the candidate has been absent from the church because of schooling, or if a pastoral change has occurred, he would be wise to reestablish relationships before moving ahead with candidate procedure. This may take from several months to a year, but a solid church base is imperative to future church-missionary relationships.

Stage two of the candidate procedure concerns the mission agency. Preferably the pastor contacts the board to ask for the Preliminary Information Questionnaire. Many agencies use this form as a means of getting acquainted with the potential candidate. At this point decisions are made about the advisability of proceeding further with the application. Because they are experienced in dealing with many potential applicants, the mission board's input should be valued by both the home church and the candidate. We need checks and balances in such life-changing decisions. Griffiths observes:

> It is not always easy for a small congregation to be sufficiently objective: they may be starry-eyed about their own protege. All their eager geese are alleged to be effective swans! The missionary society

is able to compare the caliber of candidates from other churches and other countries, and provides an objective check upon overoptimistic evaluations of some congregation's local blue-eyed boy.[4]

If, after the initial step of application, all parties agree to proceed, the candidate then completes the formal application. Major factors in this step are the applicant's doctrinal position and agreement with mission agency policies. The order of the following steps in application vary from board to board, but we will consider next the interview with the agency personnel. As stated in the previous illustration, it helps to have the home church represented at this interview.

When the applicant is approved by the mission council, the candidate attends the mission's candidate classes and is officially made an appointee. Depending on the agency, these classes extend from one to four weeks. The appointee is now ready to start deputation. The deputation procedure will be discussed in a later section.

Do these steps from candidate to appointee seem too demanding? Should the mission agency really have that much to say about the worthiness of the candidate? Yes! Experience shows that each of these steps to becoming a missionary is vital. The lives of God's servants are at stake. The churches will invest thousands of dollars. The agency will expend itself in serving both church and missionary. A structure of communication must be established between the home church and misson agency. This will eliminate potential areas of misunderstanding and contribute to a successful ministry.

A word should be said at this point about the home church's approval of mission societies. Does the church simply accept any agency in which the potential candidate is interested? Does it matter to the home constituency whether or not the board is denominationally oriented? Is the board's doctrinal position sufficiently clear? And how do they handle their finances? Five key questions should be posed by the home church about mission agencies.

- *What is the agency's stated missionary purpose?* The church should know why the board exists. (And so should the board!) Are its purposes evangelism and church planting? Is it chiefly concerned with translation or with a media emphasis such as radio or literature? A clear statement of purpose is helpful to inquiring churches.

- *What is the doctrinal position of the agency?* Someone has said that a doctrinal statement is better understood by what it omits than by what it states. Is the statement precise, for example, on Scripture and eschatology? If the church is not completely satisfied, it should ask for specific clarification on these or any other doctrinal areas.

- *What are the agency's financial policies?* Perhaps they use a pooling plan for all funds. They may use an individual support plan. A church should know how its support funds are handled, so it should ask specific questions. What kinds of churches support the agency in question? A church should be doctrinally compatible with the other churches that support a given agency.

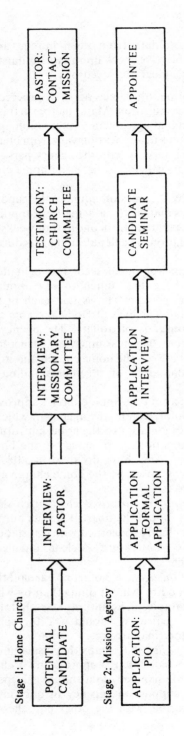

FIGURE 16

Stage 1: Home Church

POTENTIAL CANDIDATE → INTERVIEW: PASTOR → INTERVIEW: MISSIONARY COMMITTEE → TESTIMONY: CHURCH COMMITTEE → PASTOR: CONTACT MISSION

Stage 2: Mission Agency

APPLICATION: PIQ → APPLICATION FORMAL APPLICATION → APPLICATION INTERVIEW → CANDIDATE SEMINAR → APPOINTEE

Candidate Procedure

FIGURE 17

HOME CHURCH COMMISSION → AREA CHURCHES DEPUTATION → PERIODIC EVALUATION → ORDINATION → FIELD ORIENTATION

Deputation Procedure

• *What are the agency's standards of missionary acceptance?* What is their application procedure? What are their policies of screening potential candidates? Standards must be sufficiently high to ensure quality workers. Yet sensitivity to God's will in each life is imperative.

• *Does the mission agency reflect the convictions and commitment of your church?* How tragic for a church to team up with an agency that does not really hold the same doctrinal position! Does it matter whether the board is denominational or interdenominational? Does the agency cooperate with ecumenically-oriented groups? If the church knows these things first, it can avoid problems later.

The Home Church Ordains Its Missionaries

Ordination is the time a person is formally set aside to the gospel ministry. This comes through a doctrinal examination and a public confirmation. The question is sometimes raised about whether a missionary really needs ordination. Usually the missionary has the challenge of proclaiming the gospel across cultures as well as planting churches in soil culturally different from his own. Therefore, he must be well prepared biblically and theologically. Cook says:

> In reality the educational *needs* for the foreign missionary are greater than for the worker at home. He does the same work and more. But he has to do it in another language. The circumstances are much less favorable.[5]

Some pastors believe that missionaries should be considered an extension of the home church staff. Missionary personnel represent the church's ministry to a people and place to which the entire church cannot go.

The pastor of the home church should take the initiative in making necessary arrangements for ordination. Ordination normally takes place after the prospective missionary is an appointee.

Making the ordination process and requirements clear to the appointee is imperative. Let's not make him learn the ropes the hard way simply because we had to!

If the appointee will fill a support role on the field rather than that of a church planter, the home church might consider licensure instead of ordination. Some official recognition by the home church is necessary today—even in the eyes of the Internal Revenue Service. The ordination of your missionary is a significant milestone in his life and in the life of your church.

The Home Church Commissions Its Missionaries

While ordination is necessary for formal recognition of a cross-cultural minister of the gospel, commissioning is a time of church-family identification. When Barnabas and Saul were separated by the Holy Spirit for the work (Acts 13:2), the church leaders fasted, prayed, and laid their hands on them before relasing them (Acts 13:3). Identification was further reinforced when they returned to Antioch. It was in this church "they had been committed to the grace of God for the work they had now completed" (Acts 14:26).

Commissioning is a symbol of identification that applies to all missionary personnel, both at home and abroad.

Emphasis should not be placed so much on the *rite* of commissioning as on its *rightness*. Perhaps an inner circle with dedicatory prayer, laying on of hands, or another symbol of identification may be used. It is a time when the home church expresses authentication of the appointee, identification with him, and delegation of responsibility.[6] Peters states:

> By the laying on of hands, the church and the individual missionary become bound in a bond of common purpose and mutual responsibility. It is thus not only a privilege and service; it is also the exercise of an authority and the acceptance of a tremendous responsibility. The identification of the church with the sent-forth representative is inclusive doctrinally, spiritually, physically and materially. It is the constituting of a rightful representative who will be able and who is responsible to function as a representative of the church. The church, therefore, by the laying on of hands, declares herself ready to stand by and make such respresentation possible. This should include the prayers and the finances required for such a representative ministry.[7]

Most mission agencies will suggest procedures for the commissioning service.

From the standpoint of missionary appointees, commissioning is a crucial factor in their ministry. It reminds them that they are responsible to support the doctrinal position of the church, that they in turn are identified with the church, and that they are as responsible to it as any other member. Commissioning is mutually meaningful.

Ideally the home church will commission its missionaries soon after they complete the candidate procedure. This action indicates to the other churches that these people have the backing of the home church. It also assures the appointees that the home church supports their deputation efforts. Five steps constitute the deputation procedure. See figure 72.

Deputation requirements vary with the mission agency. Some expect the appointee to do very limited deputation, especially if they are in a denominational board that receives funds for the denomination's unified budget. Other agencies expect their appointees to raise all funds necessary for their support. The issue at hand is the deputation procedure rather than the pros and cons of deputation.

Usually appointees raise support in other churches in addition to their own. Both home church and mission society evaluate the appointee's progress in deputation. A tentative departure date should be set within realistic parameters. Is the deputation trail getting longer? Some mission boards say that it now takes two years or more to raise adequate support.[8] Everyone concerned must work together to bring deputation into a more realistic time period.

The home church should arrange for the appointee's ordination. He should be given plenty of time to prepare, and he should care for ordination before the final push to leave for the field.

The day does arrive when the misssionaries weigh in their baggage at the airport, say their last goodbyes, and board the plane to take their next step in the will of God. A new world and way of life awaits them. Becoming oriented to their new environment is part of the joy of doing God's bidding. When they depart, their commissioning becomes immersed in reality.

Wrap-Up

The local church must take the initiative as the sending authority for missionaries. Mission agencies perform many valuable services both for churches and misssionaries. Yet, many mission agency leaders are the first to say that the churches have usually defaulted to the agencies as the sending authority. Let us summarize some steps churches need to take in order to fulfill their sending responsibilities.

• The home church should initiate the recommendation of its candidates to the mission agency before the candidate procedure starts.

• Missions agencies can help the churches by suggesting that potential candidates seek the approval of the home church before making application.

• Specific communication channels need to be set up and implemented between the home church and the misssion agency.

• The commissioning church must follow through in the appointee's deputation ministry both by persistent encouragement and periodic evaluation.

Notes to Chapter 8

1. George W. Peters, *A Biblical Theology of Missions* (Chicago: Moody Press, 1972), p. 218.

2. Ibid., p. 219

3. George A. Slavin, "The Missionary and His Local Church," *Evangelical Missions Quarterly* 7 (Spring 1971): 171.

4. Michael C. Griffiths, *Who Really Sends the Missionary?* (Chicago: Moody Press, 1974), p. 22.

5. Harold R. Cook, *An Introduction to Christian Missions* (Chicago: Moody Press, 1971), p. 116.

6. Peters, *A Biblical Theology of Missions,* p. 221.

7. Ibid.

8. Wendell Kempton, V. Ben Kendrick, and David Marshall, "The New Missionary and Church Support," *Baptist Bulletin* 47 (September 1981): 8-9.

The Church and Its Missionaries: Material Support

9

We press on now to further commitments of the home church to its missionaries. In our study we have found that the home church co-sends its missionaries together with the Holy Spirit (Acts 13:1-4). The church also enlists, selects, authorizes, ordains, and commissions its missionaries. In addition, we will find that the home church supports, prays for, evaluates, and revitalizes its missionaries.

The Home Church Plans Its Missions Budget

A church supports its missionaries in many ways. A visit to the airport when a missionary family is leaving for their field is convincing enough. Both personal friendships and corporate concern of the home church delegation are much in evidence. At their departure the bond of Christian love is cemented anew. Yes, support has more than a dollar sign written over it. But the dollar sign *is* there and rightly so!

Financial support is a biblical concept. Paul reminded the believers at Corinth:

> I robbed other churches by receiving support from them so as to serve you. And when I was with you and needed something, I was not a burden to anyone, for the brothers who came from Macedonia supplied what I needed (2 Cor. 11:8-9).

Paul wrote to the Philippian church to thank them for their repeated gifts to his needs (Phil. 4:15-18). He reminded the Philippians, ". . . when I set out from Macedonia, not one church shared with me in the matter of giving and receiving, except you only . . ." (Phil. 4:15). Paul used financial language throughout this Philippian passage. In Philippians 4:17 he spoke of their gift as "credited to [their] account." He continued, "I have received full payment and even more; I am amply supplied, now that I have received from Epaphroditus the gifts you sent" (Phil. 4:18). They had given out of obedient hearts, and Paul viewed their gifts as a "fragrant offering, an acceptable sacrifice, pleasing to God" (Phil. 4:18). As Homer A. Kent, Jr. writes:

> Paul's readers must not suppose that he is primarily concerned with their gift as such, but rather in the development of the grace of giving among them . . . . Their spiritual growth was the fruit Paul desired, and to this end he directed his ministry.[1]

Unfortunately, the purposes of our missions giving sometimes get lost in the budgetary process. The whole matter of missionary support can become terribly mundane. We do live in a real world and must take a realistic approach to the total picture of Christian stewardship. But may the Lord preserve us from treating our giving like a tax obligation to Uncle Sam!

Three considerations are before us: budget plans, budgeting procedures, and budgetary principles. See figure 18.

FIGURE 18

Percentage Plans	Separate Budget	Faith Promise Budget

Missions Budget Plans

Three Primary Budget Plans Are in Use

The first of these is the *percentage* plan. When the yearly church budget is fixed, missions giving makes up a percentage of the total budget along with salaries, Christian education, building maintenance, administration, and other categories. Although the budget may grow in dollar figures from year to year, percentages in the different budget categories change very little. In fact it is not unusual to increase the entire budget by a given percentage. This action provides more dollars, but it leaves the percentage of the budgeted categories at status quo. We often congratulate ourselves that we are giving "more to missions this year than last," although in reality we have not increased the *percentage* of giving.

On one occasion a pastor of a church was discussing support levels with a missionary who was supported partially by that church. In the course of conversation the missionary stated that the church had started their support at 14 percent of his total need, but that currently the church's support had fallen to 8 percent of his need. And this while the dollars given to missions increased each year! Obviously the missionary's financial need had increased more than the home church's giving. There is virtually no way to "unlock" missions giving in a percentage budget.

On the other hand, we must not think of the percentage that goes to missions as some sort of "Christian magic." There is no guarantee that if we give 50 percent of the budget to missions God is honor-bound to bless us. Fifty percent is certainly a worthy goal, but we must give with proper motivation. Although percentage budgeting is perhaps the most widely practiced of any system, it is not without its problems.

The second plan is the *separate* missions budget. Two sets of books are usually kept, one for the church's missions giving and the other for the general church budget. Some churches provide a means for donors to give to missions and the general fund separately. Other churches specify certain

Sundays as "missions" Sunday, and whatever comes in that day goes into the missions budget.

However the funds come in, this plan does allow for increased missions giving more readily than the percentage plan. Aside from the fact that this plan usually calls for two treasurers instead of one, there is at least one practical problem. It is not unknown for some who are disgruntled with the pastor or with some church decision to withhold from the general fund! Their money goes to the missions fund with an air of spirituality that is hard to measure. Of course the opposite can happen, and some people give little or nothing to missions.

The third budget plan is popularly known as *faith promise*. This plan constitutes a separate budget, as does the plan above, but its philosophy of giving is quite different. A.B. Simpson of the Christian and Missionary Alliance is given credit for this concept of giving. It is said that he thought it originated with Paul! Norm Lewis provides two helpful books on the philosophy of this plan and how to implement it in the local church.[2] Many churches use this faith-promise plan today, the best known of which is The Peoples Church in Toronto, Ontario. Now pastored by Paul B. Smith, son of Oswald J. Smith who was the former pastor, the church has used the faith-promise plan for some fifty years.

Raising the budget by way of faith promise is usually carried out during the annual missionary conference. Faith-promise cards are provided with the statement: "In dependence upon God, I will endeavor to give each week toward the worldwide missionary work of (name of church) the amount checked in the column at the right." Often different cards are printed for children with realistic amounts suggested for them. All faith-promise cards are totaled at the end of the conference. This amount forms the basis for the year's missions budget.

Why is the faith-promise plan successful? Here are several reasons.

• Faith is put to work. Faith-promise giving is usually beyond a tithe. Funds are not in sight, but the giver trusts God to supply them.

• This plan challenges people to systematic and increasing participation in world evangelism. Giving is not based on whim or a missionary's emotional appeal. Systematic giving contributes to increased interest in the object of the gift.

• From children to retirees, all can have a part. All can give according to their ability, and everyone can sense the excitement of meeting individual and corporate goals.

• Good results encourage increased giving the following year. Churches practicing faith-promise giving almost invariably report increased missions budgets year after year.

• Giving is treated as a spiritual activity. The obligation, after all, is to God. People are not approached personally about keeping up on their faith promise. No one is asked to give a certain amount. And, even if people sign their faith-promise cards, names are not made public. On at least one occasion after the faith-promise cards were tallied, they were burned in an incinerator on the church steps while the congregation sang the doxology. That's anonymity!

• Faith-promise giving is in accord with the spirit of the New Testament. Paul reminded the Corinthians, "Each man should give what he has decided in his heart to give, not reluctantly or under compulsion, for God loves a cheerful giver" (2 Cor. 9:7).

• Personal commitment is the only valid basis for faith-promise giving. When Paul gathered the offering for the Jerusalem believers, he credited the Macedonian churches with giving "beyond their ability" (2 Cor. 8:3). Paul continued:

> Entirely on their own, they urgently pleaded with us for the privilege of sharing in this service to the saints. And they did not do as we expected, *but they gave themselves first to the Lord* and then to us in keeping with God's will (2 Cor. 8:3-5).

Which of these three budget plans is the best? The truth is that each of them is working remarkably well in many churches. Occasionally a church combines the percentage plan with faith promise thus opening up the possibility of increased missions giving for those who wish to give more to mission interests.

The word to eager, young pastors is—"Go slow!" That church may actually know what they are doing! At any rate, there are reasons for present practices, and it is well to find out what the rationale is. Contrary to our American way of thinking, change is not always for the better. Gain the confidence of your people, then necessary changes can be made together.

Wise Budgeting Procedures Should Be Observed

Some of the most frequent questions asked today relate to misssionary support. It costs so much to send a missionary! True, mission boards and missionaries must seek every means to econimize. But we must face the truth of the matter: missions costs money. Good stewards must be faithful (1 Cor. 4:2). They must be frugal as well. Of course, being frugal does not mean being stingy!

Whatever budget plan a church uses, certain budgeting procedures are in order. Even churches with long-established budgets can profit by a budget review. This is particularly true when changes are under consideration. The following suggestions make up a check list of budgeting procedures. We assume here that missionaries in question are responsible to raise most or all of their support through deputation.

• Survey and evaluate the missions budget as it now stands. This is a fact-finding exercise, not a means for faultfinding. Checking the balance between home and overseas missions giving is helpful at this point. A chart that shows the total missions giving helps people to visualize the situation better. Of course, it can be a disquieting experience as well. However, we must know where we are before we can decide what needs to be done.

• Whatever the budget plan, set a definite missions goal. Effective missions giving cannot be carried out simply on "whatever comes in." We do not operate this way in other financial aspects of our daily lives. People do respond to goal setting, and they should have some part in setting the goals.

• Contact each board to determine who among your missionaries may need additional support. In this age of computers, mission agencies are increasingly able to provide efficient answers to your questions. But be patient and discreet. Mission boards are there to help, but they are not omniscient.

• Contact each missionary to determine the actual need for additional support. The missionaries serve in differing economic situations. Rates of inflation vary. Special projects may be in the planning stage that do not show up on the missionary's account in the home office. All of these variables must be considered in order to plan budget changes. At this point it will be helpful to construct a graph of the church's present missions giving and to lay over against it a graph of the actual need of each missionary unit. Visuals of this nature accentuate actuality in situations that we have only vaguely understood.

Perhaps you are saying at this point, "This is a lot of work!" Or, "We never did it this way before!" (These are the famous seven last words of the church, you know.) Yes, it takes work, and it may well be that we have not taken these steps in the past. However, we must be both knowledgeable and honest in missions budget making. Sometimes we seem to be more concerned about the color of the carpet than we are the quality of our missions outreach.

• When increases in support levels are called for—and this seems almost inevitable these days—should these increases be in equal amounts for each missionary unit? For example, should we increase the entire missions budget 10 percent for all missionaries? This is certainly the easiest way to handle the situation, and, alas, we often do it this way! Reginald L. Matthews observes:

> Many churches desire to give equal support, if possible, to the members from that church who serve on the mission field. However, equality is not necessarily a matter of giving the same amount of money to each one. Equality is determined by the purchasing power of the dollar on the respective fields at a particular time. Consider these examples. For years the purchasing power of a dollar in Africa was double that in Japan. Inflation in Brazil produced a condition in which a veteran missionary was lacking $200 a month in adequate support. The missionary committee can determine the factors involved by keeping close contact with one or more agencies operating in various areas of the world.[3]

As we mentioned above, contacting missionaries as well as agencies about current and anticipated needs is in order.

• Review the missions budget regularly. Some church missions committees review their giving on a quarterly basis. Certainly we need at least an annual review and update of the missions budget. It demands constant vigilance.

• Consolidate all missions giving into the church budget. Sunday School classes or other interest groups in the church often give to special projects such as an outboard motor, typewriter, or radio for an airplane ministry. These projects do enhance missionary interest and take care of real needs. However, these in-church groups should not take responsibility for regular monthly support for missionaries. When this is the case, missionary interest in the church soon fragments, and the overall missions picture in the church may be lost. These small groups usually do not have the financial stablility or strength to give more than token support.

• Do not delay taking on new missionaries, but in adding them start at a realistic amount of support. Tunnel vision should have no place in our missions giving. We know and love our presently supported missionaries, and their needs *are* great. But new recruits are in the wings, and we must not neglect them. What is a "realistic amount"? As we will see later, we need to think in terms of a percentage of their total need rather than a dollar figure. A better question is, "What *percentage* of their support can we give?" Of course, if the giving church is itself a mission church, the people will be limited in their budget. This situation is understood, but it should be the exception rather than the rule.

• Consider monthly support for mission agencies. Faith mission boards, whether denominational or interdenominational, have no financial resources aside from the churches or the missionaries themselves. Some churches set aside a dollar amount to go to various mission agencies each month. Better yet, other churches set a percentage figure to go to a given mission board with which their church-supported missionaries serve. For example, if missionaries serving with Missions Everywhere, Inc. receive a yearly total of $25,000 through a given church, that church might earmark another 10 percent, or $2,500, to go to the board. These funds help offset the cost to the mission of servicing the church's missionaries.

Unfortunately, most churches do not give in this way to the agencies. Increasingly the mission boards find it necessary to ask the missoinaries to include mission "service funds" in the support package. The mission may set a given amount for the missionary to raise for these service funds. Or the mission agency may make the amount voluntary for the missionary. Either way, the funds come out of the supporting churches!

Are the mission agencies careful about their overhead costs? What percentage of total annual income goes into home office expense? Depending on the financial policies of each agency, these expenses will vary a great deal. The church may wish to make this factor a part of their investigation of mission board financial policies. Certainly many agencies are highly conscientious in keeping their operating costs to a minimum. Some boards are known to operate on less than 10 percent of the total funds handled in a year's time.

• Consider establishing a scholarship fund for students preparing for career Christian service. Students are certainly in favor of this help! This should not be limited to those preparing for career *missionary* service. Just to know that the home church cares means a great deal to students whether the amount they receive is large or small.

• Help appointees contact area churches in their deputation process.

This help usually occurs at the pastor-to-pastor level. Area pastors need to know from the home-church pastor that the church is squarely behind the appointee. Hopefully the home pastor can tell other pastors to what extent the home church plans to back the appointee financially. Sometimes a faithful pastor will accompany appointees from the home church to introduce them to area pastors and to encourage the support of their churches. Any expressed interest and help from the home-church missions committee and pastor are especially helpful to single women who sometimes find it difficult to make contacts for their deputation ministry.

• Consider establishing a separate budget for needs such as social agencies and educational institutions. Many valid church activities find their way into the missions budget—such as radio or bus ministries. These are all important church programs, and they demand the full interest and support of the church. But care must be taken not to make the missions budget a catchall.

The question boils down to, "What is missions?" We established scriptural guidelines for answering this question at the outset of our study. The church must deal with the question seriously so that their missions budget is both scriptural and truthful.

Three Budgetary Principles Are Now In Focus

We have seen that budget plans and budgeting procedures are crucial to mature missions giving. Budgetary principles are very much people related and concern missionaries charged with getting church support.

An experienced church-planting missionary in Latin America makes this observation about his initial deputation experience:

> Many of the pastors I would meet were strangely quiet about missionary service. Now the story had a different tune. Now we heard how pressed the church was financially, how they didn't know how they would be able to do anything more for missions, and how it seemed that every day another missionary wanted to come to their church. . . .

> The "Great Illusion" is not a disillusionment to the missionary appointee, but it certainly must be considered a disappointment. Now one has to realize that there has been much speaking but little action.

> Must there be a "Great Illusion" for our Baptist missionary appointees? Not if pastors and laymen are as zealous in putting missionaries on the field as they are in talking about it. Not if our story is the same at our youth camps and fifteen years later when that young person becomes an appointee. Not if we remember it is good to advertise but you must be able to produce the goods.[4]

Many dedicated young people headed for the mission field today balk at deputation. They have heard how difficult it is to get meetings, how much travel is involved, how little interest is found, how many churches must be visited, and how long it takes to get the necessary support. What a future after candidate school! How can the sending churches, especially the home church, help quell the qualms of appointees?

The principles suggested here apply to those who are starting their missionary career. There is no thought of imposing a different support structure on missionaries who are established in their support system. Because of the world economic picture and the new attitudes toward deputation, we must consider new approaches to financial support.

Three principles come to view. See figure 19.

FIGURE 19

Missions Budgetary Principles

First, the home church must think in terms of *percentage* giving. How much support will they commit to their newly appointed missionary? Full support? Fifty percent? Twenty-five percent? Less? More? Every church must answer this question itself. But whatever the amount, the church must think in terms of percentage of the missionary's total support need, rather than the amount in dollars given each month. Sending out missionaries today is increasingly expensive—more than many of us realize.

If a missionary must raise $20,000 per year to cover all costs, what percentage should the home church give? In order to hold the number of supporting churches to a realistic number, each church must sit down and seriously consider the cost. What is a "realistic" number? For the sake of discussion, let us suggest seven to ten supporting churches—no more than fifteen.

Now back to the home church. The size of the church is not the primary question when it comes to full support. A church of fewer than a hundred members, for example, is known to be fully supporting a missionary family. This is an unusual case, but it is being done to the mutual blessing of church and missionary.

Other churches set their support level at 50 percent for those missionaries who are members of their church. The following statement by George A. Slavin demands attention. Pastor Slavin was then serving Faith Community Church in Roslyn, Pennsylvania.

> Our church has a missionary policy and seeks first to support our own young people committed to the mission field. If they are single this usually means full support. If married, it usually means approximately 50 percent of the support needed for the couple, because one of the couple is usually supported by another church.
>
> Periodically we make a survey of our missionaries' needs by asking them to report to us in simple form as follows:

Your need for one year as approved by your mission; support received (apart from personal gifts).

We then find out what percentage of support we underwrite, and increase accordingly, if a deficit is shown. A recent survey indicated that we had to increase our personal missionary support by $10,000 before we could consider taking on any new missionaries.

We continue our support of missionaries when retired, and we begin missionary support when they are approved as candidates.[5]

The number of "supporting" churches which some missionaries have is unfortunate, to say the least. Some have as many as fifty or sixty churches. Donald A. Hamilton tells of a missionary family supported by some forty churches spread from California to Canada and on to New England. In an effort to help this family, Hamilton spoke to the husband's home-church missionary committee:

I went into the session with the missions committee, and I told them about my conversation with the young man. I asked what percentage of the total support of this missionary family they supplied. One of the members, rather proudly, said, "He's our own member. We're supporting him at 50%." I then shocked the whole committee. I said that 50% was an excellent support level for a church's member missionary and I was very pleased that they were giving him $1,000 a month. "Oh, no!" was the reply. "Our policy states that we can't give anyone more than $200 per month." Policy, schomolicy! A 1940 policy is simply not appropriate for the 1970's, much less the 1980's. Change it.[6]

The result of Hamilton's recommendation was that seven churches assumed the support of this family. A more meaningful relationship with each church resulted, and the missionaries made better use of furlough time. Many more churches need to make changes in ther support policies. The question about missionary support revolves around the percentage of total support the church can give. To think in terms of at least ten percent of each missionary's total need is not unrealistic.

Second, sending churches need to think in terms of *geographic* giving. Why should an appointee travel 85,000 miles at a cost of $15,300 to get support? These are the figures used by David L. Marshall in his enlightening study, "Suggested Changes in Missionary Stewardship for the 1980's."[7]

In an attempt to solve this deputation dilemma, Marshall suggests that a church support missionaries whose home church is within one hundred miles of their own. He suggests also that a church avoid inviting a missionary to speak who lives more than a hundred miles away.

Some will feel that a hundred-mile radius for missionary support is a pretty tight circle. Draw the line where you will—two hundred miles, home state, or home state and adjoining states. We must put a stop to deputation globe trotting.

An innovative and pace-setting move is under way among five churches in suburban Detroit which can well be a pattern for the future. These churches are known as The Suburban Detroit Missions Consortium. The member churches are Calvary Baptist Church of Hazel Park, Covenent Community Church of Redford, Highland Park Baptist Church of Southfield, Redeemer Baptist Church of Warren, and Troy Baptist Church of Troy. Guidelines are in place for both organizational purposes and the acceptance of missionaries.

The goal of these five churches is to support fully missionaries under mission agencies recognized by all of these churches. The home church of each appointee will assume at least 30 percent of the needed support. Each of the other consortium churches will assume an equitable share of support according to their ability. A consortium of this nature is an appointee's dream!

Third, sending churches must follow the principle of *discerning* giving. Inflation, energy crisis, economic and political uncertainties all demand that we send and support only those who are clearly called, well prepared, and qualified to go. These factors take us back to the principle of selectivity, or corporate confirmation. Both home church and mission agency bear heavy responsibility here. We can afford no drones.

One four-year term of service by a missionary family today can cost the churches as much as $80,000 to $100,000. The value of people lost and dying without Christ cannot be measured in terms of money, of course. On the other hand, we must be good stewards, both as those who send and those who go.

Wrap-Up

In these days of economic uncertainty, missionary support is a growing concern for churches. Wise stewardship must be practiced by churches, mission agencies, and missionaries. The following guidelines summarize our thinking.

• Churches must not be intimidated by the past in planning their missions budgets. Although change for change's sake is not valid, churches must be willing to make their missions giving as effective as possible.

• The faith-promise budget plan has a good history of helping churches realize more of their potential in missions giving. However, this plan may not be a cure-all for every situation.

• Whatever the budget plan may be, careful budgeting procedures are crucial to the wise use of funds earmarked for missions. The church's missions budget must be carefully monitored. This budget should not be allowed to become a catchall. Other valid projects should be in a separate fund.

• The three principles—percentage giving, geographic giving, and discerning giving—must govern all mission-budget planning.

• The consortium idea serves as a concrete pattern that can be adapted for percentage and geographic giving.

Notes to Chapter 9

1. Homer A. Kent, Jr., "Philippians," *The Expositor's Bible Commentary,* ed. Frank E. Gaebelein, 12 vols. (Grand Rapids: Zondervan Publishing House, 1978) 11:156.

2. See Norm Lewis, *Faith Promise for World Witness: A Challenge to Every Church* (Lincoln: Back to the Bible Broadcast, 1974). He has also written *Handbook Faith Promise for World Witness: How to Do the Work* published by Back to the Bible Broadcast, 1974.

3. Reginald L. Matthews, *Missionary Administration in the Local Church* (Schaumburg, IL: Regular Baptist Press, 1970), p. 85.

4. Larry D. Smith, "The Great Illusion." An unpublished essay.

5. George A. Slavin, "The Missionary and His Local Church," *Evangelical Missions Quarterly* 7 (Spring 1971): 173.

6. Donald A. Hamilton, "Straight Talk on Bigger Slices of Pie," *ACMC Briefing* 2 (December 1979), n.p.

7. David L. Marshall, *Suggested Changes in Missionary Stewardship for the 1980's.* (Kokomo, IN: Evangelical Baptist Missions, 1979), n.p.

The Church and Its Missionary:
Personal Support

10

The apostle Paul was convinced that the prayer ministry of believers was essential to the success of his witness. In Romans 15:30 he states, "I urge you, brothers, by our Lord Jesus Christ and by the love of the Spirit, to join me in my struggle by praying to God for me." The basis of his request was the honor of Christ's name and the love of the Spirit. In asking them to join him in his "struggle," he was appealing to them to *agonize* or wrestle with him in prayer. The original compound expression occurs only here in the New Testament (*sunagonizomai*), and it is clear proof that Paul took the prayer ministry of the saints seriously. In this passage Paul pleaded with the church at Rome that their prayer might preserve him from the unsaved (15:31), and that he might have a joyous ministry among them on his arrival (15:32). Prayer was always specific for Paul.

Prayer is a vital part in *sending* messengers of the gospel (Matt. 9:36-38; Acts 13:3). Prayer also plays a key role in *sustaining* God's servants who go out to proclaim the Word. Paul wrote, "And pray for us, too, that God may open a door for our message, so that we may proclaim the mystery of Christ, for which I am in chains. Pray that I may proclaim it clearly, as I should." (Col. 4:3-4). Paul repeatedly asked the churches to pray for him (2 Cor. 1:11, Phil. 1:14; 1 Thess. 5:25; 2 Thess. 3:1-2; Philem. 22).

The Home Church Prays for Its Missionaries

Today, a home church can do three things to follow the patterns for prayer found in Scripture. See figure 20.

First, the home church can intercede more effectively by praying for *particular missionaries*. Missionaries supported directly by the church should be the primary focus. The people should be able to identify these missionaries by their names, fields, and types of ministry. The saints of Rome prayed for Paul in this manner. Some church members have missionaries who are family friends in whom they have a close interest. Perhaps they have entertained these missionaries in their home. Others will have missionary relatives or personal acquaintances whose burdens they share. These kinds of ties are natural bridges to pray for missionaries on a personal basis.

Second, God's people must pray for *particular missionary needs*. Paul was careful to tell the believers what his specific needs were (Rom. 15:31-32). We sometimes find it very difficult today, however, to keep up with

FIGURE 20

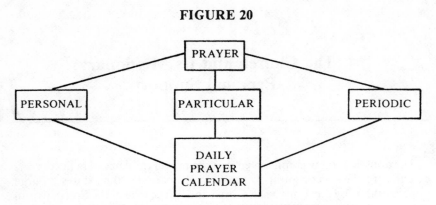

Structured Prayer in the Local Church

missionary prayer requests. The problem is twofold. Situations change so quickly on many fields that it takes constant effort to keep up an intelligent prayer ministry. Then, too, the missionaries, under pressure of urgent responsibilities on the field, sometimes find it difficult to keep the church informed about their specific needs. But the more specific prayer is, the easier it is to measure the answers.

In addition to current prayer needs, all missionaries have *standing requests* for which they always need prayer. These requests relate to political and economic situations, family, language, churches being planted, health, and other needs. Then of course missionaries have *emergency needs.* Word reaches the church about an accident, emergency surgery, border closings, or a military coup. These situations serve to galvanize the people into earnest praying brothers and sisters in Christ.

Third, *particular times* need to be set aside to pray for the specific needs of specific missionaries. In both the church and the home, this time must be scheduled in, lest carelessness result in little or no prayer at all. In special interest groups such as Sunday School classes and youth groups, in the worship services, and in the weekly prayer meetings, time can be given to meaningful missionary intercession. Prayer prompters, reminders in the church bulletin, and spot announcements from the pulpit will serve to prompt people to pray for missionary needs.

Some churches publish a prayer booklet, a prayer calendar, or a bookmark that includes the church-supported missionaries. These prayer reminders are ideal for family prayer. In family devotional times it is possible to pray purposefully for missionaries on a regular schedule. Current prayer letters are good reminders as well. But do keep them updated.

Some churches encourage their people to pray daily for a particular missionary by signing a faith promise card for prayer. The missionary's name is on the card with the caption: I promise to pray at least once daily for this missionary for one year. People making the faith promise sign the card giving their address. The card is in triplicate and is color coded; one copy goes to the church office, the second to the missionary, and the third to the signer.

Prayer for particular missonaries with particular needs and at particular times will result in particular blessing to all. Careful, purposeful planning and implementation are required for the attainment of these prayer goals.

The Home Church Evaluates Its Missionaries

Paul and Barnabas took seriously their responsibility to the home church. After all, they were commissioned and sent out by the believers at Antioch. Now, after their first missionary journey, they needed to report. Acts 14:27 states, "On arriving there, they gathered the church together and reported all that God had done through them and how he had opened the door of faith to the Gentiles." Reginald L. Matthews summarizes the significance of this scene concisely, "Missionaries are accountable to the commissioning church or supporting churches."[1] Accountability applies to all who serve in or through the local church. Paul and Barnabas gathered the *entire* church together for their report. These missionaries recognized their accountability to the whole church.

Paul and Barnabas reported *both* the good and the bad. The text states they "reported *all* that God had done through them." John Mark's defection, Jewish opposition at Antioch in Pisidia, Paul's stoning at Lystra, as well as the conversion of Sergius Paulus, believing Jews at Antioch, great multitudes of believing Jews and Greeks at Iconium—all this and more were included in the report. As our family prepared to return to the States after our second term, a fellow worker pleaded, "Be sure to tell them the whole story." How many missionaries "tell the whole story"? The missionary is responsible to relate both victories and defeats. Accountability is a vital part of Christian service.

The Gentiles were the particular objects of Paul's evangelism and church planting, and they were given special attention in the report. God "had opened the door of faith to the Gentiles." Paul's goals had been attained. As the apostle to the Gentiles, his mission to that point had been accomplished.

Ken Kilinski poses the question:

> How can be apply this principle today? In our church we have weekly staff meetings and monthly board meetings to provide accountability. We are responsible to each other for success as well as failures. Should our missionaries be any different? If they are simply an extension of the church staff, the church needs their regular reports, monthly letters, tapes, periodic visits, so they can be accountable for their performance.[2]

We need further evaluation in addition to Kilinski's suggestions. The missionary committee, or a comparable group, together with the pastor, need to talk with the missionary at least at four transition points: (1) in the

initial interview for recommendation to a mission agency, (2) before the
missionary's departure for the field, (3) upon the missionary's return from
the field, and (4) prior to the missionary's return to the field for another
term. See figure 21.

FIGURE 21

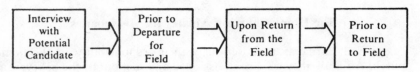

Missionary Evaluation Schedule

Churches must be careful not to interview their missionaries "to death."
We sometimes send lengthy questionaires to the field asking questions that
were previously settled—the answers to which are on record in the mission
office. Let us exercise Christian grace in demands we put upon our
missionaries. Here are some valid areas of inquiry: (1) current support
level, (2) specific problems they face in their work, and (3) progress toward
attaining their yearly or term goals. Let missionaries evaluate the
performance of the home church toward the missionaries themselves also.
After all, evaluation should work both ways.

Some missonaries wisely make it a policy to share their yearly and term
goals with their home churches. Periodically they report their progress and
their problems in prayer and news letters.

Mutual evaluation should be a regular feature in the home church-
missionary relationship. The process will be of benefit to all parties
concerned.

The Home Church Revitalizes Its Missionaries

A good deal is being said today about missionaries spending "quality
time" with their home churches. Michael C. Griffiths devotes an entire
chapter to the subject.[3] Only if the number of supporting churches is kept
within reason can this kind of time be enjoyed in the home church. This
number of churches is determined by initial deputation practices.

Paul and Barnabas had quality time in Antioch after their first trip. Acts
14:28 tells us, "And they stayed there for a long time with the disciples."
Depending on the chronologer followed, they were there for twelve to
eighteen months. Their reporting time was not a frantic weekend or a fatal
Wednesday night stand. Question time was more than a thirty-minute
Sunday School panel discussion.

On behalf of misssionaries, we must say that they do need rest and
recuperation. They must be allowed to readapt to American culture. They
will have other churches to visit. Time must be set aside for this ministry.
They need spiritual "retreading," too. Perhaps a mutually agreed-upon

number of months can be set aside for service in the home church, with the balance of furlough given to other matters. Edwin L. Frizen states:

> One of the best ways for a missionary to build relationships with the church is to spend time with the church and its members. To listen, and to learn of the current congregational concerns and interests. The missionary should seek to serve the church in every way possible. Participation in local church programs and functions with the church membership is very important. This is not an easy assignment.
>
> Research and planning for participation is essential in order to be effective, especially in view of the limitations of furlough, family obligations, multiple church involvement, continuing education opportunities, the need for additional support, and a host of other factors. Who is sufficient for these things?[4]

Really now, how can the missionary meet the expectations of the home church, constituency, and mission agency without becoming a furlough basket case? There must be mutual understanding concerning these varied furlough duties between the home church and their missionary. Marjorie A. Collins lists seventeen reasons for furlough.[5] High on the list is the kind of spiritual and emotional refreshing that can best be supplied by an understanding home church.

Furlough is a time of mutual ministry—the missionary and the home church both ministering to each other.

Wrap-Up

Praying, evaluating, and revitalizing: these are activities in which churches and missionaries can engage to their mutual benefit. Who can understand or measure the power of prayer? Evaluation that is borne out of mutual concern will benefit both church and missionary. Building one another up in the faith should be our constant concern. Missionaries want to give back to the church. Let us allow them to minister in even more effective ways than with slides and curios.

- Missionaries can minister in power only when people in the churches exercise fervent, meaningful prayer on their behalf.
- Evaluation should be welcomed by churches and missionaries alike when it is carried out in Christian love.
- Furlough time should be viewed as a time of ministry that is mutually beneficial to both churches and missionaries.

Notes to Chapter 10

1. Reginald L. Matthews, *Missionary Administration in the Local Church* (Schaumburg, IL: Regular Baptist Press, 1970), p. 31.

2. Ken Kilinski, "How Churches Can Follow Antioch's Model,"*Evangelical Missions Quarterly* 15 (January 1979): 22.

3. Michael C. Griffiths, *Who Really Sends the Missionary?* (Chicago: Moody Press, 1974), pp. 24-33.

4. Edwin L. Frizen, Jr., "Missionaries and Their Sending Churches" *Evangelical Missions Quarterly* 16 (April 1980): 75-76.

5. Marjorie A. Collins, *Manual for Missionaries on Furlough* (South Pasadena: William Carey Library, 1972), pp. 1-2.

The Missions Policy of the Church

11

It is estimated that 85 percent of "all American churches do not even have a missions committee."[1] For this reason, we must give serious attention to formulating a working committee charged with the oversight of the church's missions policies. A written missions policy is imperative.

Guidelines for a Missions Policy

For the sake of discussion we will use the outline of a policy of an actual local church.[2] Minor changes in some of the headings help clarify their intent. Although it is impossible for one church to adopt another church's exact missions policy, guidelines are helpful. See figure 22.

FIGURE 22

```
ORGANIZATIONAL GUIDELINES FOR A MISSIONS POLICY: Part 1

     Statement of Purpose
     I.   Missions Committee
          A. Composition
          B. Qualifications
          C. Chairman
          D. General Statement of Duties
          E. Specific Statement of Duties
          F. Committee Relationship to Church Board
          G. Procedure for Recommendation
```

Statement of Purpose
This written statement sets the pace for the entire missions policy of the church. What is "missions" as defined by your church? What is included and what is excluded? The *Missions Policy Handbook* explains:

The purpose statements should give a clear sense of direction to the committee. It should be the ultimate criteria around which the rest of the policy centers. Around these purpose statements, a unified effective policy can be developed for all the issues.[3]

When formulating a statement of purpose, the ultimate question to ask is What is missions as defined in Scripture?

The Missions Committee

The first question relates to the committee's *composition*. Your church's size will influence the size of your committee. In many churches this committee is elected by the congregation and often includes the chairperson, a representative from the women's missionary organization, a Sunday School officer, an elder or deacon, and a trustee, according to the church's leadership structure. Often both a man and a woman are elected at large by the congregation. Of course, the policy practiced in each congregation will influence the composition of the committee. The length of term varies, but elected commiteeᵉ members usually serve for two years on a rotating basis. The pastor should be an *ex offico* member. If the church has a minister of Christian education, this person could also be included.

Selecting the chairperson of this committee is crucial. Instead of making this an elected office, some church leaders believe this person should be appointed by the pastor and the church board, the appointment being ratified by the congregation. Others suggest that the entire committee be appointed. Reginald L. Matthews states:

> Perhaps the best method of selection is that the pastor and deacon board make appointments subject to ratification of the church. Time for prayer and consideration of a person's qualifications can be better assured this way than by popular election.[4]

Authority is delegated to the chairperson to oversee the entire missions program of the church. This person is responsible to the committee, the church board, and to the congregation. The election or appointment of this person must be carried out prayerfully and thoughtfully.

The length of term must be decided. A three-year term allows for more continuity in the committee and is preferred by some church leaders.

The second consideration relates to the *qualifications* of committee members. These must be spiritually mature people who demonstrate a concern for missions in the church. They will face many problems and must be able to deal with them objectively and fairly. Agreement with the church's missions policy is imperative.

A third factor is a *general statement of committee duties*. These will vary with each church. Some duties common to most churches will be administrative oversight of the missions policy, and recommendations concerning missions policy and the annual missions budget. The committee will work with the pastor in selecting missionary speakers and in planning the missionary conference.

Fourth, a *specific statement of committee duties* must be formulated. Again, these duties are determined by each church. These responsibilities relate directly to investigating potential candidates, evaluating supported missionaries and mission agencies, communicating missionary needs to the congregation, and coordinating all missionary activities and projects. Educating the church constituency about missions in the church is often overlooked by the missions committee. Specific means should be determined and put into practice.

Fifth, the *committee's relationship to the church board* must be spelled out. All decisions relating to financial matters come to the church board from the committee. Upon recommendation from the board these matters then come before the church for congregational action. The committee is responsible to the church body through the church board.

Sixth, the *procedure for recommendations* must be clear. Written recommendations go from the committee to the board. Upon approval by the board, the committee is authorized to carry out the recommended action.

The Missions Policy Delineated

The work of a missions committee is greatly enhanced by a written missions policy. Many hours of painful deliberation are saved by clearcut guidelines. See figure 23.

FIGURE 23

ORGANIZATIONAL GUIDELINES FOR A MISSIONS POLICY: Part II
II. Missions Policies

A. Qualifications
        1. Missionaries
        2. Mission agencies

B. Acceptance Procedure

C. Support Priorities
        1. Missionaries
        2. Mission Agencies

D. Support Policies

E. Expectations
        1. Missionaries
        2. Mission Agencies
        3. Church Corporate
        4. Church Members

F. Termination of Support

First, *qualifications* of both missionaries and mission agencies demand careful attention. *Missionaries* must reflect the convictions of the local church. Of course, if the missionary in question is a member of the church, this will be a foregone conclusion. All missionaries must give evidence of the new birth, confidence in God's call on their lives, participation in evangelism, and concern for spiritual growth.

The type of ministry the church is willing to support is delineated in the statement of purpose. If church-planting ministries are a high priority, for example, the church will seek out missionaries engaged in these ministries. This does not mean that other ministries will be bypassed.

The missions committee must keep in mind a balance between overseas and home missions. A balance of overseas areas will also have some bearing on selecting missionaries. However, do not refuse to support a missionary going to Brazil simply because you have two missionaries there already!

If your church is denominational, you will no doubt give priority to missionaries with your own group. By the same token interdenominational churches will not support many, if any, denominational missionaries.

Your church will no doubt want to make other determinations relative to the missionaries and type of ministry you wish to support. Carefully defined statements make it easier to say yes or no.

Qualifications are also important for *mission agencies*. These qualifications, too, must reflect the convictions of the church. The types of ministries in which the agency engages will be a determining factor. The agency should be willing to supply to the church its doctrinal statement, financial policies, and its principles and practices. If the church takes a stand concerning affiliation with ecumenical groups or activities, the agency must be in accord with this stand as well. Otherwise the agency does not really reflect the convictions of the church, and serious problems will arise.

Second, the *acceptance procedure* should be delineated. If appointees, missionaries, or agencies that are being considered met the qualifications set forth by the church, the missionary committee will make a recommendation to the church board. Assuming that the church gives a percentage of total support need, the committee will also recommend the support percentage. If the board approves the recommendation, the church is asked to take congregational action, or whatever procedure is appropriate according to the church's own policy.

Third, the policy must articulate *support priorities*. Support priorities for *missionaries* are often based on membership. Priority goes to those missionaries who are members of the church. Next the church considers those who have taken part in the church's ministry, but who are not members. An example of people in this category is students who work in a church while attending school away from their home church. A third category is those missionaries who are nonmembers and who have not served in the church.

Priorities for *mission agencies* must also be set. Perhaps the church has denomination affiliations. In this case, the church will give priority to agencies of their own affiliation. Other missions may meet the standards set down in the missions policy. If this is true, they may be considered as well.

Fourth, the church must spell out its *support policies.* All support of missions should go through the church rather than through organizations within the church. The entire church should support the entire missions budget.

As discussed elsewhere concerning the support of missionaries, it is preferable to give in terms of a percentage of the missionary's total support need rather than a stated dollar figure. Some churches may wish to settle on 50 percent support for missionaries who are members of their church and 10 percent to 25 percent for those who are not. The church may even wish to strive for 100 percent of the support for those who have grown up in the church. Whatever the percentage, it should be stated in the policy.

Perhaps the church can give to the agency a percentage of the total amount sent to missionaries annually with that agency. Ten percent of that total figure would be a great help in meeting the board's costs for servicing missionary needs.

The policy should state how soon support will start after the misson agency approves the missionary. Preferably support should start as soon as the missionary is placed on the budget.

It should be expected that medical and life insurance needs be included in the missionaries' stated support needs. This should also be true of retirement funds. A statement should be included in the church's policy concerning the needs of retired missionaries. It seems only right that some support continue for retirees, but each church should declare its own intention.

Fifth, certain *expectations* need to be included in the written policy. One of the principle items for *missionaries* is a reporting and evaluating procedure. The following schedule provides an example.

Report to the church concerning the progress of the work in the following manner:
   (1) At the beginning of each year draw up goals for that year.
   (2) Report progess throughout the year.
   (3) Evaluate the year's work at the end of the year.
   (4) Spend some time on furlough reporting to the church activities during past term of service.
   (5) Meet with the missionary chairman to report on activities and discuss their needs and plans for the future.[5]

Other expectations of the missionaries are to maintain regular communication with the church, and to inform the church of their specific and emergency needs.

In writing a missions policy we must keep in mind expectations of the *mission agencies.* They are expected to function as a liaison between the church and the missionary. This may be particularly necessary during times of political or economic stress. The agency should forward information to the church that it could not otherwise obtain. The board can often suggest missionary speakers for missionary conferences. In some instances, the agency can furnish all the speakers needed for a conference.

The *corporate church body* also has some expectations to meet. These need to be included in the missions policy. Responsibilities of corporate prayer and financial support rest upon the church. Providing assistance for the missionaries as they leave for their field and as they settle in for furlough are special times when the church can express their love and concern.

Expectations of individual *church members* should be included in the policy. The home is a key place for Christian parents to educate their children about missionaries and their work. Willingness to serve in the church's missionary program often brings unexpected rewards. Members of the congregation should expect to give systematically to the missions needs of the church. Regardless of age or vocation, all believers should be open to God's direction in their lives with respect to short-term service. The option of "tentmaking" (self-support) is also open to many.

Sixth, the policy must contain guidelines for the *termination of missionary support*. Occasionally a church must sever their relation with a missionary because of doctrinal deviation, improper conduct morally, failure to function effectively, or differences that arise between the missionary, the church, and the agency. The church may wish to identify other reasons.

Every effort must be made to rectify the problem. If it is not possible to correct the situation, certain guidelines are in order. It is best not to terminate support while the missionaries are on the field. However, if they refuse to return to the States or to make things right, it may be necessary to withhold their support.

Missionaries should be encouraged to communicate with the home church so that every effort can be made to settle the issue in a scriptural manner. Even though the missionary may be in the wrong, a vindictive spirit on the part of the church or the agency is never biblical.

It is quite obvious that a church cannot hammer out a missions policy overnight. Many months, even a year or longer, will be necessary to assemble a workable policy. It may be necessary to write several drafts before coming to a final policy statement. Even then, the door must remain open to revision and updating. Of course, the congregation must be kept informed and have a voice in final ratification.

Gordon MacDonald gives us a final word of caution in writing policy:

> Avoid the tendency to make your policy so detailed that you leave no breathing room for reasonable exceptions. A policy should cover 80 or 90 percent of all decisions. Beyond that, the committee makes decisions on the individual merits of each case.[6]

A well-known missions policy will help the local church perform its mission role in a Christ-honoring manner.

Wrap-Up

The purpose of this chapter has been to describe a workable missions policy for a local church. In the stewardship of both lives and giving, a church's missions program represents a significant outlay. Administering this stewardship with care is, therefore, doubly important. These concluding observations are in order.

• The discipline of working out a written missions policy helps the church to define what it understands missions to be.

• Provided with proper guidelines, a mission committee gives substance and direction to the church's missions program.

• A written missions policy simplifies the decision-making process in missionary personnel and support matters.

• The entire congregation needs to understand both the content and intent of the missions policy.

Notes to Chapter 11

1. *Missions Policy Handbook* (Pasadena: Association of Church Missions Committees, 1977), p. 16. This handbook is the best source of information currently available on forming a local church missions policy.

2. This outline of a missions policy is from Northland Baptist Church, Grand Rapids, MI. The general structure is helpful for our discussion.

3. *Missions Policy Handbook*, p. 16.

4. Reginald L. Matthews, *Missionary Administration in the Local Church* (Schaumburg, IL: Regular Baptist Press, 1970), p. 53.

5. Adapted from the *Northland Baptist Church Missionary Policy*, p. 5.

6. *Missions Policy Handbook*, p. 11b-4.

Missions Promotion in the Church

12

Constant attention and diligent work are required to maintain an up-to-date, dynamic missions environment in a church. If the last missionary conference was poorly attended, can we lay all the blame on spiritual lethargy? Do the people in the church understand that missions is not an option but an obligation? How have we helped them? Perhaps the women's missionary organization now attracts only those who "have the time"—the retirees. Again, is lagging interest a spiritual problem only?

To be sure, good advertising is not the only answer to maintaining a high level of missionary interest in the church. But good promotion does help. The purpose of this chapter is to provide reminders and guidelines for more effective missions promotion. The following figure demonstrates this:

FIGURE 24

Missions Promotion in the Local Church

Means of Promotion

Use Informational Aids for Missionary Understanding

Three kinds of informational aids are at our disposal, namely, the bulletin, the bulletin board, and if you will, the back wall.

Make the church bulletin come alive with missionary information through listing a missionary-of-the week, current prayer requests from church-supported missionaries, and periodic biographical sketches of the missionaries. These sketches can be made as attractive bulletin inserts and should consist of both personal and field data. Someone with writing skills can prepare a series of bulletin inserts featuring all of the supported missionaries.

Many churches maintain a bulletin board where missionary information can be gathered at a glance. The information must be up to date and displayed in an imaginative and attractive format. Responsibility should be given to someone who will spend time making this board a viable part of mission-related publicity. Being bulletin board chairperson is a rather unheralded position, but this ministry is very important. Church-sponsored missionaries need the best representation possible.

The third means of maintaining a dynamic missions atmosphere is to give careful attention to the back wall, or, more specifically, the missionary map. These come in all shapes and sizes, some attractive and others less than adequate. Perhaps in our changing world the map needs to present only the continents in outline form, indicating the approximate location of the missionaries. This type of map eliminates purchasing a new one every few years to keep up with the changing country names and boarders. If pictures of missionaries are used, they should be updated every furlough. Woe to the missionary whose picture has not been changed for ten years!

Speaking of the back wall, some churches highlight the missionary-of-the-week by using an easel placed near the missionary map. An enlarged picture of the missionary or missionary family is attractively mounted on the easel together with a brief account of their ministry.

Invite Missions Resource People

The systematic utilization of missions-related people will broaden missionary understanding in the church. Four categories of speakers are available.

The first, and most widely used, are the furloughing missionaries. For an in-depth understanding of a particular country of ministry, the experienced missionaries hold the day. They can provide wise counsel to those looking for God's guidance in their lives. Pastors can gain insight into current problems and needs that only the seasoned missionary provides. In turn, this affects the entire missions program of the church. When possible use furloughing church-supported missionaries. They are particularly helpful in the church's missionary conference.

Second, mission board administrators add breadth to a congregation's understanding of missions. These people know the programs and problems being experienced on many different fields. This information adds a dimension that many churches need in order to broaden their vision beyond the few missionaries in whom they have a personal interest.

Third, the missionary appointee brings a new dynamic into the church's understanding of missions. Unfortunately these recent recruits are sometimes looked upon as mere fund raisers for their particular ministry. However, they have a ministry to a local church that even an experienced missionary or mission administrator does not have. The appointee's evident commitment to God's will and his proximity in age to the youth in the church give him entree that other speakers do not have. These new missionaries may well challenge some of the ingrained ideas we all seem to have about what a misionary should be. Even though churches cannot promise immediate or even eventual financial support, pastors and missionary committees should utilize these new missionaries in the scheduling of missionary speakers. Their presence is always a powerful reminder that God is still calling people into career ministry both here and abroad.

Fourth, a word should be said about the ministry of a missions professor in the local churches. His constant contact with young people gives him insight into the thinking and commitment of today's prospective missionaries. Because of the demands of his teaching ministry, he is in touch with current issues and missions-related literature. His insights complement and bring a new dimension to the contributions of the other categories of mission speakers.

Provide Missions Resources for the Library

Readers deserve meaningful, up-to-date mission books and periodicals. Much good material is being written today in mission biographies, strategy, stories, local church responsibilities, issues and trends, growing churches, and the biblical basis of missions. There is something for every interest. A well-informed church librarian who promotes missions reading is a gift to any church. Harold R. Cook, however, issues a warning:

> The biggest mistake in the choice of books is to get the ones you think the people ought to read rather than those they really want to read. It is all right to have a certain number of reference books, but most of the books should be of the sort that nearly everybody is interested in reading. When one person likes a book he is sure to recommend it to someone else. But remember that tastes differ. You will have to make allowance for this.[1]

A word of caution also needs to be said about keeping the missions books current. Out-of-date books need to be ruthlessly eliminated. A few missions classics should be on the shelves. Books on the history of missions and mission policy need to be constantly updated.

Other media are available today for promoting missions understanding such as video tapes, films, filmstrips, slide-tape presentations, cassettes, and flannelgraph stories. These can be used to good advantage in various departments of the Sunday School as well as in other groups in the church. The church librarian can be of great help in promoting missions interest by making resources available. Some of these media presentations can be obtained on a rental basis from mission agencies.

Plan Missionary Conferences with Care

A great deal of creative thinking is needed to keep missionary conferences from being "the same old thing" year after year. Conferences should provide inspiration, information, and instruction. These aspects can be provided when well-defined goals are kept in mind. Those people who plan the conference need to keeep these principles in mind. See figure 25.

FIGURE 25

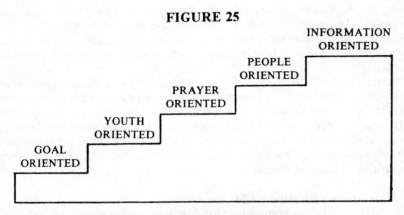

Planning the Missionary Conference

First, conferences must be *goal oriented.* One goal, for example, may be related to the missions budget. This is particularly true if the church is using the faith-promise plan of giving. Other goals may relate to attendance, or commitment to missionary service. Each conference committee needs to think through what they really want to accomplish and set faith goals accordingly.

Second, conferences need to be *youth oriented.* Local churches should be the chief source of missionary recruits. Effort must go into making the conference program attractive to the young people in the congregation. If possible, invite one or two of the young people to serve on the conference planning committee. Involvement at this level will help ensure youth participation in the meetings. Keeping the conference youth oriented can be helped by providing some separate meetings for adults, youth, and children. Rotating the missionaries among these groups gives the missionaries better acquaintance with the entire church family.

Scheduling is important if the youth are to attend. The conference must not be scheduled at the same time as the football game of the year or basketball playoffs. This has happened!

Third, a well-planned conference will be *prayer oriented.* Why is it that praying for missionaries is so mundane to many of us? Is such a state of affairs of our own making? Even when we know the needs of the church-supported missionaries, they sometimes seem so unreal and unlikely to have an answer. And missonaries are usually so far away. In short, identifying with the missionary's needs is all but impossible. Yet we limit God by our unbelief! Sounds familiar, doesn't it? Reginald L. Matthews emphasizes the importance of prayer in preparing for the conference:

> Emphasis upon prayer is a significant part of preparing for the missionary conference. In addition to the regular prayer meeting, other times of prayer should be planned. For example, Sunday School classes may take five minutes at the opening of the teaching

period for this purpose. Cottage prayer meetings may be arranged for the week before the conference begins . . . . The missionary conference should be a matter of daily prayer for two or three weeks before conference at all the family worship periods in the home.[2]

In preparation for the conference every effort should be made to determine specific needs of the church's missionaries. Then during the conference special prayer times can be planned in each service to pray for these needs unitedly. Distributing prayer prompters to all who attend will remind people to pray for these needs in their own devotional times as well.

Fourth, a conference should be *people oriented.* Naturally, missionaries participating in a conference are anxious to explain everything they can about their field. However, unless there is opportunity for interaction with the hearers, the missionaries will not know what information people need and want. One needs only to open the meeting for discussion after a presentation to find that all questions have not been answered! Features such as penal discussions and workshops will provide interaction between missionaries and the people. These will prove to be a learning experience for all concerned. Many of God's people *are* concerned for the life and work of their missionary friends. When armed with facts and reasons as to why things are as they are, these people in the church will enter into their support role with new and enlightened vigor.

Sunday School classes are sometimes charged with the task of providing displays for the conference. This activity involves many more people, and gives them a keener interest in the conference.

This leads us to the fifth principle to observe in planning a conference. Our conferences should be *information oriented.* We said earlier that churches need inspiration, information, and instruction. Conferences are often geared to inspire the saints, but information about missions may be lacking. Conferences should be an exciting time of updating the local church on current opportunities, problems in developing countries, and demands on missionaries working in today's exploding populations. Opportunities for short-term missionaries need to be explored. Open doors for tentmakers, or nonprofessional missionaries, should be investigated. The economic realites of world missions must be faced and solutions sought by the missionary and his supporting churches. Missionary conferences provide a platfrom for the prayerful consideration of these needs and others.

Organize for Missions Promotion

The organization in the local church with the longest and most illustrious history of missions promotion is the women's missionary group. Even when the missionary interest of others in the church has waned, some women have stayed by the stuff and provided a focus for missionary outreach.

Too often the women's missionary organization is remembered only for its quilts and bandages. Certainly they provide such necessities, but this caricature is unfair. They focus on the needs and activities of missionary women who are supported by the church. Furloughing missionary women are given opportunity to share information about their work and their needs. These groups often provide clothing and household items for missionary families. Missionary doctors and nurses have many needs met through these women's organizations.

Through the combined efforts of denominationally and regionally related women's missionary groups, projects are financed amounting to thousands of dollars.

Few churches have been successful in organizing permanent men's groups with a missionary purpose. But this does not mean that men are disinterested in missions. Teams of men with building skills have served short terms on various mission fields putting up medical facilities or missionary housing, saving missionaries money and much valuable time. Men should have specific needs presented to them with which they can identify. Groups of men often rally to the needs of a missionary preparing to go overseas. Some men find real delight in building crates and welding steel drums. These kinds of task forces need to be encouraged among the men in our churches.

Some churches have a vision committee charged with the task of planning for the church's future. A vital part of this planning should be projections for the church's missions program.

Wrap-Up

Promotional goals include providing a dynamic missions environment through up-to-date informational aids, utilizing mission-related speakers, maintaining meaningful library holdings, planning creative missionary conferences, and organizing for greater missions outreach. A few summary thoughts are in order.

• Missions promotion in the local church is not mere gimmickry. Whatever its form, good promotion will inform, inspire, and instruct the congregation.

• Promotion demands forethought. Planning for special speakers and missionary conferences must be correlated with the entire church calendar year.

• Adequate funds for promotion must be planned into the missions budget.

• Promoting gifts to the library can provide needed funds for missions-related books. Providing a book list with prices may encourage some in the congregation to purchase books.

• Appointing capable people to take responsibility for specific aspects of promotion is imperative.

Notes to Chapter 12

1. Harold R. Cook, *An Introduction to Christian Missions* (Chicago: Moody Press, 1971), pp. 234-35.

2. Reginald L. Matthews, *Missionary Administration in the Local Church* (Schaumburg, IL: Regular Baptist Press, 1970), p. 60.

Part 3

Strategic Role of the Mission Agency

The Mission Agency Serves the Church

13

Little did William Carey dream in 1792 that the newly formed English Particular Baptist Missionary Society would be a pacesetter for many mission societies in ensuing missions history. Today North America alone is home base for over 700 mission agencies.[1]

Essentially the terms *mission board, mission agency, mission society,* and *mission council* each refer to an organization that helps both local churches and missionaries implement Christ's commission to the church. Local churches, as we have seen, are the hub of the missions wheel, while mission agencies are spokes in the wheel helping churches extend their work of world missions. Our aim in this chapter is to discuss the purpose of mission agencies, their position in relation to their church constituencies, and the types of mission agencies serving churches today.

Purpose of the Mission Agency

The mission agency is a *service* organization aiding the local church in its task as the *sending* agency. The mission board accomplished its purpose through (1) its organizational structure, (2) its outreach resources, and (3) its consulting role.

The Agency's Organizational Structure

The mission agency provides organizational structure for both churches and missionaries to implement their work.

1. *Leadership capacities.* Because of their personal life commitment and their daily handling of field affairs, mission leaders provide insights into world missions that are otherwise unavailable to local churches. Many of the people who lead our mission agencies are those who have had field experience. Through close contact with missionaries, travel, reading, and sometimes advanced studies, these leaders keep abreast of current missionary developments around the world. Pastors and their people need the ministry of mission leaders not only at headquarters but also in their churches.

2. *Administrative capacities.* Both local churches and missionaries look to the mission board for the proper handling of their business affairs. With the multiplicity of government red tape, legal requirements, and worldwide unrest, churches and missionaries need the mission's help as never before. Little do many of us realize how many missionary hours are

devoted to these matters even by field business managers.

The number of missionaries in which a local church has an interest also contributes to the necessity of a misson agency to handle the volume of detail that is generated. Few, if any, churches have the staff or expertise to handle international matters without the assistance of mission agencies.

3. *Promotional capacities.* Churches need adequate promotional materials to publicize missionary work to their people. Many missions maintain a professional promotional staff who provide literature and multimedia productions for use in the churches. Mission agencies can present either a panoramic view of missions or spotlight specific fields and types of ministry. The breadth of their resources far exceed those of the local church. Mission agencies indeed possess unique abilities to serve the churches.

The Agency's Outreach Resources

By their very nature, mission agencies have a broader view of world needs than local churches do. Resources available to churches through the mission board are information, orientation, and exploration. See figure 26.

FIGURE 26

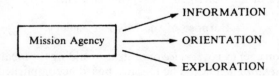

The Agency's Outreach Resources

1. *Resource for information.* Requests for information pour into mission headquarters daily. When a political or economic crisis strikes a country, supporting churches are anxious to know the status of their missionaries. Usually information is readily available either directly from the field or through the embassy or consulate in the country. If information is not immediately available, the mission will continue to seek it until a satisfactory answer is found.

Churches working on their annual missions budgets can often obtain helpful information on the financial needs of their missionaries through the agency. The increasing use of computers facilititates the process of finding needed information quickly.

People interested in a missionary career find mission agencies ready to share field needs and possibilities. Boards are anxious to share their needs for personnel on any given field.

When students do research on missions-related subjects, they use mission agencies as a ready source of information. Mission executives welcome opportunities to help students gain a better understanding of various fields.

2. *Resource for field orientation.* One of the purposes of a mission board is to provide a channel through which missionaries can carry out their life ministry. For people who are preparing to be missionaries, the agency is the primary source for orientation to a specific field. For example, if a person is going to France to engage in church planting or student ministry, the mission will have resources for orientation to those specific ministries. Not only are field surveys available, but personal contact with people who are working in these ministries will give the prospective missionary help that is unavailable elsewhere. There is no need for a rookie to arrive on a field "not knowing what to expect."

Mission personnel also stand ready to advise prospective missionaries about specialized preparation for a ministry. If a person, for example is headed for a support ministry such as medical work, literacy, or teaching MK's, the mission agency is a prime source of advice for the requirements for these ministries. How much better to have this information in hand during the preparation process!

3. *Resource for new field exploration.* Mission agencies are often concerned about growth not only in terms of missionary personnel, but also in new fields. These new fields may be new types of ministry such as translation, literacy, or university students. Mission agencies have the resources and personnel to conduct the necessary research for these new possibilities. Reliable boards will take careful fact-finding steps before launching out into a new country or ministry. Research is conducted to determine real need. The mission agency contacts government officials to establish their openness and requirements to enter their country.

The outreach capacity of a mission agency is a positive asset for local churches and prospective missionaries. Their resources need to be used to the fullest extent.

The Agency's Consulting Role

Information is one of the most sought out commodities in our busy world. Somehow we believe that if we have the right information, we can make the right decisions. Although this is not necessarily true, we do need the help of others in finding advice for life's decisions. One of the purposes of the mission agency is to provide counsel both for churches and for missionaries in their mutual missionary outreach. The mission plays a threefold consulting role.

1. *On behalf of sending churches.* Many circumstances arise in a church's missions program that demand outside help. A missionary may request to change fields. Health problems arise on the field necessitating an early furlough. Political uncertainties dictate the withdrawal of missionary women and children. Or should entire families evacuate? A missionary wishes an extended furlough for further study. All these situations and many more necessitate joint action and understanding by church and agency. Both must keep the channels of communication open. The mission can provide valuable input.

2. *On behalf of field missionaries.* Decisions often arise on the field that demand attention from the agency. These decisions may involve the purchase of new property, the launching of a new ministry, or the seemingly irresolvable tensions between missionaries and national leaders. Mission board field secretaries serve as liaison between the missionaries and the board and are often consulted for board opinion and direction. Field secretaries make periodic visits to mission fields to help with present or potential problem solving. Indirectly this consultation process also assists the sending churches. The board is in a better position to help missionaries with field needs. This service is a part of their delegated authority.

3. *On behalf of potential missionaries.* Who is in a better position than the mission agency to help those who are seeking direction for future missionary service? Pastors and teachers have valuable input, but in the final analysis mission board personnel have at their fingertips the specific opportunities available on many fields. Some mission agencies publish lists of needed personnel on their various fields. Periodically the Interdenominational Foreign Missions Association (IFMA) lists missionary opportunities in all of its member agencies. People committed to a missionary career should be encouraged to tap the consulting resources of mission personnel.

Position of the Mission Agency

Mission boards have served churches for less than 200 years. Some scholars hold that in the missionary teams of the first century we have the antecedents of a mission agency. The close relationship of Paul and Barnabas with the church in Antioch, their mutual confidence, the detailed reporting of the missionaries to the church (Acts 14:27), and their mutual concern for God's will are looked upon as setting precedents for mission societies today. In speaking of Paul's growing leadership, Harold E. Amstutz states, "There was need for someone to act apart from any one local church, but in harmony with all the churches who enthusiastically endorsed the work."[2]

Whatever precedents we may find for mission agencies in the New Testament, sending missionaries today is not as simple as it was when Paul said Yes to God on the Damascus road. Mission societies provide valuable services for sending churches.

The Agency's Authority
Mission agencies carry out their work under the authority delegated to them by the sending churches. Delegated authority was practiced in the first century. Christ delegated authority in the apostles (Matt. 28:18-20). The church in Antioch delegated authority to Paul and Barnabas (Acts 13:3). Paul delegated responsibility to Timothy, Titus, and others on the missionary team (1 Tim. 1:3-4; Titus 1:5). Ian M. Hay observes:

The Mission Society, whether denominational or inter-denominational, really performs the same function. In each case the local church has delegated to the society the authority and the responsibility of the church to get the job done. The Mission therefore is the Agency through which the local church exercises its sending authority. In each case, however, there must be accountability on the part of the Mission to the local church. There must be openness of communication and understanding.[3]

Normally the local church *initiates* the sending of missionaries and the supplying of funds for their work. The mission agency in turn *implements* this sending procedure. Historically, however, the church has not always played the part of initiator. Student movements such as members of the Haystack Prayer Meeting in the early nineteenth century and the Student Volunteer Movement in the late nineteenth century have prodded the churches to missionary action. Again in the late twentieth century students are showing unusual vitality in their desire to reach hidden-people groups for Christ. If parachurch organizations such as mission agencies have assumed the initiating authority of the local church, they have done so by default. Local churches must prove themselves to be the sending authority.

The Agency's Principles and Practices

The principles and practices of the mission agency should represent the convictions of the sending churches. Three factors demand our attention, namely, compatability, communication, and control.

The mission agency through which a church works must be *compatible* in doctrine, in finances, and in ministry goals.

First, denominationally affiliated mission agencies and churches will usually reflect compatible doctrinal positions. But problems do arise, and churches need to be alert to changes that take place. For example, the modernist/fundamentalist controversy of the early twentieth century spilled over into church/mission relationships. As a case in point, the foreign board of the Northern Baptist Convention (now American Baptist Churches of the U.S.A.) instituted the inclusive policy in which missionaries of both modernist and fundamentalist persuasion were accepted. As a result, both the Regular Baptist and the Conservative Baptist movements began, fueled in part by the desire of churches to cooperate only with agencies with whom they could agree doctrinally. Whether denominational or nondenominational, churches must seek out agencies in whom they have unreserved confidence doctrinally.

Financial compatibility between church and agency is crucial. Some boards use a personalized support plan for missionaries. In this plan all funds are raised by the individual missionary, and these funds are channeled into his account in the mission office. Other agencies use a pooling plan. In this system all gifts go into a common fund from which the missionaries share. Adjustments are made, of course, for family size, type of ministry, rate of inflation, and other changing factors. Obviously there are advantages and disadvantages to both plans. In order to be good stewards, a church needs to undertand and agree with the support plan practiced by its agencies.

Compatibility between church and agency in ministry goals is also essential. The ministries, of course, are represented by the missionaries being supported by the church. Both priorities and balance must be kept in view. In its worldwide outreach, what does the church want most to accomplish? How can these goals be reached? The church should first look at its own goals, and then seek out those agencies that will help them attain those goals. Mission agencies can help the sending churches by spelling out the ministries in which they are involved. Churches should be encouraged to investigate the extent to which the agency is attaining its goals.

The second aspect of the mission agency's principles and practices is *communication*. Two communication loops are in view as illustrated in figure 27.

FIGURE 27

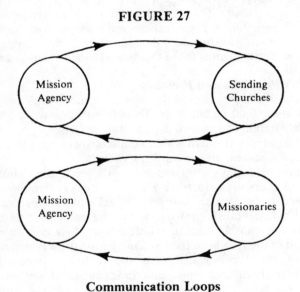

Communication Loops

First, an ongoing exchange of information between the agencies and the home churches should be encouraged. Second, a communication loop between the agency and its missionaries aids greatly in mutual understanding. Although a mission agency may service scores, or even hundreds of missionaries, their home churches need the best communication network possible. Missionaries should not bear sole responsibility to keep their churches informed about their work.

Failure to listen when the other person speaks is one of our greatest problems in communication. The agency often speaks through letters, publications, film media, and other means. Let us in the home churches listen and respond. Surely we do not need a life and death situation on some distant field to catch our attention.

Field missionaries sometimes find mission headquarters to be a very distant place. On occasion decisions are made that missionaries do not understand simply because the lines of communication are not in good repair. A major motel chain advertises its services with "no surprises." Missionaries appreciate this kind of relationship with their mission. Of course, missionaries must remember that communication is a loop, with the mission home office expecting the same courtesy from the field. A mission agency that is a good communicator will have a happy constituency of churches and missionaries.

In addition to compatibility and communication, the question of *control* arises. Two aspects are in view: (1) the supervision of missionaries, and (2) the management of funds. We have established the principle that the churches delegate authority to the agencies to carry out their mutual purposes. See figure 28.

FIGURE 28

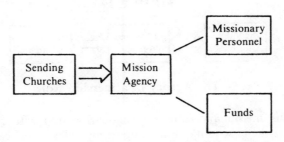

Delegated Authority to the Agency

First, supervision of missionaries and their activity is delegated to the mission agency. To whom are missionaries *ultimately* responsible? Amstutz responds, "the missionary is answerable to the church in all matters pertaining to life and work."[4] George W. Peters adds, "The missionary remains the representative of the church first and foremost, only secondarily that of the society. The church does not sign over the missionary to the society."[5] Although missionaries are primarily accountable to their sending churches, the mission agency must be recognized for the scope of its delegated responsibilities. The boards are faced with the constant necessity of maintaining harmony with both missionaries and churches. Amstutz states:

> The mission board is accountable to the missionaries and the churches in maintaining a service ministry. The services include partnership with the home church in carefully screening personnel as Paul did in Acts 16:1-3 and Acts 18:24-27; the supervisor of every aspect of the missionary ministry and the necessary communication.[6]

Second, mission agencies are charged with the responsibility of overseeing the collection and disbursement of funds from the churches. Because they are not-for-profit organizations, the Internal Revenue Service requires that mission agencies exercise careful surveillance and control of funds in order to maintain their nonprofit status.

Reliable mission societies have an annual audit of their financial affairs. In this manner, the churches are assured of proper financial procedures. For example, mission agency membership in the Interdenominational Foreign Mission Association (IFMA) is granted only if the agency meets the Association's standards. Two of these requirements are that the agencies "exercise control over missionaries" and that they "publish audited financial statements annually . . . ."[7]

The Agency's Partnership Role

The mission agency's partnership role is twofold: (1) partnership with the sending churches, and (2) partnership with the national churches. See figure 29.

FIGURE 29

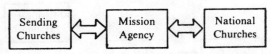

The Agency's Partnership Role

Paul and his missionary team enjoyed partnership with first-century churches in their sending and supporting roles. For example, his relationship with the church at Antioch continued with mutual concern and compatibility. Paul launched his three missionary journeys from Antioch (Acts 13:3-4; 15:40-41; 18:22-23), and he gave them full acount of his ministry (Acts 14:26-28). The church at Philippi supported Paul and his companions (Phil. 2:25; 4:15). He looked to the church at Rome to assist him on his trip to Spain (Rom. 15:24).[8]

Today the sending church and mission agency complement each other in their partnership roles. Peters observes:

> The mission agency ought to be the church's provision, instrument, and arm to efficiently expedite her task. It can neither displace nor replace the church, though it may be called upon to act in the place of the church.[9]

The mission agency also maintains a partnership role with the national churches. Mission-church relationships are undergoing rapid changes today. J. Herbert Kane describes the volatile nature of mission-national church tensions:

> The tensions are heightened by the fact that the national leaders want change and want it in a hurry, while the missions many times

are satisfied with the status quo and consequently have a tendency to drag their feet.

The moral responsibility rests heavily with the missions. They, more than the churches, are to blame for the present impasse. It is therefore up to them to take the initiative to bring about peaceful change.[10]

W. Harold Fuller describes four stages of development in mission-church relations, namely, (1) pioneer, (2) parent, (3) partner, and (4) participant.[11] Those missionaries who have been pioneers and parents sometimes find it difficult to function now as partners and participants. Some may find greater use for their gifts by again pioneering among people who have yet to hear the gospel. With whatever adjustments need to be made, missions must seek ways to realize partnership with national churches. Organizational structures are less important than mutual attitudes. As Fuller states, "The most ideal structure can be ineffective if there is lack of mutual respect, trust, and cooperation."[12] Mission-church partnership roles will continue to demand mutual humility and prayerful wisdom.

Types of Mission Agencies

Denominational Agencies

There are different types of mission agencies. First, some agencies are an integral part of a *denominational* structure. Funding is provided through the denomination's unified budget. The mission agency is usually located at the denominational headquarters, and it administers both funds and missionary activity for the denomination. An example of this type of agency is the Foreign Mission Board of the Southern Baptist Convention.

Independent Agencies

Second, other mission agencies are *independent* of denominational control. These agencies cooperate with local churches, but they maintain their own organizational structure. Some of these agencies are *denominational*, whereas others are *interdenominational*. Baptist Mid-Missions is an example of an independent, denominational mission agency. This mission is approved annually by the General Association of Regular Baptist Churches, although it serves other Baptist churches. Five other independent Baptist mission boards have this same affiliation with the GARBC. These agencies are "faith" missions in that they have personalized support plans and have no access to a denominational unified budget.

Independent, interdenominational mission agencies represent a strong contingency of missionaries. These agencies are recognized as "faith" boards, because they must depend upon local churches to meet their budget needs voluntarily. These mission boards screen potential candidates, and churches channel funds through these agencies to support missionary ministries worldwide. Both missionaries and funds come from

Bible-believing churches, most of which are interdenominational or nondenominational. One of the best-known independent, interdenominational agencies is The Evangelical Alliance Mission (TEAM). See figure 30.

FIGURE 30

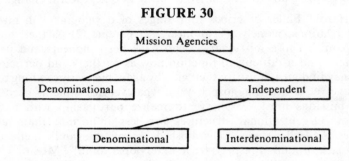

Types of Mission Agencies

Wrap-Up

The first objective in this chapter was to delineate the purpose of the mission agency. Second, the position of the mission agency in relation to the sending churches was described. In conclusion, the types of mission agencies were defined. Some of the highlights follow.

• Mission agencies constitute a valuable resource tool for churches as well as for both practicing and potential missionaries.

• The supervisory capacity of mission boards is delegated to them by the sending churches.

• Mission boards function as service agencies rendering valuable assistance to sending churches and missionaries.

• The selection of a mission agency is as important to a sending church as its selection of missionaries.

• The mission agency is a crucial communication link between sending churches and their missionaries.

• The mission agency's partnership role is an expression of mutual respect and responsibility between the mission and both the sending and the national churches.

• Sending churches need to understand the types of mission agencies available to them in carrying forward their missions programs.

Notes to Chapter 13

1. Samuel Wilson ed., *Mission Handbook: North American Protestant Ministries Overseas,* 12th ed. (Monrovia, CA: Missions Advanced Research and Communication Center, 1979), p. 19.

2. Harold E. Amstutz, *The Gospel Yoke* (Cherry Hill, NJ: Association of Baptists for World Evangelism, 1982), p. 17.

3. Ian M. Hay, "Participants Study Paper No. 1," *Missions in Creative Tension: The Green Lake '71 Compendium*, ed. Vergil Gerber (South Pasadena: William Carey Library, 1971), p. 90.

4. Amstutz, *The Gospel Yoke*, pp. 36-37.

5. George W. Peters, *A Biblical Theology of Missions* (Chicago: Moody Press, 1972), p. 226.

6. Amstutz, *The Gospel Yoke*, pp. 36-37.

7. Samuel Wilson, ed., *Mission Handbook*, 12th ed., p. 125.

8. Frederic Louis Godet, *Commentary on Romans* (Grand Rapids: Kregel Publications, 1977), p. 483. Godet states that the verb *propempo* has two ideas: "to be accompanied by some of theirs, and to be provided with everything necessary for the journey."

9. Peters, *A Biblical Theology of Missions*, p. 229.

10. J. Herbert Kane, *Life and Work on the Mission Field* (Grand Rapids: Baker Book House, 1980), p. 204.

11. W. Harold Fuller, *Mission-Church Dynamics: How to Change Bicultural Tensions into Dynamic Missionary Outreach* (Pasadena: William Carey Library, 1980), Appendix G, p. 272.

12. Ibid., p. 42.

Functions of the Mission Agency

14

"Really now, what does a mission board do for us?" This question was raised by a layperson who was thinking about his church's relationship to mission agencies. This is a valid question that we all need to ask.

As we have seen, the mission agency serves the local church in a partnership role, and its authority is delegated through the sending church. But what are some of the *specific* functions of a mission agency that are of particular benefit to churches and missionaries? The purpose of our study at this point is to delineate some of these benefits. See figure 31.

FIGURE 31

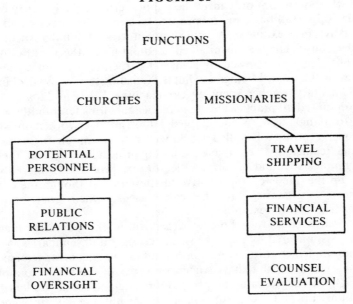

Functions of the Mission Agency

The above question concerning the actual functions of mission agencies deserves serious consideration. How *do* mission agencies serve their church constituency? Let us seek some answers to this question.

Functions Relative to the Churches

Potential Personnel

Mission agencies benefit the churches by serving three categories of potential personnel.

1. *Implementation of candidate procedure.* Because of its expertise in dealing with mission candidates, the mission agency serves the local church by implementing questionnaires and testing such as health histories, physical exams, doctrinal statements, and psychological testing. Add to these the oral examination before the board, as well as candidate classes. Although candidates may not always cheer the procedure, churches can be grateful for mission agencies that take seriously the call of God in the lives of His people.

2. *Sponsorship of short-term and apprenticeship programs.* Mission agencies provide an avenue of service for many laypeople in short-term service. An increasing number of Protestant mission organizations in North America provide opportunities for short-termers, and these adventuresome people continue to make up an increasing percentage of overseas missionary personnel.[1]

By matching spiritually committed and skilled people with specific field needs, the boards not only meet their short-term needs, but they provide unique opportunities for laypeople to serve effectively and grow spiritually. For example, a skilled architect and builder spent many months constructing a hospital clinic building in the Central African Republic. He was followed by a master carpenter who left a successful business in Jackson, Michigan to put the finishing touches on the building. An elementary teacher spent a year teaching MK's in Japan. A busy surgeon turned his practice over to his colleagues for a few months while he went to Bangladesh to share the load of an overworked missionary surgeon. A group of skilled workmen from a church in Annandale, Virginia teamed up to complete a building project in Brazil. All these and many more have found a fruitful outlet for their professions and skills while lifting up the hands of appreciative missionaries. Although these people are not "missionaries" in the career sense, their contribution to missionaries is immeasurable.

Another avenue for short-term service is the summer internship programs sponsored by many Christian colleges and seminaries. Mission agencies implement these work opportunities, making arrangements with missionaries who wish to have students for specific tasks. For example, the director of a rugged camping program in England found students to be able counselors and sports supervisors, to say nothing of their being good dishwashers! A missionary pilot in Brazil hosted a student who had building skills, and together they built a much-needed floating hanger. A missionary involved in student work near the University of Bordeaux found student interns who had a knowledge of French to be a great asset in outreach both on the campus and in the summer camping program. When missionaries provide occasions for both witness and work, the summer internships can be a life-changing experience. Many missionaries today point back to their summer missionary experience as the turning point in their career decisions.

3. *Sponsorship of volunteer programs for youth.* Many sincere young people make serious life decisions in their teen years. Mission agencies recognize that there is often a gap between making a decision for career missionary service and the application procedure. Baptist Mid-Missions, for instance, encourages high schoolers to participate in summer apprenticeships on the home front. BMM also provides a periodic news sheet, "Vision," as a missions information source for youth. With the college and seminary crowd in view, the publication, "Classified," is provided by the Association of Baptists for World Evangelism. All mission agencies are prepared to help those who have an interest in missions, either as a career or in a short-term capacity.

Public Relations

Mission boards find that funding for effective public relations is hard to schedule into an already tight budget. The work of public relations, however, demands not only funds, but dedicated people who are knowledgeable in this area. Adding another dimension to the challenge is the number of publics a mission board serves—sending churches, national churches, schools, and prospective missionaries, as well as missionaries and their families. Three areas of public relations will illustrate this point.

1. *Extensive communication with their constituency.* Mission executives learn to be good letter writers! Mail time brings in a variety of requests and questions that would challenge Solomon himself. Each request is welcomed and every question is prayerfully answered. Mission personnel are to be commended for the Herculean task of responding to constituency. Hundreds of hours and thousands of dollars each month go into vital communication.

2. *Production of promotional materials.* The public relations budget is stretched to the limit. Four-color brochures are expensive even when the mission does its own printing. People with layout abilities and writing skills are a great asset to a mission but are not always available at salaries that the mission can afford.

Quality missionary films and audiovisuals are needed in churches and schools. Indeed quality is *expected* by Christian audiences. Some agencies contract a professional company to produce films or audiovisuals. Other agencies have their own skilled personnel who give time and talent to produce high-quality media presentations. These missions offer their professional services to appointees and missionaries to help them prepare their personal audiovisuals. For example, the Association of Baptists for World Evangelism is particularly effective in high-quality presentations.

Most mission agencies publish their own periodical. The readership is largely their constituent churches and donors, although schools are sometimes included. One of the best mission periodicals is *Wherever* magazine published by The Evangelical Alliance Mission. Its articles find good response among college and seminary students.

Provision of a deputation program. Mission executives are among the first to know that people like to listen to a "real, live missionary." Even the executive's account of his recent trip among the Bongo Bongos does not have the same ring as the missionary's message who *lives* among these people. Yet mission administrators do have a vital message that needs to be heard in the churches and the schools. Deputation departments vary from mission to mission. Often home office executives are in demand for weekend ministries and conferences in the churches. They also have an effective ministry in the schools. Their missions perspective is different from that of the field missionary, and it must be heard.

Sometimes a mission agency will set up an entire missionary conference for a local church including executives, missionaries, and appointees. Such a conference can be of great help to a church that wishes to learn about the work of one particular mission.

Those people who serve as mission representatives in the schools have a special challenge. They must be good communicators and enjoy interacting with students. Students appreciate someone who will level with them and tell them "like it is." The mission representative in turn must give students a respectful hearing and straight answers to their searching questions. Candor on both sides will help ensure a hearing for world missions.

Deputation representatives among the churches have a special task as well. They acquaint the people with the mission board's purposes and outreach. Their presence and willingness to share information is more effective than literature or letters. Mutual understanding and trust are more quickly built by personal representation.

Financial and Legal Oversight

The delegated oversight of the agency again comes into focus in the financial picture. Most funds come through churches, individual donors, and the service funds of missionaries. Three functions of oversight are in view.

1. *Management of incoming funds.* Whether the mission agency practices the individual support plan or the pooling plan, all incoming funds are handled according to the wishes of the donors. Numbered receipts are issued for gifts received and the funds are designated to their proper accounts. For legal purposes, the mission agency exercises control over funds received for missionary work. Agencies submit their books for an annual audit.

If the agency operates on the individual support plan, all funds designated for the work of John and Sue Brown, for instance, are receipted and placed in their account. The Browns may choose to set up a special fund as well, such as a Building Fund or a Vehicle Fund. In these cases, the mission places in those accounts the amount that is designated by the Browns or the donors. Each month the mission forwards a mutually agreed upon amount for the Browns' work and family needs.

2. *Provision of guidelines for support levels.* Some knotty problems

surface at this point. On the one hand, we must not simply try to go the cheapest way possible with our missionary dollar at the expense of high-level productivity. On the other hand, with inflation in many countries driving costs up and up, boards and missionaries must seek ways to keep costs down to a reasonable level. Economic belt-tightening is not a popular exercise, but that is the crossroads to which we have come in missionary support. The mission board works together with field-based missionaries to determine recommended support levels for new appointees. While agencies and missionaries strive to hold the economic line, we at home need to admit that our missionary giving does not always make headline news. "Sacrifice" is a word people do not like to hear. Sending churches, mission agencies, and missionaries must work out the solutions to this economic challenge together.

3. *Provision of legal representation before governments.* In some countries career missionaries must be affiliated with a mission organization in order to establish residence. The mission assumes responsibility before the host government for the missionary's conduct and work. The mission agency agrees to repatriate the missionary in the event of political unrest or other emergency situations. Some host countries require that property be purchased in the name of the mission organization rather than the individual missionary.

Functions Relative to the Missionaries

The mission board also provides many helpful services for missionaries. After candidate classes and deputation are completed, what can missionaries expect from the mission?

Helping the missionaries get to the field is the first service rendered by the mission agency.

Travel and Shipping
If a person has never been west of the Mississippi, the thought of traveling to the Philippines can be traumatic! Passports, visas, and immunizations loom as formidable obstacles. And what about shipping all that equipment? Steel drums? Containerized shipping? And triplicate lists of *everything?* Help is provided by the mission agency for these travel and shipping needs. They seem to stay super calm—almost nonchalant. After all people *have* been traveling around the world for centuries.

For many rookie missionaries packing their goods and shipping them are major hurdles. The secret to sanity is to ask lots of questions. Mission office personnel can answer these questions or refer them to experienced missionaries.

Financial and Legal Services
1. *Management and accounts for all missionaries.* The missionaries' accounts are kept up to date daily. For example, in mission organizations that use the individual support plan, all monies received are listed by date

of receipt. Both income and disbursements are recorded and a monthly account statement is sent to each missionary. Also at the missionary's request the mission pays insurance premiums and other standing financial obligations directly from his account.

2. *Transmission of funds to missionaries.* What is the dollar worth against the world's currencies on any given day? The mission treasurer will have the answer. Monies are transferred a number of ways depending on the country to which they go. In some Third World countries, for example, the funds for all missionaries on a field are transferred in one sum to a bank in the country. The field business manager is notified of the transfer and the funds are then distributed to the account of each missionary. Exchange rates constantly fluctuate, a fact of life missionaries learn to live with.

3. *By implementing purchase of equipment and supplies.* Although missionaries try to buy locally as much as possible, needs inevitably arise that involve purchases from the homeland. Perhaps a mainspring breaks on the pick-up truck. None is available in the country. The missionary cables his need to the home office. Someone is assigned the task of ordering a replacement spring and having it shipped air freight on the next plane out. Costs are cared for from the missionary's account in the home office. Sometimes the mission is able to get discount prices on necessary supplies, and the savings is passed on to the missionary.

4. *Provision of tax and legal services.* The mission agency stands ready to help the missionaries in ascertaining their tax obligations. Some countries today require the missionary to pay income tax while residing in the country. Income tax liability in the homeland varies as to the length of time the missionary has been in or out of the country. Some agencies will assist the missionaries in filing their income tax returns. Lawyers are retained by many mission organizations to help them determine the requirements of the tax laws.

Counsel and Evaluation

1. *Provision of counsel for field problems and projects.* Mission agencies differ in their administration of field affairs. Some agencies grant a great detail of autonomy to their fields, which are usually organized into field councils. Other agencies are more authoritarian in directing mission business at the field level. In either case, the mission can provide beneficial counsel in many instances. Changing political and economic situations necessitate close cooperation between mission headquarters and each field. Policies for advance need to be set with mutual agreement. Financial and personnel goals also need mutual consideration. Home office and field need each other's help.

2. *Review and evaluation of the missionary's work.* In addition to counsel, encouragement, and direction in the missionary's work, the mission does review and evaluation. Missionaries need to be commended for work well done. The vast majority of missionaries stand in the "well done" category. On the other hand, sending churches need to be informed when a particular missionary is not serving adequately. Perhaps he or she

needs encouragement and guidance. Perhaps another missionary is not suited to the assigned task and needs a change of ministry. Or perhaps corrective measures need to be taken for the welfare of a missionary and the work in which he or she is engaged. Every possible means of counsel and assistance should be given before a missionary is replaced in a given task. The work at hand is larger than any one missionary, however, and the grievous decision for dismissal occasionally needs to be made.

Wrap-Up

This chapter is a survey of some of the specific functions fulfilled by the mission as a service agency. The list is by no means exhaustive. These tasks relate to both the sending churches and the missionaries. Here are some of the key ideas.

• The mission agency is the candidate's link to future ministry. That link will only be as strong as the mission's candidate procedure.

• Short-term service and apprenticeship programs are here to stay for the foreseeable future. Mission agencies are and will continue to be the implementers of these avenues of ministry.

• The primary emphasis of the mission agency's public relations lies in the churches and schools.

• Management of funds for both churches and missionaries is a major mission-agency responsibility.

• The mission agency's supervision and evaluation of missionaries on behalf of the sending churches must be administered with love and courage.

Notes to Chapter 14

1. Samuel Wilson, ed., *Mission Handbook: North American Protestant Ministries Overseas,* 12th ed. (Monrovia, CA: Missions Advanced Research and Communication Center, 1979), p. 21.

Mission Agency Affiliations

15

A review of associations of mission agencies is now in order. Actually the idea of agencies forming themselves into associations for mutual benefit goes back to the late nineteenth century. In 1893 the Foreign Mission Conference of North America was organized. This association has been reorganized and five more have been added. The study at hand will identify the six associations and will assess their current contribution to the missions picture in North America.

Also, mission agencies that are not affiliated with any of the associations have a growing influence. The growth of these unaffiliated agencies will be traced as well.

The Mission Advanced Research and Communication Center (MARC) has performed a monumental task of gathering missions-related data and of making their research available through the *Mission Handbook: North American Protestant Ministries Overseas.* This handbook is published every three to five years. Although precise statistics are dated, trends emerge that sketch the current missions picture in North America.

The twelfth edition of the *Mission Handbook* identifies the current associations:

> Six associations of mission agencies represent about 40 percent of the total missionary force, with the three largest (DOM, EFMA, IFMA) representing about 39 percent. The six associations are the Commission on World Concerns (CWC) of the Canadian Council of Churches; the Division of Overseas Ministries (DOM) of the National Council of the Churches of Christ in the U.S.A.; the Evangelical Foreign Missions Association (EFMA), an affiliate of the National Association of Evangelicals; the Interdenominational Foreign Mission Association (IFMA); The Associated Missions (TAM); and the Fellowship of Missions (FOM).[1]

The Canadian Council of Churches Commission on World Concerns (CCC-CWC)

The Commission on World Concerns was first organized in 1928 as the Canadian Overseas Missionary Conference. The Commission merged with the Canadian Council of Churches in 1948.[2] Member churches in Canada give toward ecumenical projects through the CWC. One of the member churches is the Anglican Church of Canada. In 1979 total personnel serving with the CWC were 315. Their total income was nearly eleven million dollars.[3]

Division of Overseas Ministries (DOM)

This association is a Division of the National Council of Churches of Christ in the U.S.A. (NCC). Its member agencies are an integral part of their parent denominations who are members of the NCC. The Division of Overseas Ministries was first organized in 1893 as the Foreign Missions Conference of North America. Members of the National Council of Churches represent the "main line denominations," sometimes spoken of as "conciliar." They are liberal in their theological tradition and ecumenical in their affiliations.

For over two decades the DOM has posted continual losses in missionary personnel. In the years 1975-1979 the DOM recorded a 22 percent change in personnel.[4] For many years their finances declined, but the 1979 figures showed a 6 percent increase. Samuel Wilson observes:

> Of the some thirty-one agencies affiliated to the DOM, 69 percent (2185) of the DOM overseas personnel are involved with agencies whose stated primary tasks include relief or development without mention of evangelism, church planting, and/or extension. The agencies that major in relief and development far outweight, in both absolute gross numbers of dollars and percentage increases, those that include evangelism.[5]

The two largest DOM agencies, and those who showed the most increase in the 1979 report, were the United Methodist Committee on Relief and the United Methodist World Division of the Board of Global Ministries.

Evangelical Foreign Missions Association (EFMA)

Organized in 1945, this association consists of both denominational and interdenominational agencies. EFMA is affiliated with the National Association of Evangelicals. This does not indicate, however, that all EFMA-member missions are in turn affilated with the NAE. A case in point is the Foreign Missionary Society of the Fellowship of Grace Brethren Churches that maintain its affiliation only in the EFMA.

From 1968 to 1976 EFMA-affiliated mission agencies were in a state of nongrowth. This pattern has been broken, however, and in 1979 the association showed a healthy 30 percent growth in missionary personnel and 89 percent increase in income.[6]

The association's stated purpose is to provide:

> (1) united representation before governments, (2) a basis of fellowship, (3) a channel for promoting cooperative effort, (4) information concerning government regulations and international affairs which affect foreign missions, (5) services along the following

lines: passport and visa service, processing authentication of legal documents, travel, reservations . . . conferences and seminars, information services.[7]

Generally speaking, the mission agencies affiliated with the EFMA are in the conservative evangelical tradition.

Interdenominational Foreign Mission Association (IFMA)

This association was formed in 1917 when the modernist-fundamentalist battle was in full array. Bible-believing churches who held to the fundamentals of the faith were determined to send their missionaries and their money through mission agencies of like conviction. Some interdenominational mission agencies had already been organized and more were in process of formation. The formation of the IFMA strengthened the hands of the interdenominational movement of the day.

The IFMA-related missions had gone into slight decline in the years prior to 1979. At that time studies showed a 6 percent increase in personnel.[8] Their receipts were up a healthy 39 percent.[9]

The association upholds high standards of accountability. The *Mission Handbook* states:

Member missions are governed by responsible councils or directorates; exercise control over missionaries; publish audited financial statements annually; approve each other on the field and at home in ethical practices; adhere to a strong conservative evangelical doctrinal position; and are engaged in taking the gospel of the Lord Jesus Christ to all people everywhere.[10]

The IFMA and the EFMA have much in common in their theology and in their philosophy of missions. One of their joint projects is the publishing of the "Evangelical Missions Quarterly" through the Evangelical Mission Information Service (EMIS). Both associations assume joint-leadership roles in regional committees that are concerned for worldwide missionary effort, as well as the Committee to Assist Ministry Education Overseas (CAMEO).[11] The two associations represent the majority of missionaries outside the conciliar DOM.

The Associated Missions (TAM)

This association is the mission affilate of the Interdenominational Council of Christian Churches (ICCC). Organized in 1948 as the Missions Commission of the ICCC, the association was reorganized in its present form in 1952. The *Mission Handbook* describes the organization as "An inter-mission service agency of fundamental tradition ."[12] In 1969 a number of mission agencies left TAM to establish the Fellowship of Missions. Presently TAM consists of six agencies with a total of some 200 missionaries.[13]

Fellowship of Missions (FOM)

The FOM is the most recently established mission association, having its beginning in 1969 as stated above. Both home and overseas mission agencies make up its membership. According to their publication, "Focus on Missions," there are fourteen agencies with a total of approximately 2,800 missionaries. It states:

> The Fellowship of Missions is a fellowship of fundamental, separated missions associated together for the defense of the gospel and to present a united stand to the world against apostasy in our day.[14]

Their home agencies are generating new interest in stateside church planting.

The association is nondenominational. Theologically it is in the fundamental tradition.[15]

Unaffiliated Mission Agencies

History bears testimony that associations of mission are of benefit to their member agencies. Mutual concerns such as financial integrity, government representation, cooperative efforts, and ethical issues are implemented through the united effort of the association.

However, not all mission agencies choose to affiliate with a mission association. For more than a decade the unaffiliated mission agencies have experienced continual growth in both personnel and income. Samuel Wilson reports:

> Unaffiliated mission agencies now comprise over half of the career personnel overseas, with the income of those agencies more than doubled.
>
> An increase of almost 1000 regular career personnel missionaries is accounted for by only three agencies in the "unaffiliated" ranks, although these are clearly evangelical or fundamentalist by any reasonable classification. They are the New Tribes Mission, reporting an increase of 521, Southern Baptist Foreign Mission Board (239 increase), and the Baptist Bible Fellowship (172 increase).[16]

The unaffiliated agencies show phenomenal growth in short-term personnel. Wilson states:

> Seven unaffiliated agencies account for an increase of 9053 (408 percent). Chief among them are the Southern Baptist's move upward from 153 in 1976 to 2866 in 1979, Youth with a Mission, from 1000 to 5000 (400 percent), and Teen Missions, from 748 to 1800.[17]

Unaffiliated mission agencies continue to register the highest rate of personnel growth, some 45 percent increase according to the latest survey.[18] Theologically these agencies are, for the most part conservative evangelical or fundamental. The theological traditions of current mission groupings are summarized in figure 32.

FIGURE 32

LIBERAL TRADITION	CONSERVATIVE EVANGELICAL TRADITION	FUNDAMENTAL TRADITION
DOM-NCC CWC-CCC	EFMA/IFMA Some Unaffiliated	FOM/TAM Some Unaffiliated

Theological Traditions of Mission Agency Groupings

Wrap-Up

What can be said in summary about the trends in North American mission agencies? The picture is quite clear.

• Over all, the main line denominations represented by the DOM and CWC continue to decline in personnel. Funding by these main line denominations for relief and development in the Third World has increased.

• Both EFMA and IFMA are posting growth in personnel and giving, and together they represent the largest number of missionaries from North America.

• Agencies in the fundamental tradition, particularly in the FOM, continue to field a significant missionary force. Their home agencies are increasingly concerned for church planting in North America.

• Slightly over half of the overseas personnel come from mission agencies unaffiliated with any of the mission associations. This increase is a long-term trend.

• Short-term personnel continue to increase, but not to the detriment of those committed to career missionary service. Again, unaffiliated agencies show the greatest increase in short-termers.

• At this point in history missionary sending in North America is moving ahead in both personnel and funding.

Notes to Chapter 15

1. Samuel Wilson, ed., *Mission Handbook: North American Protestant Ministries Overseas,* 12th ed. (Monrovia, CA: Missions Advanced Research and Communication Center, 1979), p. 119.

2. Ibid., p. 123.

3. Samuel Wilson, "Current Trends in North American Protestant Ministries Overseas," *International Bulletin of Missionary Research* 5 (April 1981): 75.

4. Ibid.

5. Ibid.

6. Ibid., p. 74.

7. Samuel Wilson, ed., *Mission Handbook*, p. 123.

8. Samuel Wilson, "Current Trends In North American Protestant Ministries Overseas," p. 74.

9. Ibid., p. 75.

10. Samuel Wilson, ed., *Mission Handbook*, p. 125.

11. Ibid., p. 126.

12. Ibid., p. 123.

13. Ibid., p. 135.

14. "Focus on Missions: Occasional News Supplement for Missionaries," *Fellowship of Missions* 12 (February 1983): 2.

15. Samuel Wilson, ed., *Mission Handbook*, p. 124.

16. Samuel Wilson, "Current Trends in North American Protestant Ministries Overseas," p. 74.

17. Ibid.

18. Ibid.

Part 4

Strategic Role of the Missionary

Missionary Accountability to Churches and Mission Agency

16

The idea of accountability has a sobering tone. Yet being accountable to someone is built into each of our lives. We are answerable to others at home, at work, at church, in our relationships as believers, and most of all to the Lord Himself. Missionaries also come to accept accountability as part of their calling. Two special groups of people to whom a missionary must give account are people in the sending churches and the mission agency.

When missionaries board a plan to return to their field, many concerns flash before their minds. Customs, of course. Housing, school for the kids, language refresher, new friends both national and missionary—on and on. Yet always in their thinking is the realization that they are accountable to others as well as the Lord for the ministry that lies ahead. See figure 33.

FIGURE 33

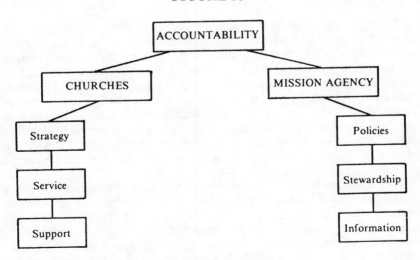

Missionary Accountability

Accountability to the Churches

Loyal friends in the sending churches have assumed responsibility for prayer and financial support so that their missionaries can serve Christ effectively. Missionaries, in turn, are responsible to their churches in a number of areas.

Accountability for Strategy

In order to give good account of themselves, missionaries need to be good strategists. The term "strategy" is often used when speaking of battle plans. A game plan in sports events is also strategy. Knowing the strengths and weaknesses of the opposition is a crucial factor in laying out a strategy. To maximize their effectiveness missionaries need a "game plan"—a strategy. Two principal ingredients in strategy making are goals and priorities.

1. *Goal setting.* Six considerations need to be kept in view when the missionary sets goals.

Missionaries' goals must be measurable so that they will know when they have arrived, or at least that they are headed in the right direction. C. Peter Wagner speaks out for measurable goals:

> While I am aware of objections which have been made to quantifying the missionary task, I have not been persuaded by them. The more I study the dynamics of the worldwide spread of the gospel, the more convinced I become that the task should be quantified, measured and monitored.[1]

Second, realistic, measureable goals help keep the missionary honest. Goals that are attainable will encourage missionaries to live and work realistically within cultural and physical limitations. If the church planter knows that it will take a four-year term to establish one church, let him plan accordingly. Of course, God can bring a more abundant harvest, making it possible to exceed the goal. If the translating team sees the possibility of preparing the New Testament for publication within the next year, the goal itself will give encouragement to complete the task within that deadline. The same realism can give incentive to goal setting in all phases of ministry—evangelism, leadership preparation, and medical outreach, to name only a few.

Third, time limits are a vital part of strategy. These limits should be set as guideposts rather than guillotines. Guideposts can be reset to meet the reality of the situation as it develops. There is a nasty finality about cutoff points. Americans in particular have problems with time. Our clock time does not always mix well with the event time of our host people. There is no merit in ulcers earned through unwise application of the clock and the calendar to our planning.

Fourth, goals must be prayerfully *integrated* with the thinking both of missionaries and of national leaders. Goals mutually set by all personnel concerned are more likely to enjoy mutual support and participation.

Finding such mutuality, however, is sometimes as elusive as a speedy halfback on a Saturday afternoon. Missionaries occasionally hear a colleague say, "You thought of it. Go ahead and do it." Pet projects are more dangerous than a pet python. If worse comes to worse the python can be donated to the zoo. Projects of one's own making can become tangential to field purposes, and they can generate more smoke than fire.

Fifth, goals must be *biblically based.* When missionaries are setting goals, they need to ask some hard questions. How do their goals measure up to God's goals? Does Scripture set its seal of approval on their plans? The motives behind their goals are fully as important as the goals themselves. Why do they want to plant three churches this term? Is it for God's glory, or is it to impress their home churches? Is their goal of 100 converts this year simply an ego trip?

Sixth, missionaries must *regularly review* their goals. Alternative ways of attaining goals need to be considered. Obstacles cannot always be anticipated. A quarterback has many options for moving the ball over the goal line. The defense would soon catch on if he were to send the fullback around left end on every play. Likewise, missionaries may need to vary their strategy.

Last term's game plan is not sufficient for the term ahead. Indeed, last year's plans are not adequate for today. Review must be built into goal setting. Opportunities and opposition shift with the passing of time.

2. *Setting priorities.* The second of the two principal ingredients in missionary strategy is priorities. Not all goals are of equal importance. The missionary's priorities demand value judgments, relational judgments, and time judgments. Again, some questions are in order.

First, which goals are the most vital? Some people find it helpful to prioritize their goals in the order of the value they place upon them. Some goals receive a "1" rating, others "2" and so on. For instance, as a missionary sizes up the next day he may see three duties demanding attention: (1) to visit a sick pastor in the hospital, (2) to prepare for the week-end ministry in a growing suburb, and(3) to keep up his translation schedule in Romans. Each of these must be cared for. The missionary will make a decision as to priority in carrying out these duties; this decision will reflect the value he places on each activity.

Second, how should the missionary's goals be ranked in priority as they relate to field strategy and to the people who are concerned (national churches, fellow missionaries, and family)? Personal priority setting always affects other people. Few Christian workers have as many other groups of people to consider as missionaries do in setting their goals and priorities.

Third, the time factor is as crucial to priority setting as to our goals. How should missionaries invest the precious time God has put at their disposal? What task must be cared for now? What can be postponed? How will these time factors affect fellow workers? Indeed, neglect may well be a part of setting priorities. Deciding what we can neglect is as important as deciding what goals should have priority. We all need the divine viewpoint.

Missionaries must inform their sending churches of their goals and priorities. We will discuss this accountablity further in the following section.

Accountability for Service

The express purpose of Christ-honoring missionaries who are serving around the globe is to proclaim the person and work of Christ so that people may hear and believe in Him. Missionaries must give account of their ministry to believers in their sending churches.

When Paul and Barnabas returned to Antioch after their first journey, they reported to the whole church about their work. Luke states, "On arriving there, they gathered the church together and reported all that God had done through them and how He had opened the door of faith to the Gentiles" (Acts 14:27). On other occasions Paul shared with the churches the progress and problems in his ministry (Rom. 15:15-20; 1 Cor. 16:7-9; 2 Cor. 8:1-6; 2 Cor. 11:28). Paul demonstrated the principle of accountability through his apostleship to the Gentiles.

1. *Missionaries inform the churches of their goals.* Many helpful seminars and books encourage Christian workers to manage their ministries by setting specific objectives. We have discussed goal and priority setting and their effect on the missionary's field ministry. People at home need to know about those goals and priorities. The missionaries' sharing of their goals with other churches will go a long way toward ensuring knowledgeable prayer and concern. By sharing their goals during furlough, missionaries can explain what they hope to do when they return to the field. For example, Larry Smith, long-time missionary to Chile, makes it a point to spell out his four-year goals to his supporting churches before he returns to his field. Understandably a missionary may tend to be a bit idealistic in goal setting while he is away from his ministry. On the other hand, he avoids the status quo that sometimes settles over his ministry while he is on the field.

2. *Missionaries inform the churches of progress toward their goals.* Let us posit that we plan a trip to Branson, Missouri in the Ozarks. We make reservations at Motel Taneycomo. We check the distance and lay out the routes. We stop a a tourist information area to see how much further we have to travel. When we see the motel sign, we will have arrived.

In like manner our missionary friends have set some specific goals. They know the routes to take in order to get there better than we do here at home. But we need to know where they are along the way. If, for example, they have set four-year goals, missionaries need to tell us at least on a yearly basis where they are toward reaching those goals. Time and distance blur our best intentions to keep up with their progress. They must remind us on a regular basis. Larry Smith uses his first news letters each year to report on the progress made on the previous year's goals.

3. *Missionaries inform the churches of problems with their goals.* The Lord knows the detours and delays along the way before our missionaries ever start down the road toward their goals. Detours and delays are no

disgrace. While the missionary halo remains in the minds of some saints at home, for the most part they want to see the missionary as a real person who is ready to share his difficulties and even defeats. Do we believe God removes road blocks through prayer? Do we believe when one member suffers we all suffer? The Bible is clear on these points. Let all of us who hold the ropes at home help our missionaries by being sympathetic listeners. Let us not expect perfection. Let us enter into the problem-solving process through believing prayer. We must remember that sometimes God uses the detours to accomplish His will. Paul's detour led him to prison, but he testified that—"what has happened to me has really served to advance the gospel" (Phil. 1:12).

4. *Missionaries inform the churches of prayer needs.* Only frequent updating of prayer needs can maintain prayer-action by friends at home. How often do we need these updates? Every month? Once a quarter? The more current the update, the more effective the prayer support. Surely it is not asking too much to hear from our missionaries every three months, or more frequently if possible. Regular briefing sessions are held in governments, industry and the military. Without them people are quick to lose touch with one another and with the task at hand. Because of the eternal issues at stake, the missionary's task needs the intelligent prayer backing of God's people. This prayer support is only possible as needs are known.

Paul was quick to share specific prayer requests. He asked the believers at Rome to join in his struggle through prayer:

> I urge you, brothers, by our Lord Jesus Christ and by the love of the Spirit, to join me in my struggle by praying to God for me. Pray that I may be rescued from the unbelievers in Judea and that my service in Jerusalem may be acceptable to the saints there, so that by God's will I may come to you with joy and together with you be refreshed" (Rom. 15:30-31).

Paul acted on the conviction that the saints needed to know exactly what his needs were, and he stated them accordingly. Accountability is mutual in the missionaries' prayer relationship with the churches. In the midst of our mechanistic age, believing prayer must find its way back into a central place in world missions.

Accountability for Support

After we have given to the missionary outreach of our church, our stewardship is fulfilled and the recipients' stewardship begins. What an awesome responsibility a missionary has in handling the gifts of God's people in a discerning manner. Paul recognized his responsibility in managing funds, and he did so with great care (2 Cor. 8:18-21). Two factors need to be mentioned in relation to the missionary's accountability for support.

1. *Missionaries express gratitude to all donors.* When Paul was preaching in Thessalonica, the Philippian Church gave "aid again and

again" when he had a need (Phil. 4:16). He was quite candid with them when he said, "Yet it was good of you to share in my troubles" (Phil. 4:14). He described their gift as "a fragrant offering, an acceptable sacrifice, pleasing to God" (Phil. 4:18). Most missionaries are not that eloquent, and if they were, some pastors and churches would wonder if they had gotten too much sun! But expressing gratitude is not an option.

While some of us may disclaim the thought, we all like to be thanked. Missionaries must take notice of this fact when it comes to thanking people for their gifts. Those of us who give must do it with the proper motive. Those of us who receive gifts for our work must thank our friends sincerely and promptly. There are no statistics on how many missionaries lose support because they neglect this vital part of their ministry, but informal reports keep filtering in. Lack of gratitude is an easy trap for missionaries to fall into. After all, they are working for God, and people *should* give. Nonsense! Thankfulness is written large across the ministry of Paul, and it must be written across our missionary's ministry as well. Interestingly, the appreciative, thankful missionary is usually a well-supported missionary.

2. *Missionaries maintain personal contact with supporting pastors.* Pastors of supporting churches are among the best friends a missionary could ever have. In many cases the missionary is receiving support from the church because of the pastor's favorable influence with his people. The pastor has seen a worthy recipient in the missionary. He has interviewed the missionary and counseled with the Missionary Committee about support. No doubt he has talked to other pastors about the advisability of supporting the missionary. If he is pastor of the missionary's home church, he has had a special interest in helping the missionary find support in other churches. Perhaps he has traveled with the missionary visiting other pastors in an effort to win a hearing and some support.

By his very attitudes and expressed concerns for supported missionaries, the pastor influences the interest of his people. Therefore, it behooves the missionary, both while he is on furlough and while he is on the field to maintain close contact with his pastor friends. The pastors should have personal letters in addition to the regular news letters from the missionaries. Sometimes problems can be shared with pastors that cannot be aired in more general letters.

Some missionaries will contend that pastors should take the initiative in contacting them. Many do. However, the missionary who is careful to communicate directly with pastors at home will reap the benefits of pastoral backing that may not be gained otherwise.

Accountability to the Mission Agency

The local-church/mission-agency/missionary complex is like a large extended family. A missionary sustains a special relationship to both the sending churches and the mission agency. Harold R. Cook holds that a prospective missionary needs to be more concerned about the choice of a mission board than the field on which he will eventually serve. Cook states:

A real missionary is seldom disappointed in his field after he gets there. But there are all too many occasions when he becomes disappointed in the mission with which he is working. It is amazing how little attention many seem to pay to this matter.[2]

Missionaries serving with a mission agency have a common bond that is not often found in other Christian organizations. Not uncommonly, missionaries develop a sense of family loyalty that exceeds natural family ties.

J. Herbert Kane comments concerning the missionary's relationship to the mission:

He should recognize that he now belongs to a team; he is a member of a family. He joins the mission; he is not *hired* by it. He is a member, not an employee. The mission is not just another organization whose members remain in good standing only as long as they pull their weight and pay their dues. He has joined a family—a very intimate and precious family where he will find sympathy, compassion, understanding, good will, and, above all, love.[3]

Within this close relationship, missionaries are accountable to the board on several fronts.

Accountability to Support Mission Policies

1. *Agreement with mission policies.* Having made the choice of a mission board, the missionary now agrees to support its policies. His choice has been made with these policies in view. He has discovered that missions vary in their policies. Is the missionary expected to raise all of his own support among the churches, or does the mission function on a pooling plan in which missionaries share and share alike? Can the missionary purchase property on the field, or must he rent? Is housing provided by the mission? Who owns his car or truck—the mission or the missionary? Does the mission have a policy on MK schooling? How rigid is it? The missionary has investigated these issues and many others in order to measure the areas of agreement or disagreement. Nothing beats open communication to clarify the reasons behind mission policy. Mission policies are not necessarily set in cement, but they should be concrete enough for all to understand them thoroughly.

It is one thing to agree with mission policies and sometimes quite another when those policies directly affect the missionary, his family, his possessions, or his ministry. If the missionary agrees that all property he held in the name of the mission, then he must support the policy when it comes to his own home. If he agrees that the title to his beloved airplane be held by the mission, so be it. If he agrees that, under normal conditions, his term of field service will be four years, let him plan accordingly. Usually mission agencies deal with scores of missionaries in multiplied fields and cultures, and policies are carefully worked out for the benefit of all concerned. The missionary's relationship to the agency is not one of object servitude but one of mutual benefit. Let it also be one of mutual respect.

2. *Cooperation with mission procedures.* Few lone wolves are left in the world. Most of us have learned to comply with application forms, questionnaires, work reports, tax returns, and other paper persecuters that we would prefer to spindle. A certain amount of paper work is necessary to keep life in order. But must the mission add its *own* round of reports?

Reports themselves vary from mission to mission. But generally speaking the missionary faces the routine of financial reports necessary for income tax purposes, periodic letters to donors, and sometimes monthly progress reports on church attendance and mission-related activity, particularly in church-planting ministries. Mission print shops must give account of literature produced, and mission hospitals and dispensaries are keenly aware of donor interest in shots and sutures.

When a missionary affirms agreement with mission policies and agrees to support them, he also assumes accountability for cooperation with mission procedures. A certain independent streak sometimes creeps into a missionary's makeup, but he must not allow this to mark his relation to the mission or the supporting churches.

Accountability to Maintain Good Stewarship
First, except for mainline d∘nominations, missionaries bear varying degrees of responsibility for raising their own support. In most cases they have developed a close tie with the sending churches, which heightens the element of accountability.

Once on the field, the missionary is expected to live within the budgeted funds available through his account at missions headquarters. Contrary to the belief of some people in some local cultures, missionaries must operate within the confines of available funds. Dollars do not continually flow out of a cash drawer at the missions office.

Under some circumstances a mission will advance needed funds to a missionary, but he must eventually pay back this amount through monies coming into his account. A case comes to mind, for instance, of a missionary in central Africa who needed an advance to build a home for his family of six. Arrangements were made with the board for a total advance of $3,000 for the project. This amount was restored to the mission reserve fund as funds came into the missionary's account.

Second, the ever-increasing cost of missionary support is causing some churches to review their missions budgets. Pastors and Missions Committees ask hard questions about the reasons behind these rising costs. Of course, some cost factors are beyond the missionary's control: continuing inflation at home and abroad, host country income taxes, and increasing travel costs, to name a few.

Third, in the light of the foregoing financial realities, missionaries must demonstrate financial integrity and ability to make ends meet with the resources at hand. Except in emergency situations, missionaries are responsible to live within their means without overdrafts in their accounts. To overdraw their accounts jeopardizes the financial integrity of both the mission and the missionary. Missionaries must have our sympathetic understanding in financial matters. They in turn must exercise careful budgetary management which will result in giving good account to their mission.

Accountability to Share Field Situations

When we sit down to view the evening news or to read the evening paper, we see only the tip of the iceberg. The events that surface today have been in formation for days, weeks, months, or even years. Our understanding of world events is very much after-the-fact. The missionary, on the other hand, is often working in the midst of rapid change politically, economically, and even religiously. He can render real service to the mission and the churches by keeping them abreast of events on his field. He can often lay to rest false impressions that sometimes come through other media.

Not all change is for the worse, of course! God is sovereign, carrying out His purpose at all times and in every place. Change is simply another way of seeing God at work. When the missionary keeps the home base informed, policies and procedures are effectively planned.

Wrap-Up

In a sense missionaries live like fish in an aquarium. Everyone seems to feel free to look in on them to see how things are going. Some of these people have a perfect right to watch the missionary at work. As we have seen, two interested groups of people are the sending churches and the mission agency. Let us review some of these areas of missionary accountability.

• Missionaries are accountable to the churches for their work plans, or strategy. Thoughtful goal setting is a part of that strategy. Every missionary must know where he is going.

• Setting priorities is crucial to missionary strategy. Some goals are primary while others are secondary. The missionary's value system will influence his priorities.

• Determining alternatives will help aid the missionary to take a flexible approach in carrying out his strategy.

• Strategy must be based on God-honoring motives.

• Missionaries need to inform their churches of projected goals and progress in reaching those goals, as well as problems encountered along the way. A sense of partnership develops when the supporting constituency is well informed.

• Well-informed people can be more effective in prayer.

• Missionaries are answerable to both the churches and the mission for the use of support funds. The changing world economy demands frugality and wise money management.

• Missionaries need to take pastors of their supporting churches into their confidence. The benefits of pastoral backing are available to missionaries who seek their help.

• Prospective missionaries need to investigate mission agencies with care and counsel before making a choice.

• Missionaries must support the policies and procedures of their mission agency with a cooperative spirit.

Notes to Chapter 16

1. C. Peter Wagner, "Goal Setting: A Key to the Growth of the Body," *Global Church Growth* 20 (March-April 1983): 256.

2. Harold R. Cook. *An Introduction to Christian Missions* (Chicago: Moody Press, 1971), p. 173.

3. J. Herbert Kane, *Life and Work on the Mission Field* (Grand Rapids: Baker Book House, 1980), p. 46.

Missionary Responsibility on the Field

17

Missionaries are among the most privileged people on earth. The Christ-centered message they proclaim has the potential to change individuals, families, tribes, villages, cities, and entire countries. As gospel bearers, many missionaries use their skills to heal the sick, to teach the unlearned, to liberate the illiterate, to translate the Word, and to relieve the hungry. These ministries manifest mercy and compassion that in turn open hearts and minds to the saving grace of God through faith in Christ. Whatever the means at their hand, missionaries by definition and calling are ambassadors of the Good News.

In their life-style and their field of service, missionaries are responsible on several fronts: sending churches, mission agency, fellow workers, those to whom they proclaim the gospel, national churches, and national leaders—to name a few. We will now survey six areas of field responsibility. See figure 34.

FIGURE 34

Missionary Responsibility

Personal and Family Welfare

Spiritual Growth

The missionary must maintain his personal spiritual growth. At no other point is there more struggle against so many odds. Satan is no fool. He strikes at the very vitals of the Christian life hoping to cripple God's servant at the source of spiritual health. Breathing the fresh air of the Word and exercising the soul in prayer are at the heart of the missionary's spiritual resources. In a hostile spiritual climate, how else can he overcome the enemy of his soul? He must maintain his guard so that the very work to which God has called him does not swallow him up in frustration and defeat. Regular, systematic devotional study of Scripture, and purposeful, disciplined prayer will help build defense against destructive waves of satanic deception. Never is the missionary more conscious of the warfare against Satan than when he is defending his own spiritual fortress.

Physical Care

Our bodies are very much a part of our stewardship. A missionary is often subjected to unusual physical stress through the buffeting of emotional and spiritual forces. When asked about body care through regular exercise and adequate sleep, the missionary may reply, "Too busy!" This sounds so spiritual. "It's better to burn out than to rust out," he says! At best this statement is a half truth. It is not necessary to burn out to please God. No one wants to rust out, of course. Are these really the only two alternatives?

The missionary, and any other Christian worker for that matter, must consider his body as a stewardship to be nurtured and cared for as a trust from God. Our body is spoken of as a temple (1 Cor. 6:19; John 2:21). The Holy Spirit indwells us. Physical care, wherever we may be, must be considered in this light.

Intellectual Alertness

Maintaining intellectual alertness is a constant challenge. Sometimes missionaries find that a certain mental inertia settles over them after they are on the field for a while. The sameness of work may have a shriveling effect. The lack of stimulating reading limits horizons. Their not being able to sharpen their minds against the thinking of others may lead to dullness. As Solomon put it, "As iron sharpens iron, so one man sharpens another" (Prov. 17:17). Culture fatigue, like the endless scrape of a fingernail across a chalkboard, can bring some missionaries to desperation.

Prefield forethought can go a long way in helping the missionary over the mental-alertness hurdle. Well-chosen paperbacks, magazine and journal subscriptions, and even thought-provoking games will serve as prods to sagging spirits. These needs can easily be supplied by interested church groups or individuals. Many books and other sources of information about the host country are available. Short wave radio is now universal so that the missionary can keep his finger on the world's pulse.

Airmail brings news magazines to remote areas today. Missionaries can tap these sources according to their own resources and needs.

On-the-field cultural studies, such as marriage customs, family structure, or rites of passage, will stretch the missionary. These studies express interest in the people and will give newcomers valuable insights into the culture.

As Spouse and Parent

Proper balance between family and ministry looms large in personal and family responsibility. Both the husband/father and the wife/mother must deal with this problem on a daily basis. Decisions they make will affect them and their families. It also affects those to whom they minister, their fellow workers, their mission agency, and their supporting churches. Missionary effectiveness will rise or fall according to the way they deal with this tension. This is at the heart of their philosophy of ministry.

For example, while settling down for story time with the family, someone knocks, coughs, calls, or claps his hands at the door. Should family time be suspended? Dad must spend days at a time away from home to visit national pastors, to evangelize, or to help with Bible translation. What happens to Mom and the kids in the meantime? The missionary mother longs to teach teenage girls or pastor's wives only to find that she must spend whole mornings teaching her children the three R's. Hasn't God called her to be a missionary, too?

Circumstances, family needs, and personal gifts will influence different decisions in different family situations at different times, but the decisions are inescapable. In discussing domestic qualifications for leadership, J. Oswald Sanders states:

> The clear implication is that, while caring for the interests of the church or other spiritual activity, the leader will not neglect the family which is his personal and primary responsibility. *In the economy of God, the discharge of one God-given duty or responsibility will never involve the neglect of another* [italics mine]. There is time for the full discharge of every legitimate duty. Paul implies that the ability of a man to exercise spiritual authority over others is evidenced by his ability to exercise a wise and loving discipline in his own home.[1]

Missionaries must realize that a sovereign God does not assign conflicting responsibilities. He does not give more than they can handle. God assigns the tasks, and He gives the enablement. Perhaps guilt trips are most abundant at this point of balance in ministry as related to family. Critics will be there on each side of any decision. Let the missionary be convinced that his decisons are God-honoring, and then let him move ahead with full confidence.

Interpersonal Relationships

In many instances a missionary does not have the luxury of choosing his friends or fellow workers. Of course, his potential friends and co-workers do not always have a chance to choose him either! Most missionary teams are formed on the field; thus guidelines as to relationships are in order.

Attitude of Humility
Paul said it well:

> Do nothing out of selfish ambition or vain conceit, but in humility consider others better than yourselves. Each of you should look not only to your own interests, but also to the interests of others (Phil. 2:3-4).

Schools missionaries attended in the States, types of work on the field, age, experience, and abilities tend to divide the troops into in-groups and out-groups. Louis J. Luzbetak observes:

> A missionary is called upon not only to adjust himself to a new cultural environment . . . but also to adjust himself to and co-operate closely with individuals having behaviors, group loyalties, and group interests that are different fom his own. Just as it is possible for a missionary to suffer culture shock so it is quite possible . . . to suffer "social shock."[2]

Maintaining both team and field unity demands constant vigilance. Local believers are quick to see pride and party spirit among missionaries. They know humility and unity when they see them, too. The missionary's humble attitude should commend his message.

Attitude of Love
Maintaining an attitude of love toward the brethren, both missionary and national, will foster Christ-honoring relationships. What makes this reminder necessary? The climate, a touch of malaria, fatigue, or someone else's cantankerous disposition come in for plenty of blame for lack of brotherly love. After all, when are people going to start thinking about *my* feelings? Yet every right-thinking missionary yearns to demonstrate daily Paul's description of love:

> Love is patient, love is kind. It does not envy, it does not boast, it is not proud. It is not rude, it is not self-seeking, it is not easily angered, it keeps no record of wrongs. Love does not delight in evil but rejoices with the truth. It always protects, always trusts, always hopes, always perseveres (1 Cor. 13:2-7).

Lines of Communication
Quarterbacks are acutely aware of the importance of good communication. The catcher calls for an outside curve. The batter looks for a signal from the third base coach. Good communication can spell the

difference between a win or a loss. Missionaries are playing in the same ball game, and they all want to win. However, communication snafus cause a fumble, a loss, or a ground ball to third. Good communication must prevail at all levels: personal, team, and field. It is tragic to lose simply because someone is not listening. Communication between missionaries is a skill that must be learned and practiced.

Team Concept

More is said today about team ministry than ever before. There is a move toward forming teams of missionaries even before they go to the field. While this approach is commendable, it is virtually impossible for those who go to already-established fields. The formation of a prefield team is more realistic in pioneer work.

At any rate, a team spirit is imperative. As used here, the team concept means to join together in a cooperative effort to evangelize, to build up believers, and to plant churches. Differing positions or roles are played by each team member. There must be a mutually-agreed-upon leader, a division of responsibility according to gifts, and accountability to the group, as well as to God.

Maintaining the team concept is another story. Even Paul and Barnabas learned this (Acts 15:36-41). Special interest groups may develop within the team. First-term members join the team. Veteran team members can be very receptive of new missionaries, or they can be very reticent to receive them.

Frequent huddles help maintain team unity. Some first termers find that they must land running before they have even seen the ball. Regular consultation preserves a unified purpose. The loner is less likely to run the ball by himself. Depending upon the matters at hand, the team needs daily or weekly reviews.

Mutually-agreed-upon leadership is crucial to a smooth-running team. No football team can function with more than one quarterback. Leadership roles must be clearly defined for the missionary team. Perhaps the leadership will rotate through various members of the team, but let everyone know what is expected of the person who assumes the position.

The question needs to be raised as to the place national leaders may or may not play on the team. This in turn surfaces the more basic question of the missionary's field role. Is he a partner with national church leaders? Does he play a servant role? Should there be a team of missionaries and a team of national leaders? Should the missionary have a place on the nationals' team or vice versa? No doubt personnel on different fields will come up with different answers for different reasons. Answers must be found for these questions.

Adaptability to Others

The ability to work with other people is a precious commodity. A missionary must have deep convictions about the direction his work should take. At the same time he must be flexible enough to include others, accept their thinking, and work harmoniously to a common end. This is as true of the new missionary as it is of the veteran. The first termer must not come to the field with his feet set in concrete. This would make it impossible for him to keep in step with the team!

Christ-centered interpersonal relationships can be some of the most satisfying rewards of missionary service. Paul wanted to see a spirit of unity in the Philippian church when he appealed to them to be "like-minded, having the same love, being one in the spirit and purpose" (Phil. 2:2).

Effective Communication

Even between subcultures in our own country, the ability to understand and to make ourselves understood can be quite frustrating. The Chicago-bred young pastor finds that his first pastorate in rural Illinois is a whole new world even though it is only 75 miles south of the Loop. A new vocabulary and life-style confront him immediately. And new value systems become quite evident. The hog market and the price of soybeans will be of more concern than where the Cubs are in the standings.

Also, in other English-speaking countries, church planters find that cultural differences are very real though subtle. Effective communication consists of more than how one pronounces "bath" or "slough." Communication is caught up in the whole life-style of a people, and it must be learned however self-sacrificing it may be.

Moving into a new-language/new-culture area of ministry, the cross-cultural communicator faces even more barriers. Whatever the cultural setting in which missionaries work, four factors are crucial to the communication process.

Understanding the Host Culture

Understanding local customs and value systems is basic to cummunication. Missionaries will not necessarily *approve* all they see in the local culture, but they must make every effort to *understand* what they see. Why do the people insist on initiation rites for their young teenagers? Should Christian teenagers be warned about involvement in these rites? If so, why and how? Should the national churches provide a substitute for them? What about the bride price that is an integral part of marriage? Why should a young man have to "pay" for his wife? Do missionaries have a right to insist that all Christian marriages be patterned after "the way we do it back home"?

Understanding the local culture and value systems is not done over a Monday morning cup of coffee with a national brother. It will be a long, agonizing process with many questions still left unanswered. Jones Kaleli, speaks out of an African context:

> . . . the missionary must listen and listen and listen. It must become a way of life. The maturity and integrity of Western missionaries often can be measured by the way they listen to feedback from the African church.[3]

Attempts to understand the culture will most certainly challenge the missionary to sort out the biblical absolutes that are transcultural from the cultural practices that are strictly local. It may come as a rude shock that some of his own cherished practices turn out to be cultural baggage stamped "U.S.A." rather than being biblical absolutes.

Empathy and Identification with Host Culture

Understanding culture is one thing. Actually *identifying* with it is quite another. It is one thing to eat, dress, and be housed in an identifable manner with the local people. It is quite another to rid oneself of one's own learned culture to the extent that the people accept the missionary as a brother or sister. The directness of Western missionaries is an affront to people in some other cultures where face-saving is a cultural priority. For instance, the manner in which a student is corrected in a classroom situation often must be handled with considerable discretion.

With few exceptions Westerners are unaccustomed to bargaining in the marketplace. Yet in many cultures arguing over prices is a part of the pleasure of buying and selling. Luzbetak says of the missionary:

> In his attempt to discourage materialism, he refuses to haggle with peddlers coming to his door and gives them the price they set; but instead of convincing his flock of the evils of greed, he merely convinces them that he is a very inefficient, not to say stupid, administrator.[4]

Two observations are in order. First, complete identification is not possible, nor do the people expect it. The missionary will always remain an outsider to some extent. Second, with the Lord's guidance the missionary must decide early on the segment of the people with whom he will identify. This will have considerable bearing on his evangelism and church planting. Luzbetak states:

> Unless the particular culture expressly requires it and unless the local people actually expect certain behavior and are pleased with its adoption by foreigners, healthy identification does not mean running around in a gee-string or sari, a fez or turban; it does not necessarily mean eating rats and beetles or restricting one's diet to rice and yams.[5]

If the missionary fails to attain an acceptable measure of local-culture empathy and identity, he will fall prey to culture shock. On the other hand, he may make vain attempts to attain a sort of psychotic chuminess with the culture commonly known as "going native." In either case, effective communication of the gospel is cut off.

The people to whom the missionary ministers quickly discern his sincerity or lack of sincerity in identifying with them. Even though his efforts are stumbling and imperfect, they will respond to his honest attempts. Universally people understand love and honesty when they see them.

Functionally Bilingual and Bicultural

The missionary must be able to communicate the gospel understandably in the local language, and he must be able to move about with ease in the host culture. The key thought here is "functional." Complete mastery of the language and complete identity with the culture are virtually impossible. But it *is* possible to be at ease in the language and culture and thereby to minister the gospel with a winsome naturalness. The ability to be at home in the culture takes serious effort. Kaleli states:

> The missionary must study and respect the African culture. Remember, the aim of missions is to communicate the gospel in another context—within the African world view. Knowing the culture will give bridges, comparisons, and illustrations that are essential in making the gospel clear. Moving from the known to the unknown was Paul's style (Acts 17). Sensitivity to the cultural wounds and scars of the past is essential.[6]

Gospel Communication in the "Heart" Language

Chaucer's *Beowulf* was written for the English reader, but it is hardly in the heart language of a twentieth-century American. Many potential Christian leaders from Asia, Africa, and Latin America go to Europe or come to America for further study, but they are not being taught in their heart language. In some multitribal situations in the Third World, students are taught in a lingua franca common to the country such as English or French. These are accommodations to situations that are less than ideal. How much better when a person hears the gospel, is taught, and then communicates the gospel to others all in his mother tongue! Though circumstances may seem to dictate otherwise, this privilege should be extended to all who hear the gospel.

Biblical Evangelism

According to the Pauline model for missions, biblical evangelism will issue in churches being established (Acts 14:21-23). Biblical, church-planting evangelism takes four factors into consideration.

Unreached People a Priority

Whole people groups such as Hindus, Muslims, and the Chinese are virtually unreached with the gospel. Pockets of tribal people remain untouched with the gospel. Occupational groups such as dock hands and restaurant workers seem so far removed from an effective witness. Then think of the thousands of refugees from war and famine whose lives are like a vacuum.

Unreached peoples may be remote geographically, though not necessarily so. Multitudes are unreached because of linguistic and cultural isolation. Minority ethnic groups, for example, may be in the midst of a highly evangelized population only to be bypassed because they are "different."

Two of the best-known missions research organizations are Missions Advanced Research and Communication Center founded in 1966 and the U.S. Center for World Mission begun in 1977. Their research teams continue to identify people groups around the world who do not have an adequate gospel witness. A people group is defined as:

A significantly large sociological grouping of individuals who perceive themselves to have a common affinity for one another. From the viewpoint of evangelization this is the largest possible group within which the gospel can spread without encountering barriers of understanding or acceptance.[7]

An unreached people group is identified as:

A people group among which there is no indigenous community of believing Christians with adequate numbers and resources to evangelize this people group without outside (cross-cultural) assistance.[8]

In referring to unreached peoples, Ralph Winter has popularized the terms "hidden peoples" and "frontier peoples."[9]

It is estimated that some three billion peole have not heard the gospel clearly enough to accept or reject Jesus Christ as Saviour. He is a total stranger to these lost people. Others have received only a garbled message. They need someone to help them sort out the meaning of the gospel so that they can believe. Many missionaries who are already the task force need a new vision of the unreached in their own linguistic and cultural background. New personnel joining the ranks must have burned into their hearts and minds the primary task of evangelism.

National churches must begin to hold forth the Word of Life as never before. They must think in terms of sending some of their own number with the message of light to others who have not heard it. One of the most significant missions trends within the last decade is the growing number of non-Western mission agencies and missionaries involved in missionary outreach. In his definitive study of third world mission societies, Lawrence E. Keyes states:

In 1972, James Wong, Edward Pentecost, and Peter Larson reported that there were at least 203 structured, missionary societies resident within the non-Western world. Eight years later, I found 368 active agencies. This represents an 81.28% increase.[10]

In his study of personnel, Keyes says, "In 1972, there were 3,404 estimated Third World missionaries. In 1980, the conservative estimate was 13,000."[11] According to Keyes, fully three-fourths of the Third World missionaries can be labeled as "evangelical."[12] Problems of support and training remain, but Third World churches are to be commended for their growing commitment to the *world* mission of the church.

Responsive People a Priority

Not all peole groups are equally responsive to the gospel, although they must all have opportunity to hear the gospel. Donald A. McGavran states:

Our Lord took account of the varying ability of individuals and societies to hear and obey the Gospel. Fluctuating receptivity is a most prominent aspect of human nature and society. It marks the urban and the rural, advanced and primitive, educated and illiterate.[13]

Forces must not be withdrawn from the unresponsive. The fields will ripen in due time. Among the responsive, however, gospel proclaimers, both missionary and national, must join forces to reap the harvest while it is ready. There are responsive people in abundance today particularly in many parts of Africa and Asia. Political and economic circumstances are less than favorable, but these people groups must hear the gospel while their hearts' doors are open. No doubt these unstable circumstances contribute to a readiness to respond to a message of hope.

Quantitative-Qualitative Evangelism

Quantitative evangelism reaches out to the very fringes of the target people. Whole communities, villages, cities, provinces and even countries are blanketed with a systematic evangelistic outreach. Quantitative evangelism, in short, seeks to saturate whole populations with the gospel. No lines are drawn between responsive and unresponsive people. These will surface soon enough. Then additional effort can be expended on the responsive. Saturation evangelism, of which Evangelism-in-Depth is a model, has proved to be an effective means of evangelism. To be sure, burnout can occur among those who participate. But the principles of church-centered, locally-led evangelism are biblically sound.

Qualitative evangelism, on the other hand, aims at the conservation of converts through church planting. The responding of great numbers of people to the gospel causes rejoicing. But ready response is only the first step. The harvest must be gathered into the granaries. Only church-planting evangelism will conserve the harvest.

Evangelism takes many forms, such as one-to-one, mass media, saturation, children's, campus, medical, educational, and mass evangelism. All of these types of evangelism, however, must result in new local assemblies of believers in order to be qualitative evangelism. These believers must be grounded in the Scriptures and rooted in the local church. The missionary can contribute much to strong national churches, but only churches made up of national believers and led by Spirit-controlled national pastors fulfill the biblical pattern. With Paul, missionaries must commend the churches into God's care (Acts 14:23).

Example-Partnership Evangelism

Converts in any place or culture tend to follow the example of their spiritual fathers. If the missionary or national pastor is active in evangelism, his followers tend to follow suit. Paul best exemplifies example-partnership evangelism. His working first with Barnabas, later with Silas, and then with Timothy demonstrates his shared gospel ministry. He speaks of Timothy as "our brother and God's fellow worker" and later admonishes him to "do the work of an evangelist" (1 Thess. 3:2; 2 Tim. 4:5). Setting the example and sharing in gospel ministry with his national brothers are two of the best ways the missionary can find to assure the on-going of a strong witness for Christ.

Biblical Church Planting

Biblical evangelism and biblical church planting go hand in hand.

Local-Culture Oriented Church Planting Consistent with Biblical Revelation

Many terms are bandied about today, such as *indigenization, accommodation, contextualization,* and even *context-indigenization,* proposing to describe what goes on in gospel communication and church planting across cultures.[14] These terms whiz about our heads like a racquet ball ricocheting from every corner of the court. Whatever term we use to describe the process, we must communicate the relevancy of the gospel within the cultural context in which we find ourselves. The gospel must be meaningful to soybean farmers in southern Iowa as well as to rice farmers in southern Bangladesh. Whether living in suburban Des Moines or in sprawling Dacca, people must hear the gospel as a meaningful, reliable message for *them.*

As gospel hearers become gospel believers, the resulting churches differ from culture to culture. Preaching styles, teaching methods, church discipline, styles of leadership, and worship patterns vary markedly. For example, will a church in culture X accept as pastor a young man who has just finished his schooling? In this particular culture only men of advanced age and experience are looked upon as potential leaders. Should the national pastor be taught to use three points and a poem? Is a worship service valid without the doxology? Are drums "proper" instruments to accompany the Sunday morning anthem? Is there only one way to take an offering? Cultural variables must be recognized and accepted as long as they do not violate the absolute truths of Scripture.

The Scriptures are supracultural, and there are biblical principles of conduct that are applicable in every culture in space and time. For example, the following relationships taught in Scripture are absolutes in any culture: (1) husband and wife (Col. 3:18-19; Eph. 5:22-23); (2) parents and children (Col. 3:20-21; Eph. 6:1-4); (3) employer and employee (Col. 3:22-4:1; Eph. 6:5-9); (4) relationships among believers (Eph. 5:21; Rom. 13:8-10; Rom. 12:9-16); (5) relationships to civil authority (Rom. 13:1-7); (6) relationships with the unsaved (Rom. 12:17-21); and (7) the believer's relationship to debatable practices (Rom. 14:1-15:3). The ways in which these principles are applied will differ from culture to culture, but the biblical principles themselves are absolute. Missionaries need extraordinary wisdom and discretion as they plant churches cross-culturally.

Regenerate, Instructed Membership

Care must be taken by the gospel bearer that his hearer understand the message he proclaims. Does the hearer have a biblical concept of God? Without it he cannot comprehend the message. Nowhere is the Holy Spirit's instructional ministry more needed. He cannot do His regenerating work until the hearer understands who God is and what He has done to effect salvation. For example, William D. Reyburn contrasts the Christian concept of God with that of the Kaka tribe in the Cameroun and the Quechua Indians of the Ecuadorean Andes.[15] The Christian believes on biblical authority that God is perfect. The Kaka tribesman believes that "God is a spider, Ndjambie. His character is impersonal, thus perfection or lack of it cannot be one of his attributes."[16] The Quechua Indian does not hold that God (Taita Dios) is perfect, rather that "he is reckoned as good or bad according to his acts."[17] These concepts of God create a dilemma for Bible translators when they are looking for ways to translate God's name. Reyburn concludes, "A conceptual transformation of God as God is necessary before man can understand and grasp the idea of God as Redeemer."[18]

What is the hearer's understanding of sin? For millions of people, sin and immorality have no relation whatsoever. For many, sin is only some local-culture taboo such as incest. For still others, sin is not sin unless the guilty person is found out. In order for the Holy Spirit to convict of "sin, righteousness and judgment," the hearer must have a grasp of the biblical teaching of these concepts. Preaching the gospel is a cooperative effort of both the communicator and the Holy Spirit to make the biblical salvation message plain. The church planter must beware of unwise haste in organizing a local assembly of believers. First he must be very sure that they *are* believers!

Again, postconversion instruction in the Word of God is vital to church planting: whether individual, small group, or congregational teaching, the Word must find its way into the understanding and life-style of the people. In order for them to be doers and not hearers only, they must be saturated in the Word.

To have a literate membership is an ideal, of course. Perhaps this is not universally possible, but it should be the goal of every cross-cultural church planter. This may involve years of translation and literacy work. In the long run, however, believers who can read and study the Word for themselves will be a stronger church body than those who are dependent on others for all of their spiritual food.

Spirit-Gifted Local Leadership

Paul, for example, planted churches, and local leaders were left in charge. He then moved on for further church planting (Acts 14:23). Because of

sovereignly bestowed spiritual gifts, no local group of believers is left
without necessary potential spiritual leaders (1 Cor. 12:7, 11; Rom. 12:6-8;
Eph. 4:11). Only in those initial pioneer stages is a missionary justified in
acting as the principal spiritual leader in a church-planting situation.
Timothy and Titus were under Paul's direction and were part of a
travelling missionary team. Paul sent them to various churches to minister,
and he asked time and again for them to rejoin him in his work. They were
never called by a church, nor did they ever resign from one.

Today's missionary best fulfills his role either as a partner with the
national brethren, or more ideally, as a servant. This attitude is the
scriptural pattern for spiritual leaders regardless of culture or time, and it
will enhance rather than hinder the missionary's work.

Area Growth through the Planting of Other Churches

During Paul's extended stay at Ephesus, the record states "that all the
Jews and Greeks who lived in the province of Asia heard the word of the
Lord" (Acts 19:10). As a result of this widespread witness through Paul's
converts it is likely that the churches at Colosse, Hierapolis and Laodicea
were planted (Col. 4:13). Paul did not have a hand in their founding (Col.
2:1). It is posible that the seven churches addressed in Revelation 2-3 found
their beginning at this time as well.

Today also churches need to be encouraged to plant other churches.
Church multiplication is the most effective means of reaching unreached
people with the gospel. Unfortunately many churches become an end in
themselves. Completely self-satisfied and finding plenty to do in the local
assembly, many soon become oblivious to unreached people who are
beyond their particular locale.

We must give serious attention to the shifting population centers of our
own country and the rest of the world. No longer does the rural and small-
town population hold center state. The sprawling cities and awesome
megalopolises continue to grow. To preach the gospel effectively to people
where they are is imperative. Time is too far spent for sending churches and
mission agencies to think that they can "go it alone."

National churches are catching the vision of evangelism and church
growth. "Each one plant one" is not an unrealistic goal for Bible-believing
churches in every culture around the world.

Leadership Preparation

Preparation of church leaders is imperative for a church-based strategy
of missions. Four considerations are in view.

Based on Demonstrated Spiritual Maturity and Gifts

Careful screening of potential students reveals that not all come with
demonstrated spiritual maturity and gifts. In some instances missionaries
still have a part in this screening process. Some students present themselves
with unworthy *motives*—family pressure, lack of something better to do,
or desire for personal advancement. The local pastor and church must help

the school find the spiritually qualified students. If there has been no evidence of spiritual growth, or development of gifts through local-church ministry, then the prospective student is a poor risk indeed. On the other hand, how meaningful it is to future church-planting ministries to prepare those who demonstrate the call of God in their life!

Compatible with the Local Culture

Woe to the missionary-teacher who constantly reminds his students, "This is the way we do it back in my country"! What are the learning patterns in the host country? Do people learn by rote memory? If so, was this imposed on them by a colonizing power? Do they have a history of aural learning? Do people in the local culture pass on knowledge through proverbs and parables? If so, does this shed any light on how to impart biblical and theological knowledge? Is it wise to shake out the old notes from systematic theology class, translate them, and impose these on eager students? Would students understand the Scriptures as well or better if theology were taught as it appears in the biblical text,that is, historically rather than logically as in systematic theology? If so this new approach could create a bit of stress for the traditionally trained teacher from Western cultures! Suffice it to say, building a study program based on the curriculum of one's alma mater is an occupational hazard of the first proportion. A person who has never taught the Scriptures cross-culturally finds it difficult to imagine the magnitude of the task.

Compatible with Levels of Ability

Differences in learning ability soon surface in any classroom. The teacher must try to meet the needs of each student, but inevitably some become bored while others find it difficult to keep up with the pace. Finding the balance between teacher expectation and student response is a continuing process in any culture.

In cross-cultural leadership preparation, the problem of meeting the needs of people with different learning abilities can become even more acute. Some with no formal education may sit in the same class with students who have had a full primary or secondary education. Basic intelligence may not differ greatly, but ability to grasp what is taught is definitely affected by previous experience in formal learning. If the school for national pastors is pegged at the primary level, what provision is made for those who are high school or college educated? Are they inescapably eliminated from ministry preparation? If, on the other hand, theological education is open only to those with advanced educational backgrounds, what can be done for those who are equally called into ministry but do not have the necessary preprequisites?

Multilevel biblical education offers the best solution to these dilemmas. In residence programs this means a significant outlay of teaching personnel and funding that may well be prohibitive. On one hand, the responsibility can be divided by committing part of the preparatory process to the national churches, while the mission agency concentrates on another level. On the other hand, national churches and missionaries may need to choose the level of preparation they should provide and concentrate their efforts at that particular level.

In the long run perhaps theological eduation by extension (TEE) can serve as an answer to multilevel leadership preparation. Self-instructional course materials lend themselves to multilevel adoption. The cost factor is reduced since buildings are not essential to the schooling process. This fact in turn also reduces the time factor necessary to get under way with the training program. For example, existing local church buildings can provide the necessary facilities for an extension program.

Flexible Methodology

Extraction-resident preparation is the traditional approach. The student leaves his family, livelihood, and familiar surroundings to pursue his education. In cross-cultural settings the provided schooling has too often been a transplant from the missionary's own homeland and educational experience. However, if the resident program is sensitive to cultural needs while maintaining faithful adherence to biblical truth, it can serve both students and churches well. Some advantages are being able to study with like-minded students under committed teachers and being able to concentrate on studies so that the time involves is lessened.

On the other hand, extension education is increasingly available to Third World leaders today. More leaders at less cost can be prepared by theological education by extension. Students are not obliged to leave their livelihood or familiar cultural surroundings. They remain a vital part of their church and community. Studies apply immediately to their local-church ministries thus enhancing the learning process. Extension education is more economical for all concerned. Existing buildings may serve as classrooms for weekly seminars. After self-instructional courses have been tested and produced, they serve many students beyond the personal presence of the teacher. Frequent seminar sessions, preferably weekly, provide application and testing of the subjects that are being studied.

Perhaps a combination of resident and extension leadership training is more advantageous than an exclusively resident or extension program. By using a common curriculum the student can have the best of both approaches. In residence he can move more quickly through the study program and have the advantages of daily teacher-student contact. On the other hand, he can shorten the time in residence by pursuing extension study and have the advantage of serving his local church. Whatever plan is used, flexibility is the key. While maintaining quality preparation, every effort must be expended to make better use of missionary teaching time and funding. Called and dedicated national leaders must move as quickly as possible into leadership roles at every level.

Wrap-Up

A review of the missionary's life and work on the field has brought to our attention some key areas of responsibility.

• The effectiveness of the missionary's field ministry is largely dependent upon the strength of his own spiritual life.

• God does not assign conflicting responsibilities to His people. Overcommitment does not originate with God.

• The missionary home should be a daily demonstration to a godless society of Christian love and devotion.

• Missionaries need a servant attitude in working with others.

• The ability to communicate the gospel in the cultural context is vital to the missionary in accomplishing his purpose.

• Biblical evangelism will reach out to new people where Christ is not known.

• Church-planting evangelism gives permanence and stability to gospel witness.

• Biblical church planting results in churches that in turn send their own missionaries to proclaim the gospel.

• Biblical leadership preparation is selective, based on demonstrated spiritual maturity and gifts.

• Biblical leadership preparation is adaptive, keeping in mind the culture, levels of ability, and effective methodology.

Notes to Chapter 17

1. J. Oswald Sanders, *Spiritual Leadership* (Chicago: Moody Press, 1967), p. 35.

2. Louis J. Luzbetak, *The Church and Cultures* (Techy, IL: Divine Word Publications, 1970), p. 122.

3. Jones Kaleli, "Pssst! Western ≠ Christian," *Wherever* 6 (Spring 1981): 7.

4. Luzbetak, *The Church and Cultures*, p. 95.

5. Ibid., p. 100.

6. Kaleli, "Pssst! Western ≠ Christian," p. 7.

7. Edward R. Dayton and Samuel Wilson, eds., *The Refugees Among Us: Unreached Peoples '83* (Monrovia: Missions Advanced Research and Communication Center, 1983), p. 499.

8. Ibid.

9. Ibid., p. 29.

10. Lawrence E. Keyes, *The Last Age of Missions: A Study of Third World Mission Societies* (Pasadena: William Carey Library, 1983), pp. 56-57.

11. Ibid., p. 61.

12. Ibid., pp. 75-77. See especially Keyes' chart on Theological Persuasion of Missionary Agencies on page 77.

13. Donald A. McGavran, *Understanding Church Growth*, Fully Revised (Grand Rapids: Eerdmans, 1980), p. 245. See his entire chapter, "The Receptivity of Men and Societies," pp. 245-65.

14. For an assessment of contextualization and related concepts see Bruce C.E. Fleming, *Contextualization of Theology: An Evangelical Assessment* (Pasadena: William Carey Library, 1980).

15. William D. Reyburn, "the Transformation of God and the Conversion of Man," *Readings in Missionary Anthropology II,* edited by William A. Smalley (Pasadena: William Carey Library 1978), pp. 481-85.

16. Ibid., p. 482.

17. Ibid.

18. Ibid., p. 485.

Part 5

Strategic Role of the Theological School

Administrators in the Theological School

18

In our study to this point we have established from Paul's model of missions the *sine qua non,* or indispensable essential, of the church's mission. This indispensable essential is threefold, namely, evangelizing the lost, edifying those who believe, and establishing local churches (Acts 14:21-23). A review of both the Old and New Testaments showed us that the Bible is a missionary book. The living God is a God of mission.

Paul's work demonstrated for us the indispensable ingredient of global missions activity: emphatic identification with people of varying cultural milieus. This includes the whole complex of cultural, social, and religious mores of the people. We observed also that the *cultural mandate* does make demands on the believers, but that these demands are corollary to the *commission mandate* rather than being integral to it.

We have also determined that the church plays the key role in God's purpose today of taking to Himself a people for His name (Acts 15:14). The task of local churches in implementing world outreach has been developed. The roles of the mission agency and of the missionary have also been described. The wheel of missions is not complete, however, without the contribution of the schools that prepare Christian leaders to serve at home and worldwide.

The theological school lays the foundation for all mission strategy. In this section of our study, the graduate theological seminary is primarily in view. However, the concepts we are discussing apply as well to Bible colleges, Bible institutes, and Christian liberal arts colleges who prepare career church leaders as a part of their purpose. Present students in these schools are the future leaders in churches, mission agencies, and mission fields, as well as in the schools themselves.

One evidence of the key position of the theological school is the need to maintain doctrinal purity. As the school goes, so go the churches and then the mission fields. The history of theological schools in both Europe and America demonstrates that institutions of higher learning are the first to fall prey to false teaching. When the cold finger of apostasy pushes over this first domino (the theological school), the church and mission field also tumble in that order. Apostasy creeps in primarily through the life and teaching of one or more of the faculty. It then works its way out through the classroom into the churches, and finally throughout the mission fields. Often the faculty member continues to sign the school's doctrinal statement each year, even though he does so with increasing mental reservations. The result is theological drift and disaster. The school that holds to the fundamentals of the faith must therefore maintain constant vigilance. If it slackens in diligence, it will share the same doctrinal downfall that has come to so many colleges and seminaries in the past.

Although an increasing number of people headed toward a missions career are seeking out seminary preparation, the majority of students in our seminaries are preparing for stateside local church ministry as pastors or as Christian education specialists. The key to world evangelization is in the hands of potential local church leaders. Some believe that the seminaries have failed to communicate the relevance of missions study as vital to future ministry. A MARC Newsletter, published by the Missions Advanced Research and Communication Center, summarized the findings of a questionnaire in mission education:

> Every response indicated a tremendous need for education at a local level. Almost every person responding mentioned that the key to such education *lies with the pastor.* But time and again comment was made how little education the average pastor receives in seminary to give him a world view. States one mission professor "it is simply a matter of record that the average pastor in our evangelical churches has no deep personal commitment to world missions." He then goes on to illustrate by noting that only 6 pastors of 196 invited showed up to a missions workshop on their campus, while 700 showed up for a Christian Education workshop. "What's the explanation? Christian Ed is relevant, missions are not."[1]

Any effort to meet the challenge must face this question squarely, "How can the theological school fulfill its proper role in mission strategy?" In this and in following chapters we will summarize the distinct responsibilities of administrators, faculty, and students in striving for excellent preparation for fulfilling the church's mission. As we do, we will keep in mind the vital importance of personal commitment and integrity in each facet of the educational process.

Responsibility of the Administrators

School administrators are defined as both the board members and the executive officers. Their individual and corporate commitment to the mission of the church is imperative. To be successful, they must fulfill the following key responsibilities in a biblical strategy for world missions.

Administrators Must Set Educational Goals That Are Biblical

A school's administrators must determine the exact answers to four basic questions: (1) What kind of person does the school want to produce? (2) What does it want its students to be? (3) What does it want its students to know? (4) What does it want its students to do?

No manufacturer begins the production of an item without planning carefully for the end result. The latest in sports cars, coffeemakers, digital clocks, and home computers are the result of detailed planning and production. The school deals with people and the direction those people will take in their life commitments. Some theological schools are known for producing theologians or philosophers; others turn out apologists or local church leaders; and some—even missionaries! Administrative leaders must determine how their school can best contribute to fulfilling God's purpose in this age (Acts 15:14; Romans 11:25).

Being, knowing, and *doing* are basic features in any educational program. Christian educators must be especially concerned about maintaining a balance in these areas that squares with their purpose. Even though administrators are not directly involved in the classroom, they do set the educational sail for the institution. The development of Christian character and commitment (being), instruction in the various academic disciplines (knowing), and development of skills in the application of acquired knowledge (doing) will be assured only as administrators grasp the rudder firmly and trim the sail accurately while they negotiate the increasingly turbulent currents of our unsettled day. It is crucial to integrate these basic education goals in order to carry them out knowledgeably. With the cross-cultural communicator in mind, the following figure illustrates the beginnings of integrated educational goals.

FIGURE 35

CROSS-CULTURAL EDUCATIONAL GOALS		
BEING	KNOWING	DOING
Evangelizers of the lost	How to proclaim the Gospel	To proclaim the gospel effectively
Teachers of believers	How to communicate the Scriptures pedagogically	To demonstrate proficiency in teaching the Scriptures
Planters of churches	How to plant a local church	To plan procedures for planting a church
Communicators across cultures	How to communicate the Scriptures cross-culturally	To demonstrate proficiency in communicating cross-culturally
Teachers/partners of church leaders ·	How to work with local culture church leaders	Internship, cross-culturally
Counselors of church leaders	How to counsel cross-culturally	To counsel with leaders cross-culturally

Administrators Must Develop a Biblical Philosophy of Education

The institution preparing men and women for the ministry must establish a scriptural philosophy of education and evaluate it regularly. This involves two aspects that complement each other: (1) preparing people *for* the ministry, and (2) preparing people *of* the ministry.

Preparing people *for the ministry* relates, of course, to preservice training. This has been the traditional role of the seminary. Dedicated people come to prepare themselves to serve God. Their basic studies center in the areas of: (1) Bible, including the biblical languages; (2) theology, including biblical theology, historical theology, and apologetics; and (3) ministries, which concentrate on the practical aspects of pastoral preparation, Christian education, or missions.

One of the basic problems in graduate education is the fact that many of these earnest young people have not been tested in the crucible of Christian service. They often do not know their spiritual gifts when they graduate, nor are they assured of the type of ministry God has for them. In recent years an attempt has been made by mission agencies to meet this need through various internship programs. Some of them, such as the Missionary Apprenticeship Program, are designed to take students into actual cross-cultural mission situations where they can learn by observation and by doing. Whether building an airplane hanger in Brazil, camping with Navajo boys and girls in Arizona, or bargaining for brass in an Eastern bazaar, the student apprentice gains firsthand insights into missionary life and work.

The traditional seminary, however, operates with an on-campus program. It must therefore find other creative ways of bridging the gap between classroom intake and ministry output. Some have done so effectively by providing internships as a part of the required curriculum. These may be taken either at home or abroad, according to the student's vocational calling. Capable and willing local church personnel or missionaries are used to make these internships valuable for the student. Evangelism, teaching, and administration are prime areas of concentration in these training experiences.

Preparing the people *of the ministry*—missionaries who have already been on the field—is a relatively new dimension of theological training in the Western nations. It is part of a developing trend in the history of theological education.[2] Continuing education is now being provided for our missionaries as well as for those involved in local church ministries. Obviously, these people come to the classroom with more maturity, with settled convictions concerning their gifts and ministry, and with deep motivation to prepare themselves further for their work. Some schools have set up both resident and extension models for continuing education. Extension courses are being offered increasingly to those active in Christian ministry. Many missionaries who have taken advantage of these courses report that they are of great benefit, both personally and in their minsitry. A number of these study programs lead to master and doctorate level degrees.[3]

Seminaries and other Chrisitan educational institutions must continue to use every acceptable means and method possible to improve the preparation they give God's chosen servants. But they must also make certain that they always stand firm on the foundation of God's unchanging Word.

Administrators Must Maintain Biblical Doctrine and Practice

School administrators are responsible for maintaining biblical doctrine and practice in their institution and training program. Three factors are significant: (1) the securing of faculty, (2) the selection of students, and (3) a sensitivity to the churches of their constituency.

Theological schools that clearly define their doctrinal position by the historic fundamentals of the Christian faith have great difficulty securing faculty members who wholeheartedly hold the same position. Their position on theological issues being debated today such as the inerrancy of Scripture, charismatic gifts, degrees of Calvinism, personal and ecclesiastical separation, and eschatology, eliminate many prospective professors. Adequate academic credentials and personal commitment to the school's doctrinal position are basic for any teacher. The attaining of the goals of a school is largely dependent on a faculty that supports those goals without equivocation.

Selecting students involves more than entrance exams and admissions procedures. The academic qualifications of incoming students are important, of course, but for the theological school their spiritual commitment is equally crucial. How refreshing it is to sit down with incoming students and share with them their dreams—and problems—as they envision preparation for a life of service! Their comprehension of and agreement with the school's goals, practices, and doctrinal position must be carefully evaluated. This is because students, both individually and collectively, exert a strong influence on the direction of the institution. Admissions procedures are based on the ideal, but they must operate in the realm of the real. Great spiritual wisdom is needed in accepting applicants.

The administrators must be extremely sensitive to the churches that support the school. Often the constituency is thought of primarily in terms of financial support, but this view is entirely too simplistic. The churches must be informed about the school's goals and made familiar with their efforts to maintain doctrinal purity. The people in the churches must be informed about the progress and the problems of the school. Only when they have this kind of open, honest information can people be expected to support the school with their prayer and finances. Administrators must be good listeners and discerners.

The Christian school and its church constituency have a mutual stake in the future. As corporate bodies of believers, churches bring people to faith in Christ and nurture them. They desire both numerical and spiritual growth in the believing community The schools, in turn, stand ready to train those believers whom God calls into career Christian work.

Administrators Must Provide an Atmosphere for Spiritual Growth

This important factor is difficult to measure empirically, but it is real nonetheless. Policies related to student life on campus, and opportunities and expectations related to Christian service, help build a positive spiritual tone. So do chapel services, conferences, and seminars related to spiritual life and missions. And the people themselves—administrators and faculty members who are sensitive and responsive to students needs— are probably the most important single factor.

Suffice it to say, the campus atmosphere of every Christian school is evident—especially to visitors who walk into the situation cold! Administrators have the responsibility of creating and sustaining a Christ-honoring climate of personal and spiritual growth, that includes students, faculty, and staff.

Administrators Must Participate in the Ministry of the Word of God

Knowingly or unknowingly, the administrators set the pattern for others by their personal commitment to Christian ministry. In their witness to the lost, their preaching and teaching of the Word of God, and their faithfulness to the local church, they are saying with their lives what they believe in their hearts. This will speak more loudly to faculty, students, and constituency than any degree or title!

Wrap-Up

Christian schools play a key role in a biblical strategy for world missions. Administrators have the potential to set the direction for the churches and mission agencies in reaching this generation for Jesus Christ. Because of this, we remind ourselves of some of the points we have made.

• Theological schools must give constant attention to doctrinal purity. They set the sail for the entire Christian movement.

• Administrators must set measurable goals so that there can be no mistaking the purposes of the school.

• Within the parameters of academic excellence and spiritual commitment, the school must prepare both people *for* the ministry and people *of* the ministry in new and innovative ways.

• The administrator's lifestyle must give credence to the school's stated purposes.

Notes to Chapter 18

1. Edward R. Dayton, "You Can't Beat the System—Part II, "*MARC Newsletter* (May 1975): 4-5.

2. Ralph R. Covell and C. Peter Wagner, *An Extension Seminary Primer* (South Pasadena: William Carey Library, 1971). In Chapter 6 the authors discuss "Forms of

Theological Education Through History." This is a helpful summary of how we arrived at today's scene of theological eduation.

3. Some of the seminaries that offer continuing education for career Christian workers are Columbia Graduate School of Bible and Missions, Denver Conservative Baptist Seminary, Grand Rapids Baptist Seminary, School of World Mission of Fuller Theological Seminary, Trinity Evangelical Divinity School, Western Conservative Baptist Seminary, and Wheaton Graduate School.

Faculty in the Theological School

19

Regardless of his particular academic discipline, every faculty member in a theological school should teach his subjects with the mission of the church in view. Every professor should be committed to filling the following areas of responsibility.

Responsibility of the Faculty

Faculty Must Foster a Total Christian World and Life View

The Christian world and life view is based upon belief in the one living and true God who is altogether holy and righteous, who reconciles and redeems the sinner, and who rewards the saint. This dimension is missing from all other world and life views. Teachers in the biblical, theological, or ministries areas find it relatively easy to relate their discipline to the Christian world and life view. However, professors in the natural or human sciences in our Christian colleges may have some difficulty integrating their field of teaching with the biblical position. More often than not, these teachers have taken their advanced studies in an academic atmosphere that ignores the Christian world and life view. In fact, some of their professors may have been openly hostile to the basic tenets of the Christian faith.

Now these professors, teaching in the field of natural or human science, are expected to view and teach their area of academic discipline in the light of the Bible—rather than looking at the Bible in the light of their academic discipline. Biology, sociology, or psychology must be judged by Scripture, rather than the Scriptures being evaluated by these various disciplines. Every faculty member must struggle with this new approach until he is able to relate his subject matter to a *total* Christian world and life view.

Stephen R. Spencer states the case as follows:

> The content of Christian education is Truth. The basis or rationale for Christian Education is Truth and its communication from one generation to the next. Christian education exists to communicate Truth—not truth about only certain selected areas of life or, certainly, not just "religious truth," if by that we mean principles of morality or spirituality *as opposed to* truths about the created realm in which we live. No, Christian education must communicate Truth in its entirety or at least in its entire scope . . . .

In short, we are to teach students the correct evaluation of all of life and reality. And, as we have seen, this correct perspective upon all of life and reality is what is called a *world-view* or a *world and life view*. The Christian world-view, then, is the basis for and the content of Christian education.[1]

Someone has observed that Christian education is education with a plus. The plus—indeed the very heart—of Christian education is an integral part of that world view.

Faculty Must Guard against Educational Provincialism

It seems only natural for a teacher to conduct his classes and to make his assignments as if no other teacher's class existed! Students know this better than anyone else. Even though the student may succeed in convincing the teacher to be a bit more reasonable, this does not expose the real issue. The basic problem is that of curriculum integration. Each academic area in a Christian institution must be integrated with all others in such a way that students see the total picture of their academic pursuits. They must not simply encounter separate areas of study that somehow do not come together in clear focus.

James M. Grier pictures a comprehensive and orderly approach to theological study. He speaks of this approach as the "theological encyclopedia," or curriculum.[2] See the Grier model in the figure below.

FIGURE 36

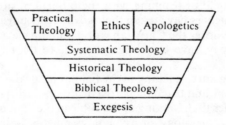

The Order and Relationship of the
Theological Disciplines

This model bases theological study on the exegesis of the biblical text in the original languages. All other disciplines grow out of this text-centered base. Integrating all the disciplines is the perennial problem of the theological school. In developing a *functional* approach to the theological curriculum, we suggest the following model. See figure 37.

Clearly our theological study needs an integrative core. Samuel Wilson made these sobering observations:

> Western theological establishment regards sound exegesis as the "pearl of great price." Hundreds of hours are spent every year in

FIGURE 37

**A Functional Approach to
Theological Study**

instruction in heremeneutics. Students, like their professors before them, are taught to approach the Word of God through the standard of objectivity. It is nothing short of a travesty, however, that this expended effort should so completely miss the mark. Exegesis is supposedly the science of leading out of the text the meaning of the given Word. Yet in many theological schools one could pursue and complete an entire theological education and never be confronted with the centrality of missions in that Word. The net effect of hour upon hour of theological and scriptural instruction is hundreds of graduates whose lives remain unaffected by the Divine command and compulsion to reach the nations of the world . . . . My point is that the real message conveyed is to be judged by the final outcome. And the final outcome seems to say rather clearly that while there may have been an occasional reference to the missionary context of the early Church as an essential to interpretation, the really *interesting* questions of interpretation have nothing to do with missionary concern.[3]

Today, God's mission in the world is carried out by the church. His mission is the church's mission. This mission should be the integrating factor in our theological education. The school must take a holistic approach to its curriculum, co-curricular activity, and the entire school community.

Achieving a curriculum that works demands faculty commitment to the school's goals and open communication between professors who teach in all areas. We must make a sincere effort to work together for the integration of the total curriculum. Upon honest appraisal we may need to drop some courses and teach others in their place. The primary concern must always be the academic and spiritual welfare of the students, and their ability to function creditably when they enter their given ministries.

Faculty Must Prepare People for This Generation

Being an effective instructor demands more than the mastery of one's academic discipline and the updating of the syllabi. Teachers must also be students of the world scene in which they live. As we saw earlier in our study, we proclaim an unchanging message in an ever-changing milieu. We must understand our changing world so that we do not fall into the trap of preparing our students for the status quo situations of the past.

As a case in point, preparing people effectively for ministry in today's churches involves relevant missions instruction. Based on a study done by Glenn Schwartz on schools and colleges offering missions courses, Robert E. Reeves states that, "Only 13 out of 216 schools . . . have a course on the subject of developing a missions program in a local church."[4]

Reeves comments further:

> The situation is clear and the problem is serious. We have produced a generation of preachers who have not been taught that missions is an important part of the local church program. And if somehow on their own they have gained a vision for developing a missions-minded church, we have not given them the tools to make their dream become a reality.[5]

The effectiveness of our theological education does not stop at home. Those preparing for international ministries need our consideration as well. The adage that "like produces like" also holds true in cross-cultural ministries. In a straightforward manner, Lois McKinney contends that:

> . . . theological schools in the States are often miseducating the very missionaries they should be educating. If missionaries have experienced a traditional kind of theological education, they are likely to communicate these values as they develop leaders overseas. If their own involvement in ministry was postponed until their seminary program was completed, they are likely to be contented to work with young, potential leaders overseas. If their curriculum was designed around traditional disciplines, they are likely to duplicate that same curriculum. If what they learned was culturally irrelevant, they are likely to be insensitive to the cultural dimensions of their teaching . . . .

> But if, on the other hand, the missonaries' experience in seminary involved learning within a committed and caring community, they are likely to create committed and caring communities themselves. If

their preparation for ministry was church-centered in their homeland, they will be likely to encourage their students to contextualize theology as well. If they learned to evangelize and disciple others in their homeland, they will teach overseas students to share and to care.[6]

Plainly, theological education cannot be divorced from a holistic approach to life. Patterns that form during student days affect one's ministry for years to come. Faculty and administrators alike must work diligently to maintain the relevance of the education process to life.

How can balance in course offerings be maintained so that the student entering an international ministry will have the necessary foundation on which to build? For example, our world is increasingly urban. Are we preparing students to think and act in terms of urban church planting and church growth at home and abroad? Is the challenge of cross-cultural communication adequately addressed? Are not those trained in the biblical languages the best prepared to translate the Word into other languages?

Charles R. Taber deals with the areas of study necessary for the training of missionaries.[7] He pleads for integration of these areas so that biblical, cultural, and communication studies reinforce and enlighten each other. Taber's suggestions are adapted and summarized below.

FIGURE 38

THE TRAINING OF MISSIONARIES			
MESSAGE	MAN	MILIEU	MEANS
Biblical Historical Theological Studies	Socio-cultural Studies	Regional Studies	Communication Linguistic Studies

These areas of study relate to the prospective missionary. They illustrate, however, how we must constantly evaluate our course offerings so that we prepare today's students in the most relevant ways possible.

Youth is characterized by idealism, even as maturity is characterized by realism. The teacher needs to make a conscious effort to understand how the students view the world around them. Students are often more sensitive than some of their elders to the needs of the lost. Historically, the student generation has stirred schools and churches to missionary action.

The missions teacher bears responsibility to serve the student well in the classroom. Edwin L. Frizen puts the onus on the teacher when he says:

Each missions professor should be the best educated man on campus. His strong points should be theology, Bible, anthropology, psychology, and education. He should have had experience as a missionary overseas. He should try to keep that experience current. He should be a coordinator of missionary information, producing selected bibliographic material for interested students of any major for directed self-study in all phases of missions.[8]

Now, there is a job description to keep a missions professor humble! Fortunate are the students who have such a person to keep them informed on current missions developments. And bravo to the school who can afford him!

Faculty Must Be Informed about Current Missions Thinking

Since God is calling out from among the nations a people for His name, and since this calling-out process will continue until Christ's return for His own, every believer needs a clear understanding of how the great commission is being carried out today.

William Carey, David Livingstone, J. Hudson Taylor, and the other nineteenth-century missionary heroes have all gone on to their reward. Paternalism is dead or dying on mission fields, and in its place has come a new partnership and servant role. The day of missionary heroes has all but disappeared.

Every-changing political and economic challenges are being thrust before missionaries, particularly in the Third World. Receptive populations are being researched and reached in every continent of the world. Concepts such as conscientization, contextualization, cultural relativity, liberation theology, saturation evangelism, church growth, homogeneous units, theological education by extension, and many more have crowded their way into the missiological scene.

Because seminary teachers in particular are preparing people to proclaim the gospel in today's world, it is imperative that they be informed about that world. This can be done to a degree through acquaintance with missionaries supported by their local church, and through conversations with mission administrators and missionaries who visit their school. But imagine what would happen if faculty members were periodically to use their expertise in a cross-cultural setting!

Much helpful information can be gained by keeping up with the missiological journals now available. Reading carefully the prayer letters of missionary friends will give personal insights into what is happening on the field. Suffice it to say, keeping informed on the current world mission scene requires more than collecting the prayer cards of your favorite missionaries.

Faculty Must Participate in the Ministry of the Word of God

It has often been said that the life of a teacher is more important than his manner of teaching or his subject matter. This is a sobering thought for the professor who is convinced that the overhead projector or the chalkboard is the key to his professional competence.

Sometimes an instructor in a Christian school is tempted to believe that his teaching ministry is the sum total of his Christian service responsibility.

After all, he reasons, this is his calling. Why should he give any further time or energy to the ministry of the Word? Administrators and students may find themselves reasoning the same way. Is this thinking valid? Absolutely not! The teacher's commitment to Christ goes beyond the classroom. It must include the home and then reach into the community where the witness is sorely needed. The local church serves as the base from which gifts can be used for God's glory, both in the community and among fellow believers.

Seminary and college professors must live and teach the claims of Christ to their families first of all. If they are to have credibility in the classroom, community, and the church, they must begin at home. Fortunate is the school whose faculty members demonstrate their commitment to Christ by their total life-style.

Wrap-Up

The faculty in a Christian school touch not only the immediate student generation of Christian leaders but those in the future. Let us review some of their basic commitments.

• The inerrant Scriptures must be recognized as the foundation of the theological curriculum.

• Exegesis of the text must not be an end in itself. Rather, exegesis must provide the basis for an integrated curriculum.

• Integration of curriculum must include structured ministry opportunities.

• We must give particular attention to preparing pastors to lead strong missions programs in our local church.

• Faculty members must demonstrate their commitment to ministry by their personal life and service.

Notes to Chapter 19

1. Stephen R. Spencer, "The Christian World-View: The Basis for Christian Education," in *Grand Rapids Baptist Seminary Theolog* (April 1982): n.p.

2. James M. Grier, Unpublished notes, 1982.

3. Samuel Wilson, "Judging Theological Education by the Outcome," *Global Church Growth Bulletin* 17 (July-August 1980): 42.

4. Robert E. Reeves, "Where Will Mission-Minded Pastors Come From?" *Global Church Growth Bulletin* 17 (July-August 1980): 49.

5. Ibid.

6. Lois McKinney, "Why Renewal Is Needed in Theological Education," *Evangelical Missions Quarterly* 18 (April 1982): 93-94.

7. Charles R. Taber, "The Training of Missionaries," *Practical Anthropology* 14 (November-December 1967): 267-74.

8. Edwin L. Frizen, Jr. "Executives Tell Missions Profs What They Think," *Evangelical Missions Quarterly* 8 (Spring 1972): 46.

Students in the Theological School

20

We can be thankful for the idealism of youth. Each new generation has its new worlds to conquer. This should be especially true of the young men and women who pursue their studies in a Christian institution. Another new generation waits to be reached for Christ. How does this purpose relate to the Christian student? Here are five goals for students who are receiving their training.

Responsibility of the Students

Students Must Discover and Develop Their Spiritual Gifts

Many students who enter our schools to prepare for career Christian service have given little prior thought to spiritual gifts. How many have considered their talents and abilities in the light of Romans 12, 1 Corinthians 12-14, or Ephesians 4? How many have tested their gifts in their local churches? How many are serving the Lord in some kind of outreach ministry? One of the key responsibilities of schools is to help students in this crucial area of their lives.

In the midst of academic pursuits and vocational preparation, it is imperative that we help students sit down and take stock of their spiritual gifts. The Holy Spirit distributes the gifts (1 Cor. 12:11), and believers must discover and develop them. What better place to determine and improve them for God's glory than the Christian school?

Students Must Discover the Will of God for Them

Knowing God's will for one's life seems to be an elusive goal for today's student generation. Perhaps this has always been true. If only God would write out His will for us on a 3x5 card!

When we speak of God's will in this way, we are really talking about guidance. God's will is made known in a multitude of ways throughout the Scripture. The Bible is filled with specific commands and principles to be obeyed. When it comes to guidance in our lives, however, the path does not always seem so clear. Should I prepare for a future in business, or study for a Christian service career? Should I become a career missionary, or enter a "tentmaking" profession overseas? Whom should I marry? Or should I remain single? Questions like these plague all of us at one time or another. They sometimes become overwhelming for those who are looking forward to a life of service.

In determining God's direction in our lives, two *preliminary questions* come to mind. First, "Am I willing to do God's will, whatever it may be?" Without considering the consequences of his question, Paul asked on the Damascus road, "What shall I do, Lord" (Acts 22:10)? Not in his wildest dreams did this fire-breathing Pharisee expect God to appoint him to be the Apostle to the Gentiles (Acts 9:15; Rom. 11:13; Gal. 2:7-9). In determining God's direction in our life, the first step is to be available.

The second question takes us a step beyond the first: "Is God leading me into a career Christian ministry?" When a person pursues a Christian ministry *career*, that is how he expects to earn his living (1 Cor. 9;13-14). Martin E. Clark states:

> While every Christian is to serve Christ and minister to fellow believers, some are called to do so in a career sense, and they earn their living by their ministries. These we are calling "Christian service careers." "Secular careers" are those in which one's living is earned by functions other than ministry . . . . "Secular careers" are neither less spiritual nor less sacred than Christian service careers . . . , for the spirituality of one's work is determined not by the content of the work, but rather by the spirituality of the worker.[1]

Paul was certain that God had called him into his apostleship (1 Cor. 1:1; Rom. 1:1; 1 Tim. 1:12). That call was made abundantly clear to Paul in his Damascus road experience (Acts 9:15-17; 22:12-15; 26:16-18). God calls many of us into a career ministry today, but not in the same sense of Pauline apostleship. Although the Lord always leads us in accordance with the propositional truth of His Word, that does not mean that we must always have a specific verse for each specific decision that we make. Many of us can point to times when God's Word *has* brought assurance about the rightness of decisions-in-formation. However, we must guard against the "hunt and point" system of finding biblical confirmation for things we have already decided we want to do! In speaking about God's call in our lives today, Clark states, "A preferable approach would be to define this calling as *God's personal guidance through which He enlightens us regarding His plan for our lives.*"[2]

Generally, the order of God's direction in our lives is first vocation, then location. This was certainly true for Barnabas and Saul. The Holy Spirit said, "Set apart for me Barnabas and Saul *for the work* to which I have called them " (Acts 13:2). As these men "put their foot in the road," God led them to various places of ministry throughout their missionary careers.

Second, in discovering God's will, some *precautions* are in order. The first of these relates to *misconceptions* about the "missionary call." J. Herbert Kane goes so far as to say that, "The term *missionary call* should never have been coined."[3] Several misconceptions must be cleared up about this "call." It does not rest on need alone, although need may be a contributing factor. It is not a "special" call in that we must have some sort of exotic experience. Certainly it is not the "Macedonian call." (Acts 16:6-10). As Harold R. Cook observes:

Paul was already a missionary; he had been a missionary for some years . . . . He was already in a foreign land when the vision came. And it came, not to call he and his companions to missionary service, but to call them to extend their operations beyond Asia Minor to Europe.[4]

Nor is the call necessarily to some definite location. God did not impose on Paul the same geographic criteria that we often require of missionaries today—one place of service for life. Strange, isn't it, that we do not make this same requirement of pastors! God's leading is continual, step-by-step guidance, not all revealed in one glamorous moment of time.

Another precaution relates to our *motivation* for Christian service. Is this someone else's will imposed upon us because they believe it would be a "wonderful thing" for us to do? Is there a bit of spiritual pride involved? Or are we motivated to serve God on the basis of the unchanging truth of His Word? In life's valley experiences, as well as the mountain tops, we must assure ourselves that we are where we are, and doing what we are doing, as a result of obedience to God's will.

Still another precaution concerns *marriage.* Scripture is clear that it is God's will for some to marry and for others to be single (1 Cor. 7:1-9). In marriage the issue is the choice of a mate. We must marry "in the Lord," of course. Beyond that, *mutual* commitment to God's will about vocational Christian service is absolutely essential for fulfilling His purposes in the individuals involved.

Third, there are *prerequisites,* or conditions, for guidance in our lives. Briefly, these relate to (1) our admitted need for guidance, (2) our willingness for God's guidance in our life, and (3) a close walk with the Guide. In seeking God's will for our life, we must prepare our hearts through submission, study of the Word, and supplication at the throne of grace.

Fourth, the *principles* of guidance are the subject of much discussion today.[5] Suffice it to say, God always directs us in accordance with His Word. We can never say, "This is God's will," when our proposed action clearly contradicts scriptural truth. It is equally clear from the Bible that the Lord uses the confirmation of godly fellow believers and wise counselors to help us determine God's will for our lives (Prov. 11:14; 12:15; 15:22; 20:18; 24:6; Acts 16:1-3).

God has promised to guide us (Prov. 3:5-6; Psalm 32:8; Isaiah 30:21). Students, indeed all of us, must walk close to the Guide in a holy and obedient life. When we do, His divine direction is manifestly clear. He may or may not lead us into career Christian ministry. It is safe to say, however, that we must not move into any vocational choice without first considering (and settling) God's direction for career service—whether at home or abroad.

Students Must Pursue Excellence Academically and Spiritually

God does not pass out medals for mediocrity. Students must never be satisfied with achieving anything less than their potential. To use the figure of engines, some of us have four cylinders, some six, and others eight. We have nothing that we have not received from God (1 Corinthians 4:7). Therefore, we must live up to our full potential both academically and spiritually. We may well have built-in limitations academically, but our spiritual limitations are self-imposed. What a tragedy to have 8-cylinder potential and 4-cylinder achievement.

Think of some of the students of the past who pursued excellence academically and spiritually—Adoniram Judson, Samuel Mills, and Luther Rice. Consider Borden of Yale or, more recently, Jim Elliot and his comrades. They all had different capacities and callings, but they shared the same commitment.

We generally concede that prospective pastors need seminary preparation for future ministry. We will even give the nod to would-be Christian education directors. However, when missionaries-to-be seek seminary training, it is sometimes a different story. A knowing nod of the head and a mumbled word like, "Here we go again! Another young person sidetracked from the will of God!" Or, "Seminary? To go out and work with a bunch of natives?" Thankfully, times are changing. But the old ideas about missionary training die slowly.

And missionaries should keep their families small, too! After all, too much schooling and too many kids can bring a promising missionary career to ruin! Does this common idea prove to be true?

Craig Hanscome, missionary with the Christian and Missionary Alliance, conducted an enlightening study of the effect of advanced schooling and family size on the drop-out rate among missionaries. He conducted a study of Christian and Missionary Alliance missionaries serving between the years of 1962-1972. He found that the drop-out rate of those without graduate work was 33.3 percent. By contrast, the drop-out rate of those with graduate work was 14.7 percent. Hanscome continues:

> Those with 0-1 child had a drop-out rate of 31.5 percent, while those with two or more children had a drop-out rate of 16.1 percent.

> When both education and children are used together, the following percentages of drop-out were found.

> No graduate work and 0-1 child, 37.7 percent.
> No graduate work and two or more children, 18.2 percent.
> Graduate work and 0-1 child, 15.7 percent
> Graduate work and two or more children 13.0 percent.[6]

In their pace-setting book on mission strategy, Edward R. Dayton and David A. Fraser compare missionary training with medical training.[7] On their way to becoming practicing physicians, students move through premedical preparation and medical school. During these years they have increasing hands-on medical experience. Then come the years of residency in a specialty. To this may be added training in a subspecialty. Doctors gradually function on their own more and more until they finally enter their own practice.

Many years have passed by then, of course. But the more crucial factor is the experience gained in the process. On-the-job training is an area we must shore up in preparing practicing missionaries. Dayton and Fraser state, "It is our contention that the 'doctor of souls' requires just as much preparation as the one who cares for the body."[8]

Providing this on-the-job training is the *combined* responsibility of school, church, and mission agency. We must come to a new mutual realization, obligation, and implementation in the responsibility of preparing missionaries. What should the career path be for a missionary? As we visualize this path, we will assume that the hypothetical student has completed his undergraduate studies in a Bible college, Christian liberal arts college, or state university. We will also assume that he has a basic understanding of Scripture, and that he has studied a language. See figure 39 on page 190.

As we observe in this suggested career path, the person has a number of options along the way. But hands-on ministry experience is no option; it is imperative! The theological school cannot do the job alone. The local church and the mission agency can help students who are preparing for excellence in ministry get first-hand experience.

Students Must Be Informed about Current Missions Developments

Direct involvement in missions is more available to students today than ever before. Apprenticeship programs are open to qualified students through many mission boards. Either at home or in a cross-cultural situation in another country, students have found meaningful service, adjusted their attitudes, and oftentimes changed their goals. Classroom instruction must be accompanied by field experience if the learning process is to be most effective. The testimonies of students who have participated in these programs are overwhelmingly favorable. Some of their ministries have been building projects, street evangelism, manuscript preparation for translation, church-planting assistance, and camping programs.

On campus, missions information is readily available to students through visiting mission representatives. Mission agencies are sending men and women to the campuses who can communicate well with the present student generation. Student-planned missions conferences usually invite missionaries who can bring information and inspiration that is available through no other means. Some agencies are leading the way in producing multimedia presentations of high professional quality that appeal to today's student population.

Students Must Participate in the Ministry of the Word of God

As we have seen, this responsibility is a common factor related to administrators, teachers, and students. Scripture reminds us that we are "created in Christ Jesus unto good works" (Eph. 2:10).

Student attitudes toward Christian service range from indifference to enthusiastic involvement. Undoubtedly, the degree of spiritual maturity is a key factor. On the other hand, schools must be careful to provide

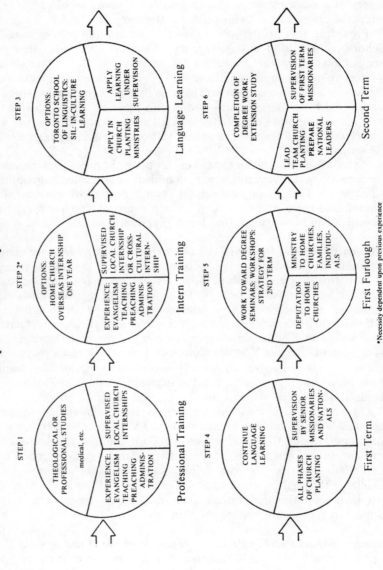

FIGURE 39
Steps in a Missionary Career Path

STEP 1

THEOLOGICAL OR PROFESSIONAL STUDIES

medical, etc.

SUPERVISED LOCAL CHURCH INTERNSHIPS

EXPERIENCE: EVANGELISM TEACHING PREACHING ADMINIS- TRATION

Professional Training

STEP 2*

OPTIONS: HOME CHURCH OVERSEAS INTERNSHIP ONE YEAR

SUPERVISED LOCAL CHURCH INTERNSHIP OR CROSS- CULTURAL INTERN- SHIP

EXPERIENCE: EVANGELISM TEACHING PREACHING ADMINIS- TRATION

Intern Training

STEP 3

OPTIONS: TORONTO SCHOOL OF LINGUISTICS: SIL IN-CULTURE LEARNING

APPLY LEARNING UNDER SUPERVISION

APPLY IN CHURCH PLANTING MINISTRIES

Language Learning

STEP 4

CONTINUE LANGUAGE LEARNING

SUPERVISION BY SENIOR MISSIONARIES AND NATION- ALS

ALL PHASES OF CHURCH PLANTING

First Term

STEP 5

WORK TOWARD DEGREE SEMINARS: WORKSHOPS: STRATEGY FOR 2ND TERM

MINISTRY TO HOME CHURCHES, FAMILIES, INDIVIDU- ALS

DEPUTATION TO HOME CHURCHES

First Furlough

STEP 6

COMPLETION OF DEGREE WORK: EXTENSION STUDY

SUPERVISION OF FIRST TERM MISSIONARIES

LEAD TEAM CHURCH PLANTING PREPARE NATIONAL LEADERS

Second Term

*Necessity dependent upon previous experience

meaningful opportunities for service that will challenge the young people to discover and develop their spiritual gifts. Students in our Christian schools are guaranteed help along the road to spiritual maturity if a purposeful program of study and service is offered.

Wrap-Up

Administrators and faculty members have their obligations in the educational process. They can instruct, counsel, encourage, befriend, and pray for students. But they cannot determine God's will for each student. Students must master the assigned course work. They must gain experience in ministry. Students are responsible for their own spiritual growth. We will summarize some further areas of student concern.

• Students must strive to fulfill their academic potential. Priorities will need to be set. For example, employment schedules must yield to class schedules and study time. When God leads a person into preparation for ministry that preparation time is as much in God's will as the future.

• Students must strive to fulfill their spiritual potential. Who can measure the possibilities of a life fully committed to God? With few exceptions, what we are in student days anticipates what we will be in ministry.

• Students are the reason for the school's existence. The school must lead them into a closer walk with God, a clearer understanding of His word, and a commitment to serve faithfully until Jesus comes.

• The school, church, and mission agency must seek specific ways to reinforce each other in the total preparation of those entering international ministries.

Notes to Chapter 20

1. Martin E. Clark, *Choosing Your Career: The Christian's Decision Manual* (Phillipsburg, NJ: Presbyterian and Reformed Publishing Company, 1981), p. 91.

2. Ibid., 92.

3. J. Herbert Kane, *Life and Work on the Mission Field* (Grand Rapids: Baker Book House, 1980), p. 4.

4. Harold R. Cook, *An Introduction to Christian Missions* (Chicago: Moody Press, 1971), p. 83.

5. Two sources worthy of in-depth study in decision making are: Martin E. Clark, *Choosing Your Career: The Christian's Decision Manual* (Phillipsburg, NJ: Presbyterian and Reformed Publishing Company, 1981) and Garry Friesen with J. Robin Maxson, *Decision Making & the Will of God: A Biblical Alternative to the Traditional View* (Portland: Multnomah Press, 1982).

6. Craig Hanscome, "Predicting Missionary Drop-Out," *Evangelical Missions Quarterly* 15 (July 1979): 153-54.

7. Edward R. Dayton and David A. Fraser, *Planning Strategies for World Evangelization* (Grand Rapids: Eerdmans, 1980), pp. 245-50.

8. Ibid., 245.

Part 6

The Divine Imperative in Missions Strategy

The Imperative of the Holy Spirit

21

Without the dynamic power of the Holy Spirit, missions strategy is dead. The Holy Spirit gives the church's world mission the imperative of urgency.

What is the work of the Holy Spirit in missions? Why did the Holy Spirit descend with power upon the disciples on the day of Pentecost? The purpose of this chapter is to answer these questions. We will observe the dynamic of the Holy Spirit (1) in proclaiming the gospel, (2) in perfecting the saints, (3) and in planting churches. Paul used this threefold model for missions in his own ministry as we saw in chapter One (Acts 14:21-23). In speaking of the Holy Spirit's work in missions, Michael Green states:

> But there can be no doubt from a candid examination of the New Testament accounts that the prime purpose of the coming of the Spirit of God upon the disciples was to equip them for mission. The Comforter comes not in order to allow men to be comfortable, but to make them missionaries.
>
> This is so contrary to our general assumptions (namely that of the Holy Spirit, however vaguely we conceive him, is an internal gift for the faithful, appropriate only to be mentioned in church) that it is important for us to see the crucial link between the Spirit and mission which is presented to us in the pages of the New Testament.[1]

Harold Lindsell adds a sobering note:

> The doctrine of the Holy Spirit is the lost dynamic of the church. The hard times which have fallen on the missionary enterprise *en toto* may be traced to this elimination of the Holy Spirit, without which no missionary work can be successful or endure.[2]

Yet the Scriptures are plain: the Holy Spirit is the prime mover in missions. Indeed, A.T. Pierson entitled one of his books on Acts, *The Acts of the Holy Spirit*.[3] The Holy Spirit must be restored in our thinking to the role He filled in first-century missionary outreach. He is the power source in the church's witness. See figure 40.

FIGURE 40

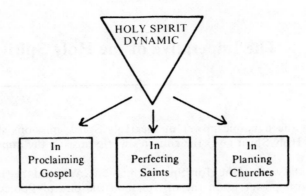

The Dynamic of the Holy Spirit in Proclaiming the Gospel

The Holy Spirit Empowers Believers to Proclaim the Gospel

Luke records Christ's promise to send the Holy Spirit (Luke 24:49; Acts 1:4-5). Christ explained, "For John baptized with water, but in a few days you will be baptized with the Holy Spirit" (Acts 1:5). The baptizing work of the Spirit is unique to the New Testament, and signals the beginning of the church, the body of Christ (Acts 2:1-11; 1 Cor. 12:13).

With the Spirit's coming, the believers were enabled to witness with power (Acts 1:8). Harry R. Boer states:

> Pentecost made the Church a *witnessing* Church. Her witness was spontaneous, immediate. She did not need a basis in reflection for the discharge of her kerugmatic task, for she had been naturally constituted to be kerugmatic community.[4]

The Spirit-empowered witness of the church continues to take her "unto the uttermost part of the earth" (Acts 1:8 KJV). J.A. Alexander remarks, "This and other kindred phrases are employed in the Old Testament, to signify all nations, not excepting the remotest. (See Ps. 2,8. 19,4. 67,7. 72,8. Isa. 48,20. Zech. 9,10)."[5] The church's continuing worldwide witness is only possible because of the power of the indwelling Spirit.

The witness of the early church was characterized by Spirit-given boldness and obedience. How else could the God-fearing Jews in Jerusalem at Pentecost have heard the gospel message (Acts 2:1-12)? How else could Peter have spoken with such boldness at Pentecost? Speaking of Jesus, Peter said, "This man was handed over to you by God's set purpose and foreknowledge; and you, with the help of wicked men, put him to death by nailing him to the cross" (Acts 2:23). At the invitation, three-thousand were added to the number of believers (Acts 2:40-41).

Peter was equally bold in his second message after the healing of the beggar. He first accused his hearers of killing "the author of life" (Acts

3:15), then went on to call them to repentance (Acts 3:19). As a result, "the number of men grew to about five thousand" (Acts 4:4).

Peter and John witnessed with boldness to the religious leaders. Peter was filled with the Holy Spirit as he gave witness to Christ's resurrection (Acts 4:8-12). Peter and John reported back to the believers, and "they were all filled with the Holy Spirit and spoke the word of God boldly" (Acts 4:31).

Stephen's witness was borne through the Holy Spirit's power. He was "a man full of faith and of the Holy Spirit" (Acts 6:5). Stephen's hearers "could not stand up against his wisdom or the Spirit by which he spoke" (Acts 6:10).

The coming of the Holy Spirit had, indeed, made the difference in the disciples' witness. Many believed on Christ in Antioch through the witness of those scattered from Jerusalem (Acts 11:19-21). The church at Jerusalem sent Barnabas to Antioch to investigate this new outreach. Barnabas was "a good man, full of the Holy Spirit and faith, and a great number of people believed and turned to the Lord" (Acts 11:24). The Spirit of God was on the move, using the disciples in ever-widening circles of witness.

The Holy Spirit empowered Paul and his companions, although this was not always explicitly stated. Paul reminded the Thessalonians, "Brothers loved by God, we know that he has chosen you, because our gospel came to you not simply with words, but also with power, with the Holy Spirit, and with deep conviction" (1 Thess. 1:4-5). The Thessalonians in turn "welcomed the message with the joy given by the Holy Spirit" (1 Thess. 1:6). The Holy Spirit prepared both the messengers and the hearers, and the Thessalonian church was soon recognized among other churches for its concern for gospel witness (1 Thess. 1:7-10).

We must appropriate the power of the Holy Spirit in our witness today both individually and corporately in the local church. We are sometimes prone to substitute organization, education, methods, or finance to provide the power for our witness. Glover warns:

> We hear much talk today about strategy, statesmanship, cooperation, and the like, in the realm of missions, and much stress is laid upon improved organization and equipment, and more up-to-date policies and methods. With no disposition to disparage these things, all of which have their proper place and value, we venture to express the fear that in these very emphases there lurks a subtle peril of substituting human mechanics for divine dynamics, and of attempting to prosecute the work of missions in the wisdom of man rather than the power of God.[6]

The Holy Spirit Convicts of Sin As the Gospel is Proclaimed

Christ's disciples were grief-stricken when they learned that He was going away. He consoled them by promising that the Holy Spirit would come to be their Counselor. "When he comes, " Jesus said, "he will convict the world of guilt in regard to sin and righteousness and judgment . . ." (John 16:8). After Pentecost the disciples understood the truth of Jesus' promise. For example, Peter pleaded in his Pentecost sermon, "Save yourselves from this corrupt generation" (Acts 2:40). As a result, "Those who accepted his message were baptized, and about three thousand were add to their number that day" (Acts 2:41). Acts 2:47 records a similar response: "And the Lord added to their number daily those who were being saved." The convicting and converting work of the Holy Spirit was evident throughout those early days of the church. Not only did people repent of their sins and believe in Christ, but they also became a vital part of the ever-growing Jerusalem church. John R. W. Stott observes:

> Salvation and church membership belong together and should not be separated. On the one hand, there was no solitary Christianity in those days: Jesus did not save people without adding them to the church. But on the other hand he did not add them to the church without saving them. He did both together, and we must expect him to do the same in our day.[7]

The regenerating power of the Spirit in the early church resulted in growing local assemblies of believers (Acts 4:4; 14:1, 23; 17:4 with 1 Thess. 1:9; Acts 17:12; 18:8).

The Holy Spirit Initiates the Proclamation of the Gospel

The Book of Acts records the spread of the gospel from Jerusalem to ever-expanding circles of people and places (Acts 1:8). Green states, "At every point in the advance, it is the Holy Spirit of God who takes the initiative."[8]

First, the Spirit led Philip in his witness to the Ethiopian. Persecution scattered the believers throughout Judea and Samaria (Acts 8:1,4). In the midst of Philip's ministry in Samaria, he was instructed to go down to Gaza (Acts 8:26). There he found the Ethiopian eunuch returning to his homeland. The Holy Spirit's instruction was clear at this point: "Go to that chariot and stay near it" (Acts 8:29). After he led the Ethiopian to faith in Christ, "the Spirit of the Lord suddenly took Philip away" (Acts 8:39). Then Philip, beginning at Azotus in Judea, preached the gospel in all the cities until he reached Caesarea in Samaria (Acts 8:40). This whole episode in the life of Philip was due to the initiating direction of the Holy Spirit.

Second, the Holy Spirit took the initiative in Peter's ministry to Cornelius and his household. God used the vision of the sheet let down from heaven to prepare Peter to preach the gospel to Gentiles. Peter obeyed the Spirit's command to go to Cornelius' home, realizing that God "accepts men from every nation who fear him and do what is right" (Acts 10:19-20,35).

Peter's message was twofold: that there is now no distinction between Jew and Gentile (Acts 10:34), and that remission of sin is promised through faith in Christ (Acts 10:43). As a result of Peter's message, the Gentiles gathered in Cornelius' house believed, and they received the Holy Spirit in the same way as the Jews at Pentecost (Acts 10:44-46). The accompanying sign of tongues was given to authenticate to the Jews that the Gentiles had the same right as they to be a part of the church. This transition point in the Book of Acts was brought about through the initiative of the Holy Spirit.

Third, the Spirit of God took the initiative in setting aside Barnabas and Saul for their ministry among the Gentiles (Acts 13:1-2; Rom. 15:16; Gal. 2:9). The church at Antioch was the first outside Palestine from which missionaries were sent to preach the gospel.

At three crucial points in the life of the fledgling church, the Holy Spirit stepped in to initiate witness. Philip, Peter, Barnabas, and Saul knew what it was for the Holy Spirit to intervene in their lives and to thrust them out into uncharted paths. The Spirit continues His initiating ministry in the church today.

The Holy Spirit Directs in the Proclamation of the Gospel

Paul chose Silas to go with him on the second journey through the provinces (Acts 15:40). Little did they realize how God would direct them in even greater outreach. Timothy joined them at Lystra, and on they traveled to deliver to the churches the decisions made at the Jerusalem council (Acts 15:40-16:4). The churches grew in faith and in numbers.

Paul's travel called for preaching the Word in the province of Asia, probably Ephesus. However, Paul and his companions were "kept by the Holy Spirit" from going into Asia (Acts 16:6). Afterward "they tried to enter Bithynia, but the Spirit of Jesus would not allow them to do so"(Acts 16:7). Important Black Sea ports were located in Bithynia, but in God's own wisdom Paul and his friends were not allowed to preach the gospel there. Turning from the northern regions, the missionary team traveled west to Troas where Luke was located (Acts 16:8). Here Paul received his vision of the man of Macedonia which took him eventually into the heart of the Roman Empire. Including himself Luke states, " . . .we got ready at once to leave for Macedonia, concluding that God had called us to preach the gospel to them" (Acts 16:10).

In describing the source of divine direction in Paul's journey, Luke speaks of the "Holy Spirit," the "Spirit of Jesus," and "God." The equation of these terms are an indication of trinitarian understanding in the first-century church.[9]

God stepped in and changed the direction of Paul's projected ministry. Although Paul himself was a good strategist, he yielded to God's leading. The geographic direction Christianity would take was determined at that point of time. Richard N. Longenecker observes:

> Authentic turning points in history are few. But surely among them that of the Macedonian vision ranks high. Because of Paul's obedience at this point, the gospel went westward; and ultimately Europe and the Western world were evangelized. Christian response to the call of God is never a trivial thing. Indeed, as in this instance, great issues and untold blessings may depend on it.[10]

The Dynamic of the Holy Spirit in Perfecting the Saints

Paul's mission model demonstrates his concern for the spiritual growth of new converts. From their ministry in Derbe, Paul and Barnabas "returned to Lystra, Iconium and Antioch, strengthening the disciples and encouraging them to remain true to the faith" (Acts 14:21-22). Spiritual growth is imperative for believers, and the Holy Spirt plays a vital role in that growth. The expression "perfecting the saints" is used here in the sense of continued spiritual growth as the believer is conformed to the image of Christ (Rom. 8:29).

The Holy Spirit Gave the Inspired Word

Peter states, "For prophecy never had its origin in the will of man, but men spoke from God as they were carried along by the Holy Spirit"(2 Pet. 1:21). The Holy Spirit has given us the entire Scriptures by divine inspiration. The reference to "prophecy" in this context refers to the divine origin of all Scripture. Benjamin B. Warifeld states:

> . . . what Peter has to say of this "every prophecy of Scripture"—the exact equivalent, it will be observed in this case of Paul's "every scripture" (2 Tim. 3:16)—applies to the whole of Scripture in all its parts."[11]

The fact that the writers of Scripture were "carried along by the Holy Spirit" shows that their writings came from God rather than themselves. Warfield observes:

> To men who spoke from God are here declared, therefore, to have been taken up by the Holy Spirit and brought by His power to the goal of His choosing. The things which they spoke under this operation of the Spirit were therefore His things, not theirs.[12]

Paul wrote, "All Scripture is God-breathed . . ." (2 Tim. 3:16). Warfield says, "In a word, what is declared by this fundamental passage is simply that the Scriptures are a Divine product, without any indication of how God has operated in producing them."[13]

The Holy Spirit has given the Scriptures to believers for their spiritual understanding and growth. Paul told Timothy that all Scripture is "useful for teaching, rebuking, correcting, and training in righteousness, so that the man of God may be thoroughly equipped for every good work"(2 Tim. 3:16-17). The Word of God is central to victorious Christian living.

The Holy Spirit Gives Enlightenment through the Word

The Holy Spirit helps believers understand the Scriptures, Paul said to the Corinthians:

> We have not received the spirit of the world but the Spirit who is from God, that we may understand what God has freely given us. This is what we speak, not in words taught us by human wisdom but in words taught by the Spirit, expressing spiritual truths in spiritual words (1 Cor. 2:12-13).

The inspired Word is the only source of absolute spiritual truth. The Holy Spirit helps us understand what He has given us in the Bible.

In the context of the above passage, Paul was contrasting human wisdom with wisdom from God (1 Cor. 2:11). He was saying to the Corinthians that his teaching was from the Spirit of God rather than human wisdom. The Spirit of God was given to them in order that they might understand spiritual truth.

Christ spoke of a similar enlightening ministry of the Spirit. In the upper room Christ said, "But when he, the Spirit of truth, comes, he will guide you into all truth. He will not speak on his own: he will speak only what he hears, and he will tell you what is yet to come" (John 16:13). The context (John 16:14-15) indicates that the coming Comforter would make clear to the disciples the full significance of Christ's person and work. When the Holy Spirit came at Pentecost, the disciples understood far more about Christ. Peter's sermon at Pentecost is clear evidence that he then understood the significance of Christ's ministry while He was on earth.

Today the Holy Spirit continues His enlightening work on behalf of believers. In some remote areas of the world where believers are limited to the Scriptures with little or no help with interpretation, they often show astonishing insights into scriptural truth. There can be no explanation of their understanding apart from the teaching ministry of the Spirit.

The Holy Spirit Is the Indwelling Helper

Jesus said to His disciples, "And I will ask the Father, and he will give you another Counselor to be with you forever—the Spirit of truth" (John 14:16-17). The expression, *parakletos,* or *Paraclete,* is used only by John (John 14:16,26; 15:26; 16:7; 1 John 2:1). The word is so full of meaning that it is difficult to find an exact equivalent. The best meaning of *Paraclete* is an advocate (as used in 1 John 2:1), an intercessor, a counselor, or helper.

The Lord Jesus sent the Holy Spirit to help the believer. We are not cast upon our own resources to carry out the commission Christ left with us (Matt. 28:19-20). The indwelling Holy Spirit is our helper in the task of world missions. We are dependent on our sovereign Helper not only for living a Christ-honoring life, but also for making Him known to our generation. We are dependent on the Spirit's wisdom and direction. In speaking of the apostles' dependence on the Spirit, George W. Peters states:

> They did not think of themselves as initiators, executors and adminstrators of world evangelism or world missions. Rather, they knew themselves to be temples of the Holy Spirit, a royal priesthood, the agents of the divine Paraclete who was residing in them to execute God's plan of salvation.[14]

The Holy Spirit, then, provides the dynamic for the perfecting of the saints by giving them the inspired Word, by giving them understanding of the Word, and by serving as their Helper in carrying out God's will. We must trust Him not only with our lives, but with the lives of those to whom we minister.

The Dynamic of the Holy Spirit in Planting Churches

The third step in the Pauline model of missions was the establishment of local churches. Luke states in Acts 14:23, "Paul and Barnabas appointed elders for them in each church and, with prayer and fasting, committed them to the Lord whom they had put their trust." Organized local churches were always the end product of Paul's evangelizing and edifying ministries. The dynamic of the Holy Spirit in church planting is evident.

The Holy Spirit Directs in Planting Churches
The Spirit of God instructed the church leaders at Antioch, "Set apart for me Barnabas and Saul for *the work* to which I have called them" (Acts 13:2). When they had completed the first journey Luke wrote, "From Attalia they sailed back to Antioch, where they had been committed to the grace of God for *the work* they had now completed" (Acts 14:26).

The work to which the Holy Spirit called Barnabas and Saul culminated in local churches. Each of the following journeys also resulted in further church planting. We must conclude, then, that church planting was a part of the Spirit's purpose in missionary work. On their arrival at Antioch, Paul and Barnabas "gathered the church together and reported all that God had done through them and how he had opened the door of faith to the Gentiles" (Acts 14:27). Church planting was a part of "all that God had done through them . . . ." The establishment of churches under the direction of the Holy Spirit is plainly in God's will in missionary outreach.

The Holy Spirit Encourages Church Growth
Beginning at Pentecost the churches enjoyed great numbers of converts joining their ranks (Acts 4:4; 5:14; 6:1,7; 9:31; 11:21; 16:5; 21:10). The churches themselves multiplied (9:31; 16:5).

The Holy Spirit played a direct part in the multiplication of churches. After Paul departed for Tarsus, Luke commented:

> Then the church throughout Judea, Galilee and Samaria enjoyed a time of peace. It was strengthened; and encouraged by the Holy Spirit, it grew in numbers, living in the fear of the Lord" (Acts 9:31).

"The church" referred to here is spoken of by Paul as "the churches of Judea" (Gal. 1:22) and "God's churches in Judea" (1 Thess. 2:14). Luke speaks of these churches in a collective sense, together with those of Samaria and Galilee. This is the first mention of churches established in Galilee. No doubt many of these churches sprang up after the first persecution in Jerusalem (Acts 8:1).[15]

During this time of peace, the churches grew both spiritually and numerically. They were "strengthened" and they "grew in numbers." There cannot be one kind of growth without the other. G. Campbell Morgan says, "Consequently if the Church is to be missionary, she must be spiritual; and if the Church is to be spiritual, she must be missionary."[16] Morgan further comments on the status of the church's growth in that era:

The Church went forth in abounding power, itself growing and multiplying because of the two facts of its life: the master-principle of the Lordship of Jesus, and the power and comfort of the Holy Spirit.[17]

We continue to need the dynamic of the Holy Spirit for the growth of our churches.

The Holy Spirit Directs in Decision Making
The Jerusalem council had decided the Gentile question, and they addressed themselves to the Gentile believers by saying, "It seems good to the Holy Spirit and to us not to burden you with anything beyond the following requirements . . ." (Acts 15:28).

Peter, Barnabas, and Paul addressed the assembly about their firsthand contact with Gentile converts. James summarized their presentations and then made his own recommendation. But through it all the Holy Spirit was presiding. The leaders who were gathered at Jerusalem were assured that they had the mind of the Spirit although we are not told how they knew the Spirit's direction. The Holy Spirit is concerned with church decision making, and He wants to have a part in it. As F.F. Bruce points out:

> This assigning to the Holy Spirit of prior authority in issuing the recommendation is eloquent of the practical realization of His presence in the early Church."[18]

Glover explains:

> What a revolution would take place in many assemblies if the sense of the Spirit's presence were thus actually felt, and everything said and done were at His prompting and under His control![19]

The Holy Spirit Appoints Church Leaders
The biblical record seldom states explicitly the Holy Spirit's part in selecting church leaders. He selected Barnabas and Saul from among the church leaders at Antioch to be ambassadors to the Gentiles (Acts 13:1-2). Again, when Paul addressed the Ephesian elders, he said, "Guard yourselves and all of the flock of which the Holy Spirit has made you overseers. Be shepherd of the church of God, which he bought with his own blood" (Acts 20:28).

The church at Ephesus must have made some sort of congregational decision about their leaders, but Paul saw it as an appointment by the Holy Spirit. Ultimately these leaders were responsible to God himself for the way they served in their appointed office.

The leaders at Ephesus are spoken of in their context as both "elders" (Acts 20:17) and "overseers" (20:28). They were to function as "shepherds" (20:28). Both position and function are in view. In the light of Paul's prediction about the coming defection from the faith, these men were assured of their divine appointment.

Whatever mode a congregation uses in choosing their spiritual leaders, they must select only people who meet God's approval.

Wrap-Up

For too long the Holy Spirit has been the lost dynamic in missions. Churches, schools, mission agencies, and missionaries need a renewed appropriation of His power. In this chapter we have touched some key ministries of the Spirit in world missions.

• The indwelling Holy Spirit provides the only valid power base for the world mission of the church (Acts 1:8).

• Boldness in witness for Christ is available to all believers through the power of the Spirit.

• Believers are completely dependent upon the Holy Spirit to make their witness effective.

• Openness to direction from the Holy Spirit will open even unexpected opportunities for witness.

• The Holy Spirit's provision of the inspired, inerrant Word of God gives the believer the only source of absolute truth in a changing world.

• The Holy Spirit helps the believer understand the Scriptures.

• The indwelling Spirit of God is the believer's helper in doing God's will.

• Church planting is a vital part of the Holy Spirit's purpose in world missions.

• The Holy Spirit brings both spiritual and numerical growth to churches.

• The Holy Spirit desires to superintend decision making and the choosing of leaders in local churches.

Notes to Chapter 21

1. Michael Green, *I Believe in the Holy Spirit* (Grand Rapids: Eerdmans, 1975), p. 58.

2. Harold Lindsell, *An Evangelical Theology of Missions* (Grand Rapids: Zondervan Publishing House, 1970), p. 195.

3. Robert Hall Glover, *The Bible Basis of Missions* (Los Angeles: Bible House of Los Angeles, 1946), p. 55.

4. Harry R. Boer, *Pentecost and Missions* (Grand Rapids: Eerdmans, 1961), p. 129.

5. Joseph Addison Alexander, *A Commentary on the Acts of the Apostles* (London: The Banner of Truth Trust, 1963), p. 12.

6. Glover, *The Bible Basis of Missions,* p. 69.

7. John R.W. Stott, "The Holy Spirit is a Missionary Spirit," *Declare His Glory Among the Nations,* ed. David M. Howard (Downers Grove: InterVarsity Press, 1977), p. 77.

8. Green, *I Believe in the Holy Spirit,* p. 62.

9. Richard N. Longenecker, "The Acts of the Apostles," *The Expositor's Bible Commentary,* ed. Frank E. Gaebelein, 12 vols. (Grand Rapids: Zondervan Publishing House, 1981), 9:457.

10. Ibid., p. 458.

11. Benjamin B. Warfield, *The Inspiration and Authority of the Bible* (Philadelphia: The Presbyterian and Reformed Publishing Company, 1970), p. 136.

12. Ibid., p. 137.

13. Ibid., p. 133.

14. George W. Peters, *A Biblical Theology of Missions* (Chicago: Moody Press, 1972), p. 303.

15. F.F. Bruce, *The Acts of the Apostles* (Grand Rapids: Eerdmans, 1960), p. 209.

16. G. Campbell Morgan, *The Acts of the Apostles* (London: Pickering & Inglis, 1948), p. 199.

17. Ibid., p. 198.

18. Bruce, *The Acts of the Apostles*, p. 303.

19. Glover, *The Bible Basis of Missions*, p. 67.

The Imperative of Christ's Coming

22

The world mission of the church will continue until Christ returns for His own. In God's time, the church's world mission will end with the sound of the trumpet (1 Cor. 15:52; 1 Thess. 4:16). Yet many of God's people seem to live out their lives as if there will always be another Monday morning.

The purpose of this chapter is to demonstrate the vital relationship between the completion of the church's world mission and the return of Jesus Chirst for the church.

Christ's command to make disciples (Matt. 28:19) is bolstered by the fact that some day the church will be complete, then Christ will return "in a flash, in the twinkling of an eye" (1 Cor. 15:52). Many of God's children expend more effort trying to determine where we are on the time line leading to Christ's return for the church than they do in getting the gospel to those who have never heard. But God's salvation purposes are interrelated with Christ's coming. Soteriology and eschatology must be viewed in proper perspective. They are not isolated disciplines. See the figure below.

FIGURE 41

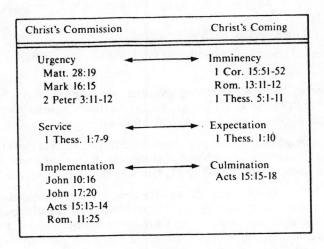

Christ's Commission	Christ's Coming
Urgency	Imminency
Matt. 28:19	1 Cor. 15:51-52
Mark 16:15	Rom. 13:11-12
2 Peter 3:11-12	1 Thess. 5:1-11
Service	Expectation
1 Thess. 1:7-9	1 Thess. 1:10
Implementation	Culmination
John 10:16	Acts 15:15-18
John 17:20	
Acts 15:13-14	
Rom. 11:25	

The Imperative of Christ's Coming

Urgency and Imminency

Urgency of the Church's World Mission

Christ's commands in the Great Commission passages give urgency to the worldwide proclamation of the gospel. He gave the command recorded in Matthew 28:19 to "make disciples of all nations." In our previous study of this passage we established that people become disciples of Christ when they come to know Him through saving faith. The universality of the imperative is plain—"all nations," or all peoples, are to be reached with the gospel. This command for universal disciple making stands to this day.

The command recorded by Mark is equally plain: "Go into all the world and preach the good news to all creation" (16:15). In order for people to know Christ as Saviour, they must hear the gospel (Rom. 10:8-13, 17). Messengers must preach the Good News throughout the world so that people may hear and believe. The urgency of the Great Commission imperatives continue to impel the church until the task is complete. We are debtors to all unreached people (Rom. 1:14-17).

In his panoramic view of future events, Peter challenges his readers: "Since everything will be destroyed in this way, what kind of people ought you to be? You ought to live holy and godly lives as you look forward to the day of God and speed its coming" (2 Peter 3:11-12). How can we "speed" the consummation of all things? An example is found in Peter's message to the Jewish leaders in his second sermon. Israel must repent so that their sins may be forgiven. Peter said:

> Repent, then and turn to God, so that your sins may be wiped out, that times of refreshing may come from the Lord, and that he may send the Christ, who has been appointed for you—even Jesus. He must remain in heaven until the time comes for God to restore everything, as he promised long ago through his holy prophets (Acts 3:19-21).

Peter told his Jewish listeners that their repentance would lead to forgiveness of sins and the coming of kingdom blessings. Charles C. Ryrie states:

> The phrase "times of refreshing" (v. 19) is evidently a synonym for the phrase "restitution of all things" (v. 21) or the millennial kingdom. But that kingdom will not come, apart from personal repentance.[1]

God is sovereign over all things including the future, and yet there is a sense in which repentance and faith in Christ hastens the coming about of future events. In speaking of Acts 3:19-21, Gordon H. Clark observes:

> Christ must remain in heaven until the time of restoration as the holy prophets have said; but men must repent *so that* times of refreshing may come and that he may send Christ who has been appointed for you. In this sense, by our repentance, our pious life, and holy conduct we bring or hasten God's day of judgment.[2]

Although divine sovereignty and human responsibility continue to challenge our understanding of future events, the fact of urgency rests upon the church to preach the gospel to the uttermost part of the earth (Acts 1:8).

Imminency of Christ's Return for the Church

Christ's return for the church can occur at any moemnt. This fact is soemtimes referred to as the imminency of His coming. Because Christ may return for the church at any moment, believers are exhorted to "watch" and to look forward to His coming with hope.

Christ's return for the church will be sudden. Paul explained to the Corinthians:

Listen, I tell you a mystery: We will not all sleep, but we will all be changed—in a flash, in the twinkling of an eye, at the last trumpet. For the trumpet will sound, the dead will be raised imperishable, and we will be changed (1 Cor. 15:51-52).

The "mystery" here, or truth not before revealed, refers to the fact that we will all be changed and to the manner in which this change will take place. This passage does not speak of a particular time. We are to live in the light of Christ's coming for the church. G. Campbell Morgan comments:

Notice that Paul does not tell us when. The New Testament never tells us when this will happen. We are always to live on the border line of this event. It may take place before this day is over . . . . The resurrection will take place at the exact and right moment in the economy and purpose and programme of God. No date is named, but the fact; and it will be sudden.[3]

This Corinthian passage is reminiscent of Paul's comforting word to the Thessalonians:

For the Lord himself will come down from heaven, with a loud command, with the voice of the archangel and with the trumpet call of God and the dead in Christ will rise first (1 Thess. 4:16).

Paul was not looking for signs. He was looking for Christ's return *at any moment*.

Christ's return for the church calls for watchfulness. Paul exhorted the Romans:

And do this, understanding the present time. The hour has come for you to wake up from your slumber, because our salvation is nearer now than when we first believed. The night is nearly over; the day is almost here. So let us put aside the deeds of darkness and put on the armour of light (Rom. 13:11-12).

"Salvation" in this context refers to our deliverance from the world scene at Christ's return. The imminency of this event calls for alertness and a life-style honoring to God. Leon J. Wood comments:

The point made is that the Christian should give attention to a change in life-pattern without delay, because this "salvation" might be brought about at any moment. In other words, Christ could come at any time.[4]

The anticipation of the church's being caught up to be with Christ must take us beyond the confines of our prophetic conferences. Our understanding of prophecy must be mixed with a holy life and an urgency to get the gospel to those who have not heard.

Another passage in which Paul urges his readers to be watchful in the light of Christ's return is 1 Thessalonians 5:1-11. The fact that Christ can come at any time is clearly in view. Paul first reminds his readers that "the day of the Lord will come like a thief in the night" (1 Thess. 5:2). The Day of the Lord is described in the Old Testament as an extended period of time that includes both judgment for sin and blessing for Israel (Isa. 13:9-11; Zeph. 1:14-16; Isa. 2:1-4; 11-16; Zeph. 3:14-15). John F. Walvoord points out:

> The Day of the Lord, as revealed in the Old Testament, indicates first a time of wrath and judgment upon a wicked and Christ-rejecting world which is followed by a time of peace in which Christ shall be in the midst of the earth and will rule over the earth and bring blessing to the nation of Israel.[5]

Paul's teaching is that the Day of the Lord will come suddenly and will catch the world unawares "like a thief in the night" (1 Thess. 5:2). Within the context Paul was teaching "that just as the translation of the church is the end of the day of grace it also marks the beginning of the Day of the Lord."[6]

Since, then, Christ may come for the church at any moment, Paul concludes:

> So then, let us not be like others, who are asleep, but let us be alert and self-controlled . . . . But since we belong to the day, let us be self-controlled, putting on faith and love as a breastplate, and the hope of salvation as a helmet (1 Thess. 5:6, 8).

Christians must live in the light of Christ's imminent coming. What better motive to lead a Christ-honoring life! What more impelling reason to obey Christ's command to be His witnesses to the very end of the earth! We are not appointed to wrath (1 Thess. 5:9), but we *are* appointed to be Christ's ambassadors until He comes (2 Cor. 5:20). The urgency of the church's world mission and the imminency of Christ's coming for the church must be harmonized in our thinking and living.

Service and Expectation

The believers in Thessalonica are a case study of the practical outworking of urgency and imminency in the life of a local church.

Serving through a Faithful Witness

The church in Thessalonica became an example to other believers. Paul states, "And so you became a model to all the believers in Macedonia and Achaia" (1 Thess. 1:7). The word for "model" is *tupos,* sometimes translated "example," "pattern," or "type." Paul, using the word *tupos* in the singular, was viewing the Thessalonians in their corporate testimony as a church. Thessalonica was the only church Paul designated as a model for others to follow. The extent of their modeling reached the other churches in Macedonia and Achaia, namely, Philippi, Berea, Corinth, and Athens.

The Thessalonian church gave evidence of their faith by sharing it far and near. Paul continued, "The Lord's message rang out from you not only in Macedonia and Achaia—your faith in God has become known everywhere" (1 Thess. 1:8). The expression "rang out" may refer to a trumpet blast or thunder.[7] No one had to guess about the clarity of their message. George Milligan translates in part, ". . . the word of the Lord has sounded out like a clear and ringing trumpet-blast in the districts just mentioned . . . ."[8] This church not only welcomed the message with joy (1:6), but they also shared it with conviction (1:8).

The believers at Thessalonica expressed their faith by forsaking their past and serving God without reserve. Paul adds, "They tell how you turned to God from idols to serve the living and true God . . ." (1 Thess. 1:9). The consistent testimony (present tense) of the Thessalonian church was that they turned once for all (aorist tense) from idols (an indication of their Gentile background) to serve whole-heartedly the living and true God. Their service was that of a slave (*doulos*). "Urgency" was written large over this early church. And their service was mixed with hope.

Expecting Christ's Return for the Church

Paul concluded this account for the Thessalonian church by saying, ". . . and to wait for his Son from heaven, who he raised from the dead—Jesus, who rescues us from the coming wrath" (1 Thess. 1:10).

The verb, "to wait," (*anamenein*) is used only here in 1 Thessalonians 1:10 in the New Testament. The present infinitive form indicates a continuing life-style. The word is intensified with the addition of "up" (*ana*) which lends the idea of waiting up for someone. As Milligan explains, "The leading thought here seems to be the wait for one whose coming is expected . . . , perhaps with the added idea of patience and confidence."[9] The picture is that of a faithful wife waiting into the night for the return of her husband from a long journey.

The Thessalonian church anticipated that the resurrected, ascended Jesus would return to rescue them from the coming wrath. In speaking of the term "wrath," Robert L. Thomas states:

> Used technically, as it so frequently is in the NT, "wrath" (*orges*) is a title for the period just before Messiah's kingdom on earth, when God will afflict earth's inhabitants with an unparalleled series of physical torments because of their rejection of His will . . . .[10]

Serving God and expecting His Son from heaven go hand in hand. The church that received the most instruction about the "at-any-moment" coming of Christ was the one that gave itself most to the proclamation of the gospel.

Implementation and Culmination

Implementaton of God's Present Purpose

God's present purpose is stated in a threefold manner. First, Jesus said, "I have other sheep that are not of this sheep pen. I must bring them also. They also will listen to my voice, and there shall be one flock and one shepherd" (John 10:16). Jesus also prayed, "My prayer is not for them alone. I pray also for those who will believe in me through their message ..." (John 17:20). Christ's obvious purpose was to bring others to Himself beyond the Jewish believers of His day.

Second, James declared at the Jerusalem council, "Simeon hath declared how God at the first did visit the Gentiles, to take out of them a people for his name" (Acts 15:13-14 KJV). The Jerusalem council had been called to consider the contention of some believer from the Pharisee group. They held, "The Gentiles must be circumcised and required to obey the law of Moses" (Acts 15:5). Peter began by explaining how Gentiles in Cornelius' house received the gospel (Acts 10:23-48; 15:6-11). Barnabas and Paul followed, telling how God had worked among Gentiles through their ministry (Acts 15:12). James summarized the matter by concluding that God is today taking out of the Gentiles a people for his name. J. Dwight Pentecost observes about God's present purpose:

> The Jerusalem council (Acts 15:14) announced that "God at the first did visit the Gentiles, to take out of them a people for his name." The "taking out of a people" thus constitutes God's present-age program . . . . The reason for this calling out is stated in Ephesians 2:7, "That in the ages to come he might shew the exceeding riches of his grace in his kindness toward us through Jesus Christ." The divine purpose in the outcalling of the church is to display the infinity of His grace.[11]

The church of Jesus Christ has been commissioned to carry out God's purpose today. We are bearers of the gospel which alone can bring saving faith. Paul said, "Consequently, faith comes frm hearing the message, and the message is heard through the word of Christ" (Rom. 10:17). People cannot hear the life-giving message without someone to tell them (Rom. 10:14-15).

Third, Paul reasoned in Romans 11:25:

> "I do not want you to be ignorant of this mystery, brothers, so that you may not be conceited: Israel has experienced a hardening in part until the full number of the Gentiles has come in."

A believing remnant of Jews is found in the church (Eph. 2:14-18). Hence, Israel's hardening is "in part" both in extent and in duration—"in part until

. . . ." The context that follows Romans 11:25 relates to Israel's salvation as nation (Rom. 11:26-27). In reference to the eschatological setting, Everett F. Harrison asks:

> Does our passage throw light on the time when Israel's national conversion is to be expected? Certainly not in terms of "that day or hour" (Matt. 24:36), but rather in terms of the time when the full number of the Gentiles has come in (v. 25). The "so" (v. 26) is apparently intended to correlate with "until" (v. 25), thereby acquiring temporal force . . . .[12]

When the world mission of the church is fully implemented, God will again step into history as He did at Christ's first coming, although we do not know the day nor the hour.

Culmination of God's Present Purpose

We now return to the decisions made at the Jerusalem council. The historical setting must be kept in mind. James drew the conclusion from Peter's account of Gentile response to the gospel that God now is taking from the Gentiles a people for His name (Acts 15:14). His quotation from Amos 9:11-12 is subject to much debate both exegetically and theologically. James uses the Septuagint version rather than the Masoretic text, but he does not always follow the form of the Septuagint.[13] The passage is set in both a soteriological and eschatological framework.

What are we to understand by this rather free paraphrase from an Old Testament prophet? In the light of other Scripture, we know that James' statement is consistent with what the Holy Spirit wants us to understand. The quotation is a part of progressive revelation evident in the Scriptures. The amillennialist holds that the restoration of "David's fallen tent" is fulfilled in the church. Premillennial dispensationalists, on the other hand, "contend that James was not claiming fulfillment but simply saying that Gentile salvation today is in *harmony* with God's aim to bless Gentiles along with an exalted Israel in the future Messianic Kingdom"[14] Promise theology takes a mediatory position between covenant theologians and dispensationalists in its interpretation of this passage.[15]

We must keep in mind that James was dealing with the Gentile question that was before the council. His recourse to Amos' prophecy, variations and all, spoke to the question at hand as well as to Israel's future. In considering the text, its eschatological implications seem plain. In his study of Amos 9:11-12, James E. Rosscup concludes:

> James quoted Amos 9:11-12, not to claim fulfillment of that passage in this age, but to demonstrate that the prophets were in harmony with the present blessing of Gentiles apart from circumcision. But, at the same time, he cited Amos to give assurance to the Jews that the present program of salvation among the Gentiles did not endanger the divine promises that Israel would be nationally restored to an exalted place in the Messianic Kingdom. Thus, despite the brevity of his address, he provided solutions to both the soteriological problem and the eschatological problems of the transitional period.[16]

In quoting Amos, then, James looked beyond other future events to the time of the messianic kingdom when both Israel and the Gentiles will enjoy God's blessing in their own relationship to Him.

The major concern to us today, of course, is God's purpose to take to Himself a people for His name. To this same purpose the church of Jesus Christ must put forth every effort to make disciples from among the peoples of the earth—even the uttermost part. One day, known only to God, the church's world mission will end "in the twinkling of an eye."

Wrap-Up

Christ will return from the church at any moment. The church's task remains unfinished. The reality of these two truths must send us forth with the gospel until the commission is complete. Let us summarize our thoughts on the imperative of Christ's coming.

• Truths taught in the Scriptures about salvation and future events must be integrated in our understanding of the church's world mission.

• God is sovereign over future events; nevertheless, He commands the church to witness worldwide until Christ returns.

• Because Christ may return for the church at any moment, we must watch and live a holy, self-controlled life.

• We must serve Christ with abandon while eagerly expecting His return.

• God's present-age purpose is to take for Hmself a people for His name, and he commissions the church to make this purpose a reality.

Notes to Chapter 22

1. Charles Caldwell Ryrie, *The Acts of the Apostles* (Chicago: Moody Press, 1961), p. 31.

2. Gordon H. Clark *II Peter: A Short Commentary* (Philadelphia: Presbyterian and Reformed Publishing Company, 1975), p. 74.

3. G. Campbell Morgan, *The Corinthian Letters of Paul* (New York: Fleming H. Revell Company, 1946), p. 201.

4. Leon J. Wood, *The Bible and Future Events* (Grand Rapids: Zondervan Publishing House, 1976), p. 79.

5. John F.Walvoord, *The Thessalonian Epistles* (Findlay, OH: Dunham Publishing Company, 1955), pp. 78-79.

6. Ibid, p. 81.

7. George Milligan, *St. Paul's Epistles to the Thessalonians: The Greek Text with Introduction and Notes* (Grand Rapids: Eerdmans, 1953), p. 12.

8. Ibid., p. 11.

9. Ibid., p. 14.

10. Robert L. Thomas, "1 Thessalonians," *The Expositor's Bible Commentary* ed. Frank E. Gaebelein, 12 vols. (Grand Rapids: Zondervan Publishing House, 1978), 11:248.

11. J. Dwight Pentecost, *Things to Come: A Study in Biblical Eschatology* (Findlay, OH: Dunham Publishing Company, 1958), p. 133.

12. Everett F. Harrison, "Romans," *The Expositor's Bible Commentary* ed. Frank E. Gaebelein, 12 vols. (Grand Rapids: Zondervan Publishing House, 1976) 10:124.

13. Richard N. Longenecker, "The Acts of the Apostles, *The Expositor's Bible Commentary* ed. Frank E. Gaebelein, 12 vols. (Grand Rapids: Zondervan Publishing House, 1981) 9:447.

14. James E. Rosscup, *The Interpretation of Acts 15:13-18* (unpublished Th.D. dissertation, Dallas Theological Seminary, 1966), p. 1.

15. See Walter C. Kaiser's article, "The Davidic Promise and the Inclusion of the Gentiles (Amos 9:9-15 and Acts 15:13-18): A Test Passage for Theological Systems," *The Journal of the Evangelical Theological Society* 20 (June 1977), pp. 97-111. Kaiser holds that "Promise theology, or epangelicalism, without setting out to be a middle way between covenant theology and dispensationalism, promises to be such, for it picks up the strengths of both systems of exegesis" (p. 111).

16. Rosscup, *The Interpretation of Acts 15:13-18*, p. 231.

Bibliography

Alexander, Joseph Addison. *A Commentary on the Acts of the Apostles.* London: The Banner of Truth Trust, 1963.

Allen, Roland. *Education in the Native Church.* London: World Dominion Press, n.d.
_____ . *Missionary Methods: St. Paul's or Ours?* Grand Rapids: Eerdmans, 1962.

Amstutz, Harold E. *The Gospel Yoke: The Relationship of the Mission Board to the Local Church.* Cherry Hill, NJ: Association of Baptists for World Evangelism, 1982.

Boer, Harry R. *Pentecost and Missions.* Grand Rapids, Eerdmans, 1961.

Bruce, F.F. *The Acts of the Apostles.* Grand Rapids: Eerdmans, 1960.

Chafer, Lewis Sperry. *Systematic Theology* 7. Dallas: Dallas Seminary Press, 1948.

Clark, Gordon H. *II Peter: A Short Commentary.* Philadelphia: Presbyterian and Reformed Publishing Company, 1975.

Clark, Martin E. *Choosing Your Career: The Christian's Decision Manual.* Phillipsburg, NJ: Presbyterian and Reformed Publishing Company, 1981.

Collins, Marjorie A. *Manual for Missonaries on Furlough.* South Pasadena: William Carey Library, 1972.

Conybeare, W.J. and Howson, J.S. *The Life and Epistles of St. Paul.* Grand Rapids: Eerdmans, 1957.

Cook, Harold R. *An Introduction to Christian Missions.* Chicago: Moody Press, 1971.

_____ . "Who Really Sent the First Missionaries?" *Evangelical Missions Quarterly* 11 (October 1975): 233-239.

Covell, Ralph R. and Wagner, C. Peter. *An Extension Seminary Primer.* South Pasadena: William Carey Library, 1971.

Dayton, Edward R. and Fraser, David A. *Planning Strategies for World Evangelization.* Grand Rapids: Eerdmans, 1980.

Dayton, Edward R. "You Can't Beat the System—Part II," *MARC Newsletter* (May 1979): 4-5.

Dayton, Edward R. and Wilson, Samuel. *The Refugees Among Us: Unreached Peoples '83.* Monrovia: Missions Advanced Research and Communication Center, 1983.

Earle, Ralph. "1 Timothy." *The Expositor's Bible Commentary* 11. Edited by Frank E. Gaebelein, 12 vols. Grand Rapids: Zondervan Publishing House, 1978.

Engel, James F. *Contemporary Christian Communications: Its Theory and Practice.* New York: Thomas Nelson Publishers, 1975.

Fleming, Bruce C.E. *Contextualization of Theology: An Evangelical Assessment.* Pasadena: William Carey Library, 1980.

"Focus on Missions: Occasional News Supplement for Missionaries," *Fellowship of Missions* 12 (February 1983): 2.

Friesen, Garry and Maxson, J. Robin. *Decision Making & the Will of God: A Biblical Alternative to the Traditional View.* Portland: Multnomah Press, 1982.

Frizen, Edwin L., Jr. "Executives Tell Missions Profs What They Think," *Evangelical Missions Quarterly* 8 (Spring 1972): 143-146.

Frizen, Edwin, L., Jr. "Missionaries and Their Sending Churches," *Evangelical Missions Quarterly* 16 (April 1980): 69-76.

Fuller, W. Harold. *Mission-Church Dynamics: How to Change Bicultural Tensions into Dynamic Missionary Outreach.* Pasadena: William Carey Library, 1980.

Girdlestone, Robert B. *Synonyms of the Old Testament: Their Bearing on Christian Doctrine.* Grand Rapids: Eerdmans, 1956.

Glover, Robert Hall. *The Bible Basis of Missions.* Los Angeles: Bible House of Los Angeles, 1946.

Godet, Frederic Louis. *Commentary on the First Epistle of St. Paul to the Corinthians.* Grand Rapids: Zondervan Publishing House, 1957.

_____. *Commentary on Romans*. Grand Rapids: Kregel Publications, 1977.

Green, Michael. *Evangelism in the Early Church*. Grand Rapids: Eerdmans, 1970.

_____. *I Believe in the Holy Spirit*. Grand Rapids: Eerdmans, 1975.

Grier, James M. "Biblical Basis for Graduate Ministry Training," Unpublished notes, Grand Rapids Baptist Seminary, Fall, 1982.

Griffiths, Michael C. *Who Really Sends the Missionary?* Chicago: Moody Press, 1974.

Gromacki, Robert G. *Stand Fast in Liberty: An Exposition of Galatians*. Grand Rapids: Baker Book House, 1979.

Hamilton, Donald A. "Straight Talk on the Bigger Slices of Pie," *ACMC Briefing* 2 (December 1979): n.p.

Hanscome, Craig. "Predicting Missionary Drop-Out," *Evangelical Missions Quarterly* 15 (July 1979): 152-155.

Harrison, Everett F. "Romans." *The Expositor's Bible Commentary* 10. Edited by Frank E. Gaebelein, 12 vols. Grand Rapids: Zondervan Publishing House, 1976.

Hay, Ian M. "Participants Study Paper No. 1," *Missions in Creative Tension: The Green Lake '71 Compendium*. Edited by Vergil Gerber. South Pasadena: William Carey Library, 1971.

Hesselgrave, David J. *Communicating Christ Cross-Culturally*. Grand Rapids: Zondervan Publishing House, 1978.

Johnson, S. Lewis. *The Old Testament in the New: An Argument for Biblical Inspiration*. Grand Rapids: Zondervan Publishing House, 1980.

Kaiser, Walter C., Jr., "Israel's Missionary Call." *Perspectives on the World Christian Movement*. Edited by Ralph D. Winter and Steven C. Hawthorne. Pasadena, CA: William Carey Library," 1981

_____. "The Davidic Promise and the Inclusion of the Gentiles (Amos 9:9-15 and Acts 15:13-18): A Test Passage for Theological Systems," *The Journal of the Evangelical Theological Society* 20 (June 1977): 97-111.

_____. *Toward an Exegetical Theology: Biblical Exegesis for Preaching and Teaching*. Grand Rapids: Baker Book House, 1981.

Kaleli, Jones. "Pssst! Western ≠ Christian," *Wherever* 6 (Spring 1981): 6-7.

Kane, J. Herbert. *Life and Work on the Mission Field.* Grand Rapids: Baker Book House, 1980.

Keesing, Felix M. *Cultural Anthropology: The Science of Custom.* New York: Holt, Rinehart, and Winston, 1965.

Keil, C.F. and Delitzsch, F. *Biblical Commentary on the Old Testament* 1. Grand Rapids: Eerdmans, 1968.

Kempton, Wendell, Kendrick, V. Ben, and Marshall, David. "The New Missionary and Church Support," *Baptist Bulletin* 47 (September 1981): 8-9.

Kent, Homer A. "Philippians." *The Expositor's Bible Commentary* 11. Edited by Frank E. Gaebelein, 12 vols. Grand Rapids: Zondervan Publishing House, 1978.

Ketcham, Donn W. *The World Hurts!: A Biblical Approach to Social Action.* Cherry Hill, NJ: Association of Baptists for World Evangelism, 1981.

Keyes, Lawrence E. *The Last Age of Missions: A Study of Third World Mission Societies.* Pasadena: William Carey Library, 1983.

Kilinski, Ken. "How Churches Can Follow Antioch's Model," *Evangelical Missions Quarterly* 15 (January 1979): 19-23.

Lewis, Norm. *Faith Promise for World Witness: A Challenge to Every Church.* Lincoln: Back to the Bible Broadcast, 1974.

_____. *Handbook Faith Promise for World Witness: How to Do the Work.* Lincoln: Back to the Bible Broadcast, 1974.

Leupold, H.C. *Exposition of Genesis* 1. Grand Rapids: Baker Book House, 1975.

_____. *Exposition of Isaiah* 2. Grand Rapids: Baker Book House, 1971.

Lindsell, Harold. *An Evangelical Theology of Missions.* Grand Rapids: Zondervan Publishing House, 1970.

Longenecker, Richard N. "The Acts of the Apostles." *The Expositor's Bible Commentary* 9. Edited by Frank E. Gaebelein, 12 vols. Grand Rapids: Zondervan Publishing House, 1981.

Luzbetak, Louis J. *The Church and Cultures*. Techy, IL: Divine Word Publications, 1970.

Marshall, David L. *Suggested Changes in Missionary Stewardship for the 1980's*. Kokomo, IN: Evangelical Baptist Missions, 1979.

Matthews, Reginald L. *Missionary Administration in the Local Church*. Schaumburg, IL: Regular Baptist Press, 1970.

McGavran, Donald A. "How About That New Verb 'To Disciple'?" *Church Growth Bulletin* 15 (May 1979): 265-270.

_____. *The Clash Between Christianity and Cultures*. Washington, D.C.: Canon Press, 1974.

_____. *Understanding Church Growth*. Fully Revised. Grand Rapids: Eerdmans, 1980.

McKinney, Lois. "Why Renewal Is Needed in Theological Education," *Evangelical Missions Quarterly* 18 (April 1982): 85-96.

Milligan, George. *St. Paul's Epistles to the Thessalonians: The Greek Text with Introduction and Notes*. Grand Rapids: Eerdmans, 1953.

Missions Policy Handbook. Pasadena: Association of Church Missions Committees, 1977.

Morgan, G. Campbell. *The Acts of the Apostles*. London: Pickering & Inglis, 1948.

_____. *The Corinthian Letters of Paul*. New York: Fleming H. Revell Company, 1946.

Morris, Leon. *The Revelation of John*. vol. 20 of *The Tyndale New Testament Commentaries*. 20 vols. Edited by R.V.G. Tasker. Grand Rapids: Eerdmans, 1978.

Mounce, Robert H. "Gospel," *Baker's Dictionary of Theology*. Edited by Everett H. Harrison. Grand Rapids: Baker Book House, 1960.

Pentecost, J. Dwight. *Things to Come: A Study in Biblical Eschatology*. Findlay, OH: Dunham Publishing Company, 1958.

Peters, George N.H. *The Theocratic Kingdom* 1. Grand Rapids: Kregel Publications, 1978.

Peters, George W. *A Biblical Theology of Missions*. Chicago: Moody Press, 1972.

Purves, George T. *Christianity in the Apostolic Age*. Grand Rapids: Baker Book House, 1955.

Reyburn, William D. "The Transformation of God and the Conversion of Man," *Readings in Missionary Anthropology II*. Edited by William A. Smalley. Pasadena: William Carey Library, 1978.

Reeves, Robert E. "Where Will Mission-Minded Pastors Come From?" *Global Church Growth Bulletin* 17 (July-August 1980): 49.

Richardson, Don. *Eternity in Their Hearts*. Ventura, CA: Regal Books, 1981.

Robertson, Archibald T. *Word Pictures in the New Testament* 3. New York: Harper & Brothers, 1930.

Rosscup, James E. *The Interpretation of Acts 15:13-18*. Unpublished Th.D. dissertation. Dallas: Dallas Theological Seminary, 1966.

Ryrie, Charles Caldwell. *Biblical Theology of the New Testament*. Chicago: Moody Press, 1959.

_____. *The Acts of the Apostles*. Chicago: Moody Press, 1961.

Sanders, J. Oswald. *Spiritual Leadership*. Chicago: Moody Press, 1967.

Saucy, Robert L. *The Church in God's Program*. Chicago: Moody Press, 1972.

Slavin, George A. "The Missionary and His Local Church," *Evangelical Missions Quarterly* 7 (Spring 1971): 169-175.

Smith, Larry D. "The Great Illusion." An unpublished essay, n.d.

Speer, Robert E. *Missionary Principles and Practice*. New York: Fleming H. Revell, 1902.

Spencer, Stephen R. "The Christian World-View: The Basis for Christian Education," *Grand Rapids Baptist Seminary Theolog* 7 (April 1982): n.p.

Stott, John R.W. *Christian Mission in the Modern World*. Downers Grove: InterVarsity Press, 1975.

_____. "The Holy Spirit is a Missionary Spirit," *Declare His Glory Among the Nations*. Edited by David M. Howard. Downers Grove: InterVarsity Press, 1977.

Taber, Charles R. "The Training of Missionaries," *Practical Anthropology* 14 (November-December 1967): 267-274.

Thomas, Robert L. "1 Thessalonians." *The Expositor's Bible Commentary* 11. Edited by Frank E. Gaebelein, 12 vols. Grand Rapids: Zondervan Publishing House, 1978.

Trench, Richard Chenevix. *Synonyms of the New Testament.* Grand Rapids: Eerdmans, 1948.

Wagner, C. Peter. "Goal Setting: A Key to the Growth of the Body," *Global Church Growth* 20 (March-April 1983): 256-258.

_____. "What is 'Making Disciples'?" *Evangelical Missions Quarterly* 9 (Fall 1973): 285-293.

Walvoord, John F. *The Thessalonian Epistles.* Findlay, OH: Dunham Publishing Company, 1955.

_____. *The Revelation of Jesus Christ.* Chicago: Moody Press, 1966.

Warfield, Benjamin B. *The Inspiration and Authority of the Bible.* Philadelphia: The Presbyterian and Reformed Publishing Company, 1948.

Wilson, Samuel. "Current Trends in North American Protestant Ministries Overseas," *International Bulletin of Missionary Research* 5 (April 1981): 74-75.

Wilson, Samuel. "Judging Theological Education by the Outcome," *Global Church Growth Bulletin* 17 (July-August 1980): 42.

_____. ed., *Mission Handbook: North American Protestant Ministries Overseas.* 12th edition. Monrovia, CA: Missions Advanced Research and Communication Center, 1979.

Wood, Leon J. *The Bible and Future Events, Grand Rapids: Zondervan Publishing House, 1976.*

_____. *The Prophets of Israel.* Grand Rapids: Baker Book House, 1979.

Subject Index

Abrahamic Covenant, 25-6, 31-2

Antioch, 3-5, 7, 9, 16, 31, 52, 59, 61-2, 65, 69, 74, 91-2, 114, 118, 142, 197, 199-200, 202-3

Athens, 5, 16-9, 211

Barnabas, 4-5, 7, 9-10, 17, 31, 37-8, 49, 52, 59, 61-2, 65, 69, 73, 91-2, 114, 142, 153, 159, 186, 197, 199-200, 202-3, 212

Bible Colleges. *See* Theological School

Bible Institutes. *See* Theological School

Budget. *See* Missions Budget

Bulletin Board, 103-4

Call, 61-2, 64-5, 86, 98, 105, 124, 139, 149-51, 161-3, 172-3, 185-7, 199, 202. *See also* Home Church, selects

Canadian Council of Churches Commission on World Concerns, 131-2, 135

Candidate Procedure, 70-3

Career Path, 188-90

Christian Colleges. *See* Theological School

Church Budget. *See* Missions Budget

Church, Definition of, local, 45-6; universal, 45-50

Church, Home, authorizes, 69-73, 75, 117, 123; commissions, 73-5, 77; co-sends, 61-2, 67, 77; enlists, 55, 60, 62-4, 67, 77; evaluates, 77, 91-3; ordains, 73, 77; prays, 51, 55, 62, 77, 89-91, 93, 143; revitalizes, 77, 92-3; selects, 65-6, 77; supports, 77-87,

89-94, 98-101, 107, 126-7, 143-4, 147-8, 182

Church, Local, 3, 6-7, 9-11, 13, 17, 21, 23, 36-9, 41, 45, 47-57, 59-67, 69-75, 77-86, 89-93, 95-101, 103-8, 111-20, 123-9, 131-5, 139-47, 149, 151, 153-4, 156, 158-64, 169-74, 179-83, 185, 189-91, 195-9, 202-4, 210

Church, Mission of, 3, 10-11, 35, 39, 41, 48-50, 52, 62, 157, 169-70, 177, 179, 195, 204, 207-8, 210, 213-4

Church, Missionary Conference. *See* Missionary Conference

Church, Missions Committee. *See* Missions Committee

Church, Missions Policy. *See* Missions Policy

Church, Missions Promotion. *See* Missions Promotion

Church, Pastor. *See* Pastor and Missions

Church Planting, 9-11, 13-4, 17, 19, 39, 48, 59, 71, 73, 83, 90-1, 98, 113, 132, 134-5, 140-1, 146, 153-6, 158-61, 164, 169, 181, 189, 195, 202, 204

Church, Relation to Mission Agency, 114-20, 123-9

Church, Relation to Missionaries, 51-57, 59-67, 69-75, 77-87, 89-94, 139-44, 146-7, 149, 151

Church, Universal, 3, 6, 23, 36-9, 41, 45-50, 157, 170, 179, 195-6, 207, 209-14

Churches, Establishing. *See* Church Planting

Churches, National. *See* National Churches

Scripture Index